Restorative Cities

Restorative Cities

Urban Design for Mental Health and Wellbeing

JENNY ROE AND LAYLA McCAY

BLOOMSBURY VISUAL ARTS
LONDON · NEW YORK · OXFORD · NEW DELHI · SYDNEY

BLOOMSBURY VISUAL ARTS
Bloomsbury Publishing Plc
50 Bedford Square, London, WC1B 3DP, UK
1385 Broadway, New York, NY 10018, USA
29 Earlsfort Terrace, Dublin 2, Ireland

BLOOMSBURY, BLOOMSBURY VISUAL ARTS and the Diana logo
are trademarks of Bloomsbury Publishing Plc

First published in Great Britain 2021
Paperback edition reprinted 2022 (twice)
Hardback edition reprinted 2022

A catalogue record for this book is available from the British Library.

Library of Congress Cataloging-in-Publication Data
Names: Roe, Jenny author. | McCay, Layla, author.
Title: Restorative cities : urban design for mental health and wellbeing /
Jenny Roe and Layla McCay.
Identifiers: LCCN 2020052674 (print) | LCCN 2020052675 (ebook) |
ISBN 9781350112872 (hardback) | ISBN 9781350112889 (paperback) |
ISBN 9781350112896 (epub) | ISBN 9781350112902 (pdf) | ISBN 9781350112919
Subjects: LCSH: City planning–Psychological aspects. | City and town
life–Psychological aspects. | City dwellers–Psychology. | Environmental
psychology. | Mental health planning. | Mental health policy. | Urban policy.
Classification: LCC HT166 .R597 2021 (print) | LCC HT166 (ebook) | DDC 307.1/216019–dc23
LC record available at https://lccn.loc.gov/2020052674
LC ebook record available at https://lccn.loc.gov/2020052675

ISBN:	HB:	978-1-3501-1287-2
	PB:	978-1-3501-1288-9
	ePDF:	978-1-3501-1290-2
	eBook:	978-1-3501-1289-6

Typeset by Integra Software Services Pvt. Ltd.
Printed and bound in Great Britain

To find out more about our authors and books visit www.bloomsbury.com
and sign up for our newsletters.

For Alice Roe and Rosalind Campion

Contents

List of Illustrations   viii

Preface   xii

Acknowledgements   xvii

1   Introduction to restorative urbanism   1

2   The green city   17

3   The blue city   41

4   The sensory city   63

5   The neighbourly city   89

6   The active city   113

7   The playable city   135

8   The inclusive city   159

9   The restorative city   191

References   205

Index   240

Illustrations

1.1 Oasia Hotel, Downtown Singapore, a re-imagined 'radiant' high-rise city 3

1.2 An urban restorative niche offers access to nature and supports mental health 4

1.3 The Restorative City Framework 13

2.1 Effects of green space on mental health and wellbeing 19

2.2 Benefits of green cities for mental health and wellbeing 22

2.3 Oasis schoolyard project, Paris, France 35

2.4 Riverside Embankment, Moscow, Russia 36

2.5 The Green City: Neighbourhood Scale 38

2.6 The Green City: City Scale 39

3.1 Effects of blue urban design on mental health and wellbeing 44

3.2 Benefits of blue cities for mental health and wellbeing 47

3.3 Cooling water mister, Shanghai Expo Park, China 52

3.4 Water park offering a daily cycle of water and lighting theatrics, Bradford, UK 55

3.5 Sheaf Square, incorporating *Cutting Edge*, a stainless-steel sculpture and waterfall, Sheffield, UK 56

3.6 Waterway in Middelfart, Denmark 57

3.7 Cheonggyecheon River Park, Seoul, South Korea 58

3.8 The Blue City: Neighbourhood Scale 60

3.9 The Blue City: City Scale 61

4.1 Effects of sensory urban design on mental health and wellbeing 66

4.2 The benefits of sensory cities for mental health and wellbeing 68

4.3 The Saanjihi Programme, West Midlands, UK 81

4.4a and b The Foyle Reeds lit up at night and controlled through an app, Derry/Londonderry, Northern Ireland 82

4.5 The use of blue light in a Japanese station to deter suicide 83

4.6 The 107-colour palette of Turin, Italy, and the schematic chromatic map of the axes of the historic city centre 85

4.7 The Sensory City: Neighbourhood Scale 87

4.8 The Sensory City: City Scale 88

5.1 The effects of neighbourly design on mental health and wellbeing 93

5.2 The benefits of neighbourly cities for mental health and wellbeing 95

5.3 A sitting-out space in central Hong Kong 104

5.4 Kalkbreite housing development, Zurich, Switzerland 108

5.5 The Neighbourly City: Neighbourhood Scale 110

5.6 The Neighbourly City: City Features 111

6.1 The effects of physical activity on mental health and wellbeing 116

6.2 The benefits of active cities for mental health and wellbeing 118

6.3 Barcelona superblock, Spain 128

6.4 The Active City: Neighbourhood Scale 132

6.5 The Active City: City Scale 133

7.1 The effects of playable cities on mental health and wellbeing 139

7.2 The benefits of playable cities for mental health and wellbeing 142

7.3 Play street, *'Crezco con mi barrio'* (I grow with my neighbourhood) urban95 initiative, Bogotá, Colombia 146

7.4 *Cloud Gate*, Chicago, United States 147

7.5 The Heidelberg Project, Detroit, United States 149

7.6 *Das Netz* (The Net), Berlin, Germany 154

7.7 Adolescents playing a location-based urban health game, *Stadtflucht* (Urban Flight), Frankfurt, Germany 155

7.8 The Playable City: Neighbourhood Scale 157

7.9 The Playable City: City Features 158

8.1 The effects of inclusive cities on mental health and wellbeing 163

8.2 The benefits of inclusive cities for mental health and wellbeing 165

8.3a and b Signs saying 'We Cater to White Trade Only' in a restaurant window in the United States, in 1938; and 'Japanese only' outside a bathhouse in Japan in the year 2000   168

8.4 Children participate in a visioning process in Boulder, Colorado, United States   183

8.5 Rickshaw rides for older people, York, UK   184

8.6 Representation of women in public art about the Holocaust, Vienna, Austria   185

8.7 The Inclusive City: Neighbourhood Scale   188

8.8 The Inclusive City: City Scale   189

9.1 The Restorative City: Neighbourhood Scale   203

9.2 The Restorative City: City Scale   204

Preface

Leveraging the urban built environment to promote good physical health and prevent injury has been a mainstay of planning and design for years. But it took a pandemic for the impact of urban planning and design on mental health to become widely appreciated. The resulting global recognition of the importance of this nexus is what makes *Restorative Cities* so timely and so necessary.

Many policies designed to protect people and communities during the Covid-19 pandemic, particularly social distancing, have had a profound effect on how we interact and live alongside each other. This impact is directly related to the principles of urban design for mental health. While millions of people were affected by physical illness, the predominant personal impact of the pandemic for the majority of the global population has been psychological. For most of us, Covid-19 was characterized by varying degrees of uncertainty, anxiety and loss – of loved ones, of livelihoods and security, of life plans and, crucially, of the ability to interact with the world unrestricted. Mental health problems were triggered and exacerbated, with mental health repercussions predicted to last for years.

The primary aim of most urban policy, planning and design measures implemented during the pandemic was to reduce transmission of Covid-19. While changes to the public realm offered protection from the virus, a side effect was the pervasive impact on our mental health. With commercial, employment, entertainment, cultural, sporting and academic facilities closed or limited, and with policy restrictions on being physically close to each other, opportunities to engage in activities that protect mental health, like socializing, playing and sports, were curtailed. Measures like social distancing floor signage, and road closures to facilitate walking at safe distance, changed how we interact with our local areas and communities. As mask-clad people took wide berths around each other and walked quickly away, so public places were stripped of their conviviality and promoted new tensions as we jostled for safe space on our streets. But the measures implemented to keep people apart also created opportunities for us all to use public space in new ways.

In no setting has this change been more jarring – and more illuminating – than in the bustling density of the city. Around the world, the pandemic paused or reduced the established rhythm of the urban commute and by doing so changed the ways people use cities. Millions were suddenly confined to homes and neighbourhoods that pre-pandemic had simply been our jumping-off point for work and leisure throughout the city. In the liminal space that arose during the various Covid-19 restrictions, the importance of the home and neighbourhood was elevated, and we became increasingly aware of how our everyday environments affect our health and how we feel.

The challenge emerging for planners and urban designers has been responding to policies demanding that they reduce virus transmission while concurrently preserving mental health: how can people be together, but apart? And how can they safely access environments and activities that help protect and restore their mental health during this difficult time, without increasing their exposure to the virus? Policymakers, planners, designers and community members alike have recognized that measures can be taken to keep us physically distanced, but if we are to flourish, we still need access to green and blue natural spaces; to engage our senses; to enjoy casual and meaningful social connections; to be able to walk and cycle and play safely; and to feel included in the life of our city, with our diverse identities, characteristics and needs all fairly reflected, respected and supported. It is no coincidence that many of the planning and design approaches required to meet these needs reflect the pillars of a restorative city that form the basis of this book. As the pandemic evolves, the key will be to build upon the positive – mostly temporary – changes that occurred (including political, behavioural and equity-challenging developments like reduced vehicles on our roads) and to sustain them as part of the future of public mental health.

The science behind how city design can support and promote mental health and wellbeing has existed for years – and is rapidly growing. But its uptake into policy and practice has historically been patchy, marred by barriers like poor awareness, stigma, low funding and a lack of demand from influential advocates. But experiencing the Covid-19 pandemic has helped distil what matters to people within the urban environment, has overcome some of the barriers and, after years of stagnation, has driven widespread progress in urban planning and design for mental health.

One marked consequence of the imposed Covid-19 restrictions was that people gravitated to local beauty spots like parks and riversides to access the positive effects of nature for our mental health and wellbeing. The surge in demand shone a spotlight on the equation of how much we value nature-based places, versus their accessibility, quantity and quality, particularly for city residents. Some parks and playgrounds become so popular that cities felt compelled to close them to prevent overcrowding. Meanwhile private access to green space, such as gardens, became a symbol of privilege and inequity, and in response, the role of public parks in upholding social justice grew in importance. A more equitable response to the demand, increasingly adopted across the world, was not to close existing parks, but to embrace placemaking strategies that expanded new and adaptable park-like spaces into the city's streets and other public spaces. In the longer term, the insights during the Covid-19 pandemic will likely create demand for more balconies/ gardens for homes, and wider local access to community parks, gardens, allotments and other green spaces; it will also hopefully increase focus on the need for equitable access to high-quality public spaces within the urban realm.

Another consequence was the remarkable expediting of infrastructure changes to enable the social/physical distancing mandated by many governments. For years, urbanists have lamented that so much potential space within the city is monopolized by motor vehicles to the detriment of the pedestrians and cyclists who make the streets vibrant. But despite ever-growing evidence of numerous benefits, including to our mental health, without a powerful catalyst for change, the car-free transformation of any inch of road has been a battleground for many cities. With pedestrians and cyclists expanding in number, and crowding together at traffic lights and public transit stops, planners and designers were faced with the conundrum that in many places, enabling people to move at a safe distance through the public realm was both essential and impossible: a person cannot, after all, achieve the mandated six feet of distance while overtaking a slower walker on a sidewalk that is only five feet wide. Covid-19 created a new need for personal space that has demanded urgent solutions. Decades of barriers to achieving more people-centred streets for walking and outdoor recreation were promptly overcome in cities around the world. Short-term urbanist strategies proliferated: the widening of sidewalks, the addition of new cycle lanes, and pedestrianized and traffic-calmed streets popping up all over the world in a matter of weeks. Some of these strategies have led to permanent change, from Paris to New York. Cities have proved that change is not the impossibility it may have seemed: where there's a will, there's a way.

This notion has proved disruptive because the Covid-19 experience has led cities to realize that their resilience, including their economic resilience, depends on their flexibility to make the most of their assets. With so many education, employment, exercise, culture and entertainment facilities traditionally located in poorly ventilated indoor spaces, cities have been compelled to think more creatively about making best use of every last inch of their streets and outdoor public and public-private spaces. Investments in movable, flexible materials that enable shared and diverse uses of space throughout the day, and weatherproofing – including temporary heating and cooling, shade and shelter – have become compellingly strategic investments. The pandemic context has catalysed the advancement of tactical urbanism as a means of testing out temporary spatial ideas to promote health and wellbeing before spending on permanent infrastructure change. Engaging communities in tactical urbanist strategies and co-design promotes empowerment and social capital, whether in redesigning streets for walking and cycling, for play, for art, for performance spaces, for dining, for socializing, even for outdoor classrooms and work meetings, and for opening up new spots for wild swimming.

As the infrastructure for outdoor amenities continues to develop, there is growing recognition that traditional urban planning approaches cannot pick up where they left off. Many cities were designed with downtown cores and other areas that purposefully convene people. These dense, vibrant places are often the parts of the city featured on its postcards: impressive urban landscapes that attract and define the identity of the city and its population; so filled with awe and energy and possibilities that they create an irresistible pull to the city, and justify the investment and sacrifices many people make to be a part of it. These sacrifices often come in the form of residential compromise. There are umpteen examples pre-Covid-19 of affordability and convenience being sufficient to attract new residents to an urban neighbourhood, regardless of its other features. This equation relies on mass transit access to compelling attractions in the city centre. With increasing home working practices, and concerns about the compatibility of gathering in central hotspots with safe social distancing, incentives to leave our own neighbourhoods may be diminishing. Instead, we may look more locally to meet our needs within walking distance from our homes. Covid-19 may have inadvertently speeded progress towards the aspirational '15-minute city' or '20-minute city', with more investment in local community spaces and amenities that promote mental health and wellbeing.

Finally, cities are often described as 'melting pots' but the pandemic showed us some of the separate ingredients. Covid-19 has given us new insights into the different ways people live, and their different needs within the city. It laid bare many of our inequalities. People who live in poverty, in overcrowded homes with no gardens, and with critical public-facing jobs, in greater need of easily accessible and regular public transport, were at more risk of catching the virus. People who could not understand the predominant language were sometimes excluded from public safety messaging. A spotlight was shone on the risk of loneliness for older people and those with certain illnesses that compelled them to stay home and take particular care. Children's social and play needs were recognized but often unmet. Deaf people experienced communications barriers caused by masks, and visually impaired people had navigational barriers due to social distancing needs. And it became clear that policy decisions affected some cultures, ethnicities, religions and other groups more than others. The Covid-19 pandemic, alongside the concurrent

#BlackLivesMatter movement in many countries, exposed our different vulnerabilities, and an understanding that there are many people in our cities whose needs are not met by current design and planning – and this affects their mental health.

But the unique context of the pandemic also catalysed community engagement in more diverse and inclusive urban design, volunteering and equitable collaboration, fairer uses of space, and testing ideas that were not previously politically possible through such tactics as short-term 'pop-ups': public art that is representative of local communities, like the installation of a #BlackLivesMatter statue in Bristol overnight; pedestrianizing roads in New York City and Paris; or expanding a regular Sunday cycle route into weekdays in Bogota.

Covid-19 may have generated uncertainty, anxiety and loss, but it also brought insight, inspiration, motivation. The pandemic has heralded a time of transition for urban planners, designers and public health professionals – and in different ways, for everyone who lived through it. Many of us, with time apart from the amenities and routines that we once took for granted, have had the opportunity to reflect on what we value most, what we miss and what, perhaps, has less value to us than we might have assumed pre-Covid. People are reevaluating their cities, and calling for their needs, and the needs of their diverse communities, to be met. Some naysayers have looked to the countryside, pronouncing the 'death' of the city. But many more have fixed our gazes expectantly upon our ever-evolving cities to be part of whatever comes next.

With a greater priority placed on the interaction between place and health, and with many of the traditional barriers overcome, urban design has incredible potential to create restorative cities that support and promote mental health and wellbeing. The demand and the imperative are finally here, and *Restorative Cities* will help empower readers to make it happen.

Acknowledgements

A number of people contributed to the completion of this book in many different ways, and we extend our thanks to them for their assistance. This includes support from the Dean's Office at the School of Architecture, University of Virginia, who generously funded the illustrations for this book. We are indebted to our illustrator, Spring Braccia-Beck, who worked so brilliantly to translate our ideas into visual images, and to Madeline Smith, our photographic assistant. We also thank the Fellows at the Centre for Urban Design and Mental Health for contributing to thinking across the themes, and to Alice Roe (Researcher, Nuffield Family Justice Observatory) for critiquing all chapters and illustrations. We extend our thanks to all those who generously allowed us to reproduce photographs from their various collections. We also thank our copy editor, Stephen Smith, who came out of retirement to edit the manuscript, and to our editorial team at Bloomsbury, James Thompson and Alexander Highfield.

1

Introduction to restorative urbanism

Why restorative urbanism?

How do you feel about your neighbours? What if there were millions of them? For many people who live in cities, this is already a reality. The world's megacities, particularly in Asia, are set for dramatic growth; Beijing's population, for example, is predicted to grow by 129 per cent to 45 million people by 2050. By 2050, 69 per cent of the world's population will live, work and play in close proximity to many millions of other people. But rates of stress, depression and mental illness are also increasing in urban areas globally. Changes in social networks (including the rise of social media) and social support systems in cities are leading to isolation and loneliness. And the Covid-19 pandemic has affected how people interact and use public open space in cities across the world. With urban growth comes an essential question: how 'well' can we really live in close proximity to 45 million other people? How can we successfully co-exist en masse and flourish as a humanity?

Imagining the city of 2050 means learning how to address the challenges of mass urbanization. This calls for careful thought about our political, economic and social fabric. A fundamental part of this is considering the mental health challenges that these massive urban populations will face – and the increasing need for infrastructure that can help support psychological wellbeing. This includes how we design our cities. Below we set out the first ever framework that specifically addresses how urban design can help tackle these challenges in a model of 'restorative urbanism'.

This is not a challenge unique to the twenty-first century. Throughout history, visionary architects and planners have crafted utopian masterplans to address similar questions about 'liveability' that continue to preoccupy today's urban designers. But not many of these former visions have materialized as intended. In the 1900s, Ebenezer Howard proposed the 'garden city' as a utopian blueprint for a new society and a direct response to London's over-crowded, vermin-infested slums. Inspired by his vision, new towns sprung up in the rural hinterlands of London (including Welwyn Garden City in the 1920s, and today, the re-launched garden city of Ebbsfleet). These new towns have been maligned as 'soulless suburbs' and 'cultural deserts' lacking any sense of place or 'soul' (Gillibrand 2015). In the 1920s, Swiss architect Le Corbusier proposed an alternative blueprint for the Ville Radieuse (Radiant City), a city of glass towers connected by sky bridges, with vast empty lawns interspersed between the towers. Similar images of multi-tier cities were proposed by Italian architect Antonio Sant'Elia, inspiring Fritz Lang's 1927 film *Metropolis*, a futuristic vision of a city with elevated walkways, elevators and monorails. These utopian visions never came to fruition – although the principles later inspired post-war public high-rise housing in the UK and the United States, and today, a re-imagined modernist vision for (largely) private and exclusive developments in China, Hong Kong and Singapore (Figure 1.1). What kind of world will these futuristic 'vertical cities' – with their verdant sky gardens – create? How will they support human belonging and draw people together? And will they succeed where their precedents have failed? Some are sceptical that these city typologies can support the social and economic fabric our cities need. Jan Gehl, a Danish urban designer, has commented: 'There is great confusion about how to show the city of the future. Every time the architects and visionaries try to paint a picture, they end up with something you definitely would not like to go anywhere near' (Kunzig 2019: 85).

This book argues that the future healthy city does not require so radical – or futuristic – a vision. By comparison, it presents a 'quieter' approach that puts mental health, wellness and quality of life at the forefront of city planning and urban design. We define this approach as 'restorative urbanism'. It builds off the principles of restorative environments research and robust, scientific evidence showing how urban design can support mental health. The 'signatures' of restorative urbanism include well-connected cities and effective wayfinding systems; high-quality aesthetics in urban form; dynamic, multi-functioning neighbourhoods that support people's everyday activities; and letting nature right into the city core (Figure 1.2). Our model also assigns importance to the smaller signatures – the settings for 'episodic' moments of city life: the experience of a richly vibrant multi-cultural market, for example; or an impromptu social interaction with a café barista. In this introductory chapter, we set out the framework for the restorative city, describe the key theoretical perspectives contributing

FIGURE 1.1 Oasia Hotel, Downtown Singapore, a re-imagined 'radiant' high-rise city. Source: K. Kopter.

to that vision (including the concept of salutogenesis and restorative environment theory) and define key words at the core of mental and social health. But first: why is it important that we prioritize urban design for mental health now?

FIGURE 1.2 An urban restorative niche offers access to nature and supports mental health. Source: Jenny Roe.

A new urban paradigm for mental health?

The burden of mental health problems is increasing everywhere amongst affluent and poorer countries alike, with rising rates of conditions like anxiety, depression and post-traumatic stress disorder, aggravated by increasing violence and trauma from natural and man-made disasters, political strife and division, and human rights violations (Patel et al. 2018). This is well-documented by the major global health agencies. Depression is the primary driver of disability worldwide (Vos et al. 2015); and one in four people will experience a mental health problem at some point in their lives (WHO 2001), although there are currently big gaps in the data, especially in low- and middle-income countries. The global economic cost of mental illness to society is huge and is predicted to reach $16 trillion (£12 trillion) by 2030 (Patel et al. 2018), mostly due to the impact on work for adults with mental health problems. Meanwhile, basic research into the biology of mental health disorders and drug development for new medications has stalled (Bulleck and Carey 2013). Access to appropriate psychiatric care worldwide is often inadequate (Patel et al. 2018). Whilst there are health advantages of urban living, particularly for the wealthy (Dye 2008), the risk of experiencing a serious mental health disorder, from depression to schizophrenia, is increased by living in the city (Lederbogen et al. 2011). It is believed that this risk is due to increased exposure to social stress in cities, including greater exposure to over-crowding, violence and crime.

Given the scale of the problem, the infrastructure available to solve it is simply not sufficient. New paradigms to support mental health are therefore needed. One area of promise, we propose, is a new mental health urbanism, which we have named 'restorative urbanism'; this book explores how urban design can foster human flourishing in a rapidly expanding world. Before setting out our new model, we first define key parameters of what constitutes 'wellness' and mental health.

What is mental health?

Mental health is a complex construct relating to a person's optimal experience and functioning (Ryan and Deci 2001). The presence of mental health (variously defined in terms of psychological wellbeing and flourishing) is a holistic and multi-dimensional concept that integrates three core components of *hedonic* wellbeing (e.g. happiness, enjoyment), *eudaimonic* wellbeing (e.g. purpose, meaning, fulfilment) and *social* wellbeing (e.g. healthy relationships, connections to others). The World Health Organization (WHO) defines mental health as a state of wellbeing in which every individual realizes his or her own potential, can cope with the normal stresses of life, can work productively and fruitfully and is able to make a contribution to her or his community (WHO 2004). This includes how well we are functioning, our emotional state, the quality of our social relationships, the variety of our interests, and how satisfied and happy we are with our lives (see Box 1).

People who have mental disorders usually experience some combination of problems with their thoughts, emotions, behaviours and relationships with other people. These symptoms cause distress, impair their personal functioning and affect the extent to which they are able to meet the WHO's definition of mental health. Examples of mental disorders include schizophrenia, depression, anxiety, dementia and disorders associated with drug abuse.

Like physical health, mental health is not binary: mental 'illness' and mental 'health' are not diametrically opposed but instead are part of a spectrum (Keyes 2002). A person can be diagnosed with a mental disorder and still be able to realize their potential, cope with the normal stresses of life, work productively and fruitfully and contribute to their community (often with medication and/or psychological support). Likewise, someone with an undiagnosed mental health problem may not be able to do this. The absence of mental illness, therefore, does not necessarily mean the presence of mental health, and vice versa; mental illness and mental health are two distinct but related dimensions (Keyes 2002).

Keyes (2007) has argued that focusing on trying to 'fix' mental health problems is a misguided approach and, alone, will not sustain a flourishing society. Clinical diagnosis of depression, Keyes argues, is just the tip of

Box 1: Definitions of mental health concepts.

Mental health: According to the World Health Organization, mental health is a state in which an individual 'realizes his or her own potential, can cope with the normal stresses of life, can work productively and fruitfully, and is able to make a contribution to her or his community' (WHO 2004). Conceived in this way, mental health encompasses the absence of *mental illness* and the presence of *psychological wellbeing*.

Mental illness (or disorder): A person's experience of a combination of abnormal thoughts, perceptions, emotions, behaviours and relationships with other people that causes distress and can affect that person's ability to flourish and function. Types of disorders include common conditions such as depression, anxiety, post-traumatic stress disorder (PTSD), dementia, attention deficit hyperactivity disorder (ADHD) and substance abuse, as well as less common but often severe disorders such as schizophrenia, autism and bipolar disorder. Different types of disorders are defined in *The Diagnostic and Statistical Manual of Mental Disorders* (American Psychiatric Association 2013) and the *International Classification of Diseases* (WHO 2017).

Psychological wellbeing: This comprises multiple mood (affective) and thought (cognitive) components (Seligman 2011), including:

- Hedonic wellbeing (happiness, enjoyment)
- Eudaimonic wellbeing (purpose, meaning, fulfilment)
- Self-actualization (accomplishments, optimism, wisdom)
- Resilience (capacity to cope, lack of maladaptive problem solving, and adaptive emotion regulation)
- Social wellbeing (healthy relationships).

For the purposes of this framework, we also include healthy cognitive functioning (e.g. attention, working memory).

Flourishing: This includes experiencing high levels of all components of psychological wellbeing, finding fulfilment in life, accomplishing meaningful and worthwhile goals and connecting with others at a deeper level, defined by Seligman (2011) as living the 'good life'.

the iceberg; supporting human flourishing is equally important for mental wellbeing (Keyes 2019). This, we argue, requires a truly 'salutogenic' (health-promoting) approach to how we design our cities, focusing on physical and social attributes that promote wellbeing, as well as treating specific mental health diagnoses. A new mental health urbanism is becoming increasingly important to address as some governments are now shifting away from measuring societal progress in terms of wealth and economic growth (gross domestic product (GDP)) to measuring gross national wellbeing, as in Bhutan, New Zealand and Iceland.

In this book, we conceptualize mental health as both the absence of mental illness and the presence of human flourishing, which are not mutually exclusive.

What is psychosocial health?

Social contact and interactions are critical factors in shaping the psychological wellbeing of individuals and their communities. Social isolation has been linked to increased mortality and lower levels of psychological and physical health (Laugeson et al. 2018; Richard et al. 2017). Loneliness and lack of social belonging are critical risk factors implicated in suicide (Joiner 2005). Social wellbeing includes feeling part of society and believing you're a vital member of that society. The role of urban design in fostering or inhibiting psychosocial health is an emerging area of interest, with evidence suggesting it can support social capital and social cohesion (see Box 2 for definitions). But the evidence is contentious currently, particularly in relation to neighbourhood density. Contact with nature in cities is associated with higher social wellbeing and increased social capital. But large parks and urban green space can act as territorial boundaries between communities and aggravate gang violence and 'postcode wars' (reviewed in The Green City chapter). The empirical evidence remains mixed and is considered separately in each chapter.

Box 2: Definitions of social health concepts.

Social wellbeing: Dimensions of social wellness include social integration (feeling part of society), social contribution (believing you are a vital member of society), social coherence (making sense of the world around you), social actualization (feeling hopeful about the future of society) and social acceptance (feeling good about the people around you) (Keyes 1998).

Social capital: This refers to the extent to which a person can leverage his or her relationships to achieve some particular aim (essentially through the reciprocity embedded in social relationships). Social capital tends to rely more on strong relationships and therefore may not be as 'mutable'.

Social cohesion describes the overall extent to which a social group is connected and harmonious and applies more to a group than to an individual.

A systems approach to mental health

Mental health is a complex problem to address and requires an integrated approach to public health using a systems-thinking perspective. This is an approach to health that recognizes the multitude of interdependent items (or variables) within a connected whole (Rutter et al. 2017). A systems approach to public health recognizes that complex health issues cannot be solved by a single intervention approach but by the reshaping of the interacting factors within the system. In the case of mental health, this includes the availability of good mental health care, fighting poverty and inequality, improving education, opposing violence and discrimination, and social prescribing (i.e. tapping into non-clinical services such as volunteering and community services in a neighbourhood) (Patel et al. 2018). Any integrated approach also needs to recognize a role for urban design in determining mental health outcomes. But too often the role of the built environment is overlooked.

The built environment is vital to reframing the mental health agenda. Contributory factors in this complex system include the provision of safe and healthy housing; reducing exposure to environmental stressors, such as poor air quality (that deplete cognitive resources); and increased opportunities for 'green exercise' (i.e. physical activity undertaken in green spaces) linked with reduced rates of depression. But these factors interact within a bigger system; there is no one cause of depression. Increasing the amount of green space in a neighbourhood may not in itself result in an immediate drop in anti-depressant prescriptions (an association identified by Helbich et al. 2018), but may do so when combined with a complex interplay of other factors – increasing the walkability of a neighbourhood, for example, which in turn increases opportunities for social interaction. The relationship between mental health and the environment, we argue, is an integral – and often overlooked – part of this system. Mental health and environment relationships, whilst not linear, play an important part within this wider complex, dynamic system.

The association between mental health and the quality of the city fabric is well evidenced. Bad housing, poor-quality neighbourhoods, crime and noise, for example, all contribute to social stress, a known risk factor for developing mental health problems. These environmental stressors are part of the wider socio-environmental nexus. This also includes a role for the salutogenic (health-improving) attributes of a city, that is, the physical, social and cultural contexts that support healthy behaviours, de-stress people and help build mental health resilience. This thinking originated in Antonovsky's (1979) theory of salutogenesis: a theoretical perspective that focuses on the creation of health rather than the prevention of disease. It asks: *how can people stay healthy despite life stressors? What creates good health as compared to what causes disease?* Rather than focus on biomedical deficits, this approach is assets-orientated, asking what individual and community capabilities and resources can actively help build health (Lindström and Eriksson 2005). Salutogenic (health-improving) properties of the city are at the core of restorative urbanism: these include a role for parks, squares and gardens; creative place-making endeavours; and interactive art installations, walkable streets and trails, play opportunities for children, youth and older people alike – any attribute that supports strong social networks and builds mental health.

Restorative urbanism

Restorative urbanism is a new concept that places mental health, wellness and quality of life at the forefront of city planning and urban design. It builds on theory and empirical evidence from a body of research called *restorative environments*, which shows how certain places foster recovery from mental fatigue, depression, stress and anxiety. It also builds on a new global urban agenda that integrates health and equity within the wider context of city planning, upon which the Covid-19 pandemic has focused even more attention.

The WHO recommends 'placing health and health equity at the heart of [city] governance and planning' (WHO 2016). For thirty years, the WHO Healthy Cities Program, established in over 1,000 cities worldwide, has promoted comprehensive and systematic policy and planning for health (WHO 2014). The movement has made significant strides (particularly with respect to advancing governance and design for the healthy ageing city and the child-friendly city), but it has paid little attention to mental health outcomes across the age span. Now, with a new global conversation on mental health (Patel et al. 2018) and the role of public open space in the context of Covid-19, there is an opportunity to capitalize on wider urban global strategies. One of the Sustainable Development Goals (SDGs) of the United Nations (UN 2016b) is to 'make cities inclusive, safe, resilient and sustainable by 2030' (Goal 11), addressing road safety, public transport, air quality and increased access to safe, inclusive green and public places. A new urban manifesto was adopted by the 2016 UN Habitat III Quito Conference, which embeds health within a vision for a better and more sustainable future (UN 2017). The UN's 2030 Agenda for Sustainable Development is to 'ensure healthy lives and promote wellbeing for all at all ages' (UN 2016a). The targets of the UN's SDGs and New Urban Agenda – setting global standards for equitable, inclusive and sustainable urban development – are supported by extensive collaboration with the WHO on urban health, and the publication of practical guidance on how to integrate health into urban planning and governance worldwide (UN-Habitat and WHO 2020).

These global policy drivers offer a supportive framework for a new 'restorative' urbanism focused on mental health outcomes. It is also important to recognize that our model of restorative urbanism operates within a bigger system that overlaps with other urban frameworks that include the 'regenerative city' (i.e. a resource-efficient and low-carbon city that enhances planetary health) and the 'resilient city' (which can adapt to and withstand future shocks, such as natural or man-made disasters, through sustainable and inclusive growth, which, in turn, contributes to mental health).

What is a restorative environment?

A restorative environment is any setting that helps us regulate our emotions and recover from mental fatigue, stress and the demands of everyday life. Restoration has been defined as the process of recovery from a depleted psychological, physiological or social resource (Hartig 2007). Two theories currently dominate the literature on restorative environments: attention restoration theory (ART) (Kaplan and Kaplan 1989) and stress reduction theory (SRT) (Ulrich 1983). ART focuses on the effect of environments on cognitive demands, whilst SRT looks at the influence of environments on emotional wellbeing and physiological stress recovery.

In the ART model, Kaplan and Kaplan posit that natural settings are inherently rich in fascinating stimuli (leaf patterns, the shape of a tree branch) and command our attention without any effort (defined as involuntary attention), a process which allows us to overcome mental fatigue. These settings, high in 'soft' fascination, provide just enough interest in the surroundings to hold one's attention but not so much as to exclude room for reflection. In contrast, man-made urban environments (such as urban streets filled with traffic and noise) grab our attention dramatically (defined as direct attention), leaving no room for reflective thought; indeed, mental effort is needed to overcome the stimulation, depleting us cognitively.

Natural settings are believed to promote restoration by creating a sense of being away: nature can create a feeling of psychological and/or geographical distance from our everyday demands. Furthermore, the extent to which it can do this is important: nature can create a setting 'rich enough and coherent enough so that it constitutes a whole other world' (Kaplan 1995: 173). Finally, natural settings offer compatibility: a good fit between our goals and the kinds of activities supported, encouraged or demanded by the setting.

The ART model proposes four successive stages in a restorative experience (Kaplan and Kaplan 1989: 196–7): first, 'clearing the head' of distracting thoughts; secondly, recovery of directed attention capacity; thirdly, a process of contemplation or 'cognitive quiet'; fourthly, a deeper state of restoration, reflection on one's life, priorities, possibilities, actions and goals. This process of reflection is defined as 'the most demanding of all in terms of both quality of the environment and duration required' (Kaplan and Kaplan 1989: 197). Hundreds of studies have shown that settings with a higher proportion of these key restorative ingredients (i.e. fascination, being away, extent and compatibility) will contribute to cognitive and affective restoration. The evidence is particularly strong for exposure to natural environments, with some limited evidence for other settings (cafés, libraries, art galleries, museums, aquariums and historic city districts) (Staats 2012).

The second theory, SRT (Ulrich 1983; Ulrich et al. 1991), posits that our immediate response to our environment is an affective and aesthetic response that triggers the body's stress response. The affective response is evoked by the visual stimuli of a setting (called 'preferenda') and involves an immediate 'like–dislike' response accompanied by physiological changes (to heart rate, blood pressure and stress hormones such as cortisol) that support recovery from stress. According to Ulrich, the preferenda (or attributes) of an environment that are believed to promote this response include the complexity of a scene and the presence of a focal point.

Most of the research on restorative environments has focused on individual-level psychological restoration (e.g. individual cognitive, stress and mood recovery). More recently, it has been posited that restoration in one individual may extend to another – that is, there is a spread of benefits beyond the person immediately affected (Hartig et al. 2013). These benefits may be in the form of a renewed relationship with another significant person (e.g. an increased sense of trust or appreciation), termed 'dyad restoration', or the benefits might spread within a group, termed 'collective restoration' (Hartig et al. 2013). It is feasible, given that a restorative environment recovers our attentional capacity, that it can make us more attentive to those around us. The benefits may extend to our 'significant others' (i.e. our friends, family or colleagues). Collective restorative benefits also accrue from chance encounters amongst people who don't know each other – for instance, from convivial interactions at cafés, whilst walking in the park, or at a festival. You might meet the same people more than once, say, getting your coffee from a regular barista. Blau and Fingerman (2009) have described the people involved in these peripheral social encounters as 'consequential strangers' and assign them a significant role in social wellbeing. The authors also posit that the quality of these encounters will also depend on the quality of the place in which they occur; for example, we might avert our gaze from other pedestrians whilst walking in a run-down neighbourhood, but walking in a pleasant urban park we may turn our gaze towards another, even say 'hello'. They define the latter as 'being spaces' (i.e. welcoming, safe spaces that encourage social connection). Hartig et al. (2013) suggest that the positive emotional contagion sparked by such settings ('mass psychogenic wellness') may also increase our relational resources, allowing us to adopt a more empathic perspective on those around us. As yet, collective restoration – or the power of impromptu encounters – has yet to be empirically studied other than in the context of vacations (Hartig et al. 2013). Understanding how these types of social encounters can help combat loneliness in those most at risk (e.g. the elderly, young people) could help advance interventions and concentrated effort at times of the year when people are most vulnerable to loneliness (e.g. national holidays, periods of confinement due to illness/quarantine).

Health inequity is an injustice that undermines our societal capacity to flourish, with wealth (and greed) at the top obstructing the human potential of those below. Globally, this is exasperated by racial segregation, poor housing, poor education and poor welfare. The consequence (in the United States, as one example) is that longevity for the poorest in society is actually shrinking. Restorative urbanism, we argue, is one way to approach health inequity. Some places appear to foster more health and social equity than others; places with a greater number of recreational and urban green facilities, for example, can reduce the mental wellbeing gap between rich and poor. In a European survey of thirty-four nations, socioeconomic inequality in mental wellbeing was 40 per cent narrower among people with good access to recreational and urban green space facilities compared to those with poorer access (Mitchell et al. 2015). This is consistent with other studies showing that the positive health effects of green areas are stronger for those experiencing greater poverty. Mitchell (2013) and colleagues have coined the term 'equigenesis' to describe the environments that help create this type of healthy equity. Whilst few studies have shown the effects of equigenic environments, it appears some attributes of place (including access to parks) could 'level up' population health more than others, supporting the health of poorer people as much as, if not more than, that of wealthier individuals. A core interest of the restorative framework presented here is, what kinds of places can make us more 'equally' mentally healthy? And what features of places might be described as equigenic?

The restorative city framework

In this book, we think about the restorative city from both a large-scale perspective (e.g. transport infrastructure) and a micro-perspective that includes our everyday 'episodic' activities (e.g. life on the bus, life in the square, life in the café). Our framework for the restorative city (Figure 1.3) integrates the

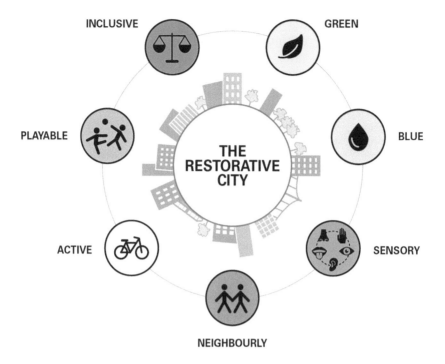

FIGURE 1.3 The Restorative City Framework.

concept of an 'inclusive city' (or equigenic city, as set out above) with six additional typologies: the green city (taking nature into the city core), the blue city (maximizing access to water settings for wellbeing), the sensory city (immersing all five senses), the neighbourly city (supporting social cohesion), the active city (supporting cognitive and emotional wellbeing through mobility), and the playable city (offering opportunities for all-age creativity and play).

Putting science into practice

The theory and ideas set out in this book are driven by research, drawing on the most up-to-date scientific evidence from a variety of sciences (psychology, public health, geography, anthropology, urban planning) for each component of the 'restorative' system. Where possible, we draw on the most recent systematic review of a topic, which summarizes the most robust existing research on that topic and provides a high level of evidence on the effectiveness of a particular environmental approach for mental health outcomes. In emergent areas of interest (e.g. the playable city), we have undertaken our own critical literature searches to inform our ideas and identify new theories and approaches to the design of cities for mental health. When applying the evidence to advance mental health practice, it is important to distinguish between evidence-based practice (EBP), which draws on the highest possible level of evidence (e.g. systematic reviews) and robust evidence from randomized control trials (RCTs), and evidence-informed practice (EIP), which draws on less robust types of evidence in combination with clinical knowledge.

Whilst this scientific evidence has largely originated in Western (and wealthier) world contexts, we incorporate research from across the world, and our recommendations are intended to help direct the physical and social fabric of cities not just in high-income countries, but also in low- and middle-income countries, particularly those facing exponential growth in Africa and Asia. By including examples from around the world, we aim to show how the ideas are translatable to a wider range of global contexts.

This book is designed with urban designers, planners, architects, landscape architects and public health practitioners in mind, but it is also intended for playground designers, artists, community groups and anyone who wants to better understand how to create places (using art, artefacts of cultural or historic interest, or social interventions) that support wellbeing. Each chapter presents, first, the theoretical framework that underpins a particular theme, followed by the empirical evidence that supports a relationship between that theme (e.g. urban green space) and mental health outcomes, and then offers broad-brush design guidelines at both a community level (smaller scale) and a city level (larger scale). This is not a 'rule' book; that is, our ideas are not intended to be prescriptive but are meant to be interpreted broadly within the special context of a place, to be considered at a local level and with a freedom of expression and creativity.

Our book begins by exploring the relationship between natural systems and mental health. In Chapter 2, we present the 'green city' and how access to urban green space can help support psychological wellbeing in the general population and help alleviate the symptom severity of serious mental illnesses such as schizophrenia and ADHD. In Chapter 3, we turn to 'blue space' and the role of urban water settings – both engineered water bodies (e.g. waterfronts, canals, urban fountains) and natural systems (e.g. rivers, lakes, ponds) – in supporting mental wellbeing. Whilst the research (and attention) on 'blue health' benefits is largely concentrated on coastal settings (particularly in the UK), we also consider land-locked locales and the potential for sustainable urban water systems (e.g. rain gardens, green roofs, swales) to deliver co-benefits for mental wellbeing and resilient infrastructure.

Chapter 4 explores the sensory signatures of a city – the smells, sounds, tastes and tactility of city life – and how these characteristics bring a place to life and feed into social (and emotional) processes that people respond to in a particular place. Hitherto not much attention has been paid to the mental health benefits that arise from the rich sensory textures of a city; here we argue that attentiveness to 'the senses' in urban design is paramount for wellbeing. This chapter also considers design for those with sensitive sensory needs, including those with autism and dementia.

Chapter 5 explores how we co-exist and live alongside others in neighbourhoods, and how this has a key role in our wellbeing and restorative health. We explore how heterogeneous city neighbourhoods embrace diversity, foster community participation and build community spirit, social capital and social cohesion. We consider some new social city models, including intergenerational co-sharing (e.g. in housing and social care), and explore how urban design interventions can help support and integrate vulnerable groups, such as the homeless or ageing populations, in the life of a city.

Next, in Chapter 6 we turn to the 'active city' and how urban design that increases opportunities for physical activity not only benefits physical health but also delivers co-benefits for mental health. By flagging these co-benefits, we aim to leverage this data to accelerate a strategic shift in thinking about 'active design' that prioritizes mental and social health as much as physical health.

In Chapter 7, we set out a vision for the 'playable city' that puts all-age play – including urban gaming – at the heart of better-connected and more socially cohesive cities. This is a new human-centred urban design approach that aims to create playful interactions with a city that surprise, inspire new thinking, and foster curiosity and engagement with place – and that benefit mental wellbeing across the age span.

Chapter 8 brings together the restorative design opportunities detailed in this framework using a lens of inclusion. We look at how diversity can be fostered so cities can span divisions and bring people from all walks of life together in the 'inclusive city'. In an increasingly polarized and unequal world, we suggest how urban design can help bridge the divide and promote equity in mental health outcomes; this includes a role for the multi-cultural city and equal access to healthcare and recreational facilities as well as access to bustling high streets and vibrant street markets.

Throughout the book, we build a comparative database of evidence for each of the above themes – or 'episodes' of a city – to present a comprehensive vision of the 'restorative city' in the final chapter. Chapter 9 draws together the complete anatomy of the restorative city and the systems that can support mental and social wellbeing.

We hope that this book will inspire imagination and creativity and a more human-centred design approach to the future city. We hope it will inspire you, your community, city mayors and those that govern our built environment to apply a creative and social imagination to thinking about city growth from the perspective of mental wellbeing and quality of life. Restorative urbanism is an incremental model; it builds in small pieces (or 'episodes') – and might include some riskier pieces that disrupt the status quo, as in the 'playable city' – that work towards a strong urban core that supports mental health. It is a vision, we believe, that is attainable in diverse local contexts, and that rests on solid scientific evidence. There is really no reason – given the forecast of increasing mental health disability presented at the beginning of this chapter – not to take action on at least one small 'episode' in your own city.

2

The green city

Highlights

- Robust scientific research has found that exposure to natural environments (green space) can help reduce depression and stress, improve cognitive capacity and help manage the symptoms of anxiety disorders, schizophrenia, ADHD and dementia.
- Nature exposure in childhood reduces the risk of developing mental health problems in adulthood.
- The impact of green space on mental health is modified by the amount of green space involved, accessibility of that green space from home, the type of green space, views of nature, perceived quality of green space, richness of biodiversity involved, usage patterns and the amount of exposure.
- There are inequalities in people's experiences of – and access to – the green city that impact mental health. Design approaches should focus on maximizing green space quantity, quality and accessibility across the city, with particular investment for children, youth, older people, and marginalized groups.

Key concept definitions

Urban green space: There is no universally accepted definition of urban green space. Here we use the term loosely to describe any urban place that includes vegetation, such as public parks, private and community gardens, streetscapes that include trees/green verges, urban woodlands, green walls/roofs integrated into the built urban fabric, sports fields, children's play areas that also incorporate grass/trees etc.

Incidental nature exposure: Contact with nature (or green space) in the community, home or workplace without consciously choosing it (e.g. catching a view of nature through a nearby window or during a work commute).

Intentional nature exposure: An active interaction with nature through consciously visiting a park or choosing to take a walk in a natural setting.

Dose–response relationship: The relationship between the amount of exposure (dose) to green space (frequency and duration of time spent there) and the resulting health outcomes.

What is the green city?

Green space and wellbeing have been intrinsically linked for centuries. This association particularly captured the attention of policymakers and planners in the 1800s, and by the late nineteenth century and early twentieth century, designing urban green space for health and wellbeing was growing in popularity – particularly in Europe and North America. Wellbeing was a key consideration driving the creation of some of the world's best-loved parks, including Hyde Park in London and Central Park in New York City. Pioneer urban planners of the early twentieth century, like Patrick Geddes and Ebenezer Howard, considered green space for health and wellbeing to be central to neighbourhood planning, manifesting in developments like the Garden City movement of the 1930s; these new towns in London's greenbelt inspired similar developments around the world. Envisaged as an alternative to the overcrowded slum conditions of London, a guiding principle was to bring nature into the heart of the city whilst maintaining a protective ring of greenbelt on the outer fringes. Despite these developments, improving mental health through green urbanism then fell out of vogue for decades, forgotten amongst other town planning and public health priorities.

But in the last thirty years, that interest has returned, accompanied by a powerful body of research demonstrating the health benefits of urban greening. This research tells us that those urban planners of old were onto something: it is increasingly clear that designing nature into cities can impact people's physical and mental health. Some of the strongest research evidence finds that urban green space is associated with reduced deaths from all causes (Rojas-Rueda et al. 2019). There is less research evidence relating to the links between urban green space and specific diseases, including mental health outcomes, but this evidence is growing. In this chapter, we set out the theory and science supporting a relationship between mental health and urban green space and present a case as to how urban green space can support public health, recreational and environmental policy.

Theory

Whether our contact with urban green space is incidental (e.g. a view through a window) or intentional (e.g. choosing to walk in a park), exposure to natural settings has the potential to affect our mental health and wellbeing. The specific impact depends on the type of encounter and the duration and frequency of that encounter (Figure 2.1), which interact with a host of individual, household and societal characteristics to influence mental health and wellbeing. Through different routes, urban green space can trigger psychological and physiological responses that bring about positive mental and social health outcomes.

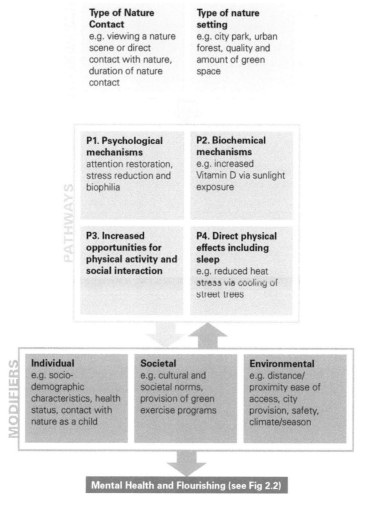

FIGURE 2.1 Effects of green space on mental health and wellbeing.

There are four key pathways by which urban green settings seem to positively affect mental health, two of which are direct and two indirect.

The first key pathway is direct impact of the nature experience itself on mental health. There are three posited theories of how exposure to nature may exert these benefits. The first, attention restoration theory (ART) (Kaplan and Kaplan 1989), attests that our response to nature is primarily a cognitive one, and that the soft stimuli of nature – the patterns created by light falling through a tree canopy, for instance – attract our involuntary attention. The amount of 'fascination' in the natural environment – the curiosity and wonder that the natural world inspires – is a critical environmental cue in the process of psychological restoration. It enables people to pay attention to the complexity of nature, allowing time for reflection without exerting any cognitive demands like concentration. This is linked with three other attributes that nature provides: a sense of 'being away', extent (a sense of a whole 'other' world) and compatibility (a good fit with our intentions and goals). The second theory, stress reduction theory (SRT) (Ulrich 1983), suggests that our response to nature is primarily an emotional one, which, in turn, triggers a response in our parasympathetic nervous system and slows down our stress response, inducing calm (see Chapter 1 for a full summary of the processes associated with environmental psychological restoration). Finally, the biophilia hypothesis (Wilson 1984) suggests that biologically, human beings have a psychological orientation of being connected to all living systems and an innate need to connect with the natural world, and that such environments are inherently associated with lower stress levels than more urban environments. This belief has led to worldwide advocacy projects for urban greening, including the Biophilic Cities network, bringing together cities around the world that emulate natural systems in all forms of cityscapes and buildings.

The second key pathway by which nature affects mental health is through biochemical mechanisms. Exposure to sunlight from being outdoors is linked to improved cognitive functioning (particularly in the elderly) and provides a vital source of Vitamin D (Gill 2005). Research has also proposed that exposure to a diverse variety of bacteria present in natural settings may bring immunoregulatory benefits and reduce inflammation (Rook 2013), and that the phytoncides (volatile organic compounds with antibacterial properties) released by trees may explain some of the health-promoting benefits of green space exposure (Li et al. 2009; Tsunetsugu, Park and Miyazaki 2010).

The third key pathway by which green space affects mental health is indirect, by providing settings in which activities that support mental health and wellbeing can take place. For instance, urban green space facilitates impromptu or organized social encounters (see the Inclusive City and Neighbourly City chapters); physical activity such as walking, jogging and cycling (the Active City chapter); and play (the Playable City chapter).

A fourth pathway by which urban green space can support mental health is by modulating the physical environment to deliver physical health benefits that, in turn, impact mental health. For instance, the cooling influence of urban street trees on surface radiating temperature (SRT) reduces heat stress (Salmond et al. 2016), and tree benefits to noise mitigation can improve sleep quality and reduce the risk of developing cognitive impairment, hypertension and cardiovascular disease, and type 2 diabetes (De Ridder et al. 2004; Sarkar, Webster and Gallagher 2018b; Wolch, Byrne and Newell 2014). Vegetation can also improve air quality by acting as a natural filter for ambient particulate matter (e.g. PM2.5) that improve respiratory health (Irga, Burchett and Torpy 2015), which, in turn, may impact mobility behaviours that support mental health.

Many of these pathways have been explored empirically; in the next section, we document the scientific evidence showing positive effects of urban greening on psychological wellbeing.

The impact on mental health

The twenty-first century has witnessed a surge in the number of scientific articles identifying links between urban green space and health. The majority of these articles have originated in Europe and North America, with an increasing number emerging from China, South Korea and Japan. A number of systematic reviews (synthesis of study results using a rigorous method) bring together the most compelling evidence for the health benefits of urban greening, including benefits to physical activity (Bowler et al. 2010; Lachowycz and Jones 2011; Twohig-Bennett and Jones 2018; van den Berg et al. 2015). Two systematic reviews have focused exclusively on mental health (Gascon et al. 2015; Houlden et al. 2018).

Urban green space exposure has a role in reducing the development of mental health disorders and in managing symptom severity of specific conditions (Roe 2016). Amongst the most powerful evidence for the positive effects of urban greening on mental health are robust large-scale population health studies capturing neighbourhoods and, more rarely, citywide or nationwide associations. However, these are mostly cross-sectional studies (i.e. describing what is happening at a given moment in time), so causation cannot be inferred (Gascon et al. 2015). Only a few longitudinal studies capture the effects of increased exposure to urban green space or of efforts to improve access over time (for a summary, see WHO 2016). Increasingly, studies have been able to use longitudinal data, which, combined with high-quality study designs, has provided more robust evidence and indications to support a causal relationship between urban greening and mental health. However, the data in these larger studies mostly relies on multiple self-report ratings using tried-and-tested psychological scales (e.g. mood scales) that run the risk of self-report bias (i.e. people respond inaccurately, consciously or not, because they are seeking social desirability or approval). More recently, studies have applied objective health indicators, including the use of anti-depressant prescriptions as a proxy for depression prevalence, along with biomarkers of cardio-vascular disease and physiological stress. Below we document the evidence for the benefits of green cities in sustaining and supporting mental health in the general population. These benefits are summarized in Figure 2.2.

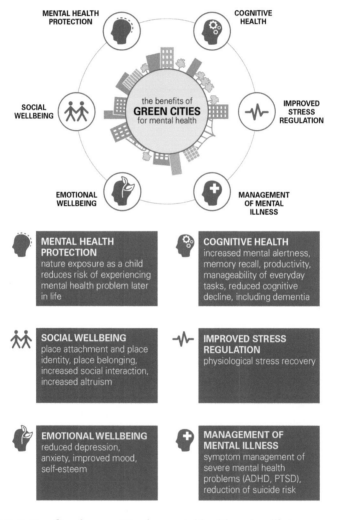

FIGURE 2.2 Benefits of green cities for mental health and wellbeing.

Green cities confer general mental health benefits from childhood

Research has shown that children who grow up with local-area green space are less likely to develop a serious mental health problem in adulthood. A Danish study mapped the amount of green space around the homes of almost 1 million Danes and showed that children living amongst higher amounts of green space were up to 55 per cent less likely to experience a multitude of different mental disorders (including schizophrenia) later in life (Engemann et al. 2019). The study showed that the risk decreases incrementally the longer a child has been exposed to green space, from birth up to the age of ten. Providing access to green space throughout childhood is therefore an important priority for urban planning. Furthermore, a Dutch study found that higher amounts of local-level green space are associated with a reduced risk of suicide (Helbich et al. 2018), with a strong geographical variation for amplified suicide risk. Both of these studies need to be confirmed in other international contexts.

Green cities help reduce depression and improve mood

A number of large-scale population health studies have shown protective effects of residential green exposure on depression and mental wellbeing (Alcock et al. 2014; Beyer et al. 2014; de Vries et al. 2016; Groenewegen et al. 2018; Nutsford, Pearson and Kingham 2013; Taylor et al. 2015; Triguero-Mas et al. 2017). All of these cross-sectional studies were carried out in high-income countries and consistently show that higher quantity of urban green space in a residential neighbourhood is associated with lower odds of people experiencing depression. Some have identified distance metrics associated with this relationship – for example, more greenness within 1 km of home was associated with 4 per cent lower odds of depression and within 3 km of home, 2 per cent lower odds of depression (Maas et al. 2009). Very few studies have scoped countrywide data, with one exception: a nationwide study of ten UK cities identified that higher levels of local-area green space are associated with lower odds of having a major depressive disorder (Sarkar, Webster and Gallacher 2018a). The benefits were strongest amongst people under the age of sixty, women, those living in poorer neighbourhoods, and those living in more compact neighbourhoods (i.e. higher urban density). Another national study, in the Netherlands, found more green space to be associated with lower anti-depressant prescription rates (Helbich et al. 2018). This is one of the first studies to indicate a dose–response relationship between quantity of green space and prescription rates. It identified a potential critical threshold value at which green space benefits may operate: 28 per cent (or more) green space in the residential neighbourhood is required for mental health gains. Whilst these findings warrant further replication and testing, they have interesting implications for the greening of towns and cities.

A novel and interesting development is the use of smartphones to collect mental health data in real time in urban green space (referred to as mHealth). A UK study (Bakolis et al. 2018) used a smartphone app to deliver ecological momentary assessments (EMAs), capturing 100 people's location, their exposure to natural features in the environment and their momentary subjective wellbeing over the course of a week. The study found that being outdoors, seeing trees, hearing birdsong and contact with nature were associated with higher levels of subjective mental wellbeing. The research also found that the effects lasted for up to 2½ hours after the original assessment and that effects were stronger for people with higher trait impulsivity (i.e. people prone to impulsive behaviours are also at greater risk of experiencing mental health problems).

Smaller quasi-experimental studies (carried out in the real world as opposed to a laboratory setting) have shown the positive effect of exposure to green space on symptoms associated with depression. Rumination (when an individual repetitively focuses on negative emotions and thoughts) is linked to onset of depression and can be reduced by contact with green space. A ninety-minute walk in a green environment has been found to decrease both self-reported rumination and cortical brain activity associated with rumination, whereas the same duration of walk in an urban setting had no effect (Bratman et al. 2015). This type of study design (i.e. juxtaposing the effects of walking in natural settings as compared to urban 'grey' environments) is common in research design in the 'green health' field.

Green cities reduce stress disorders, including PTSD

The evidence of a beneficial impact of nature exposure on stress disorders is still under review and focuses on the effectiveness of nature-based therapies – direct nature interactions facilitated by specialist staff in a range of contexts, from urban gardens to wilderness settings. A Danish study found nature-based therapy (an intensive nine-hour-per-week intervention with various individual and group components) was as effective as cognitive behavioural therapy (CBT) for treatment of stress disorders (Stigsdotter et al. 2018). Further research has identified the beneficial effect of nature-based therapy on symptom severity management in war veterans experiencing post-traumatic stress disorder (PTSD) (for a review, see Roe 2016). Collectively, these studies suggest that nature-based activity can significantly reduce PTSD symptomatology and depression. But few studies have followed veterans over time – or indeed explored other PTSD patients in different contexts using rigorous trials.

Some of the most convincing studies showing the stress-relieving effects of exposure to urban green space use physiological biomarkers, indicators of stress that can be measured in the body. These include the use of salivary cortisol, amylase, telomere length and improved cardiometabolic health (for a review, see Kondo et al. 2018) as well as biomarkers of allostatic load (a quantitative measure of the cumulative 'wear and tear' on the body resulting from stress) (Ergorov et al. 2017). A significant body of pioneering research in this field has surfaced in Japan in recent years, where *shinrin yoku* (forest bathing) is a popular practice defined as 'taking in the atmosphere of the forest' (for reviews, see Hansen et al. 2017; Tsunetsugu et al. 2010). Participants in *shinrin yoku* spend time in the forest directed by an instructor to either sit or walk slowly and consciously be mindful of nature. Forest bathing is associated with health benefits for the immune system (an increase in the count of the body's natural killer (NK) cells), cardiovascular health (reduced hypertension), the respiratory system (fewer reported allergies and respiratory disease) and psychological wellbeing (improvements in mood, stress, depression, anxiety). The extent to which these results can be applied to the wider population tends to be limited by their small sample sizes (between 8 and 120 participants), and by the fact that they have mostly been carried out with university students and are somewhat skewed by gender and age. Similar studies of conscious interactions with nature in the West that match these findings are limited.

Green cities mitigate the symptoms of schizophrenia and other psychotic disorders

Navigating busy, noisy city streets can have a detrimental effect on people with diagnosed psychotic disorders, increasing levels of anxiety and paranoia. By contrast, walking in urban green space can improve psychological wellbeing and functioning in people with schizophrenia and other forms of psychosis (Roe and Aspinall 2011a). In addition, urban walks rich in historic fascination can improve wellbeing, suggesting that walking in carefully chosen urban environments (e.g. with interesting building facades) can promote mental wellbeing in people with severe mental health problems. Neighbourhood aesthetics and the presence of street trees have also been associated with better health outcomes for people with schizophrenia, including improved cognitive functioning and increased walking activity (for a review, see Roe 2016).

Attention deficit hyperactivity disorder (ADHD) and behavioural problems in children and young people: Some of the strongest evidence for a positive effect of urban green space on mental health problems relates to attention deficit hyperactivity disorder (ADHD). Across a series of studies, a group at Illinois University have consistently demonstrated that the symptom severity of ADHD is reduced when playing in 'green' settings as compared to play sessions in 'hard' landscapes (Taylor and Kuo 2011). This team has investigated 'dose' effects of nature in children with ADHD, comparing a twenty-minute walk through an urban park with walks through less green settings; children with ADHD performed significantly better after walks in the park, exhibiting higher levels of concentration than after walks in the other settings. The authors suggest that a regular 'dose' of daily nature might serve as a safe, inexpensive and easily accessible tool for managing ADHD. Research carried out in Europe has also reported higher levels of emotional wellbeing and cognitive functioning in children with ADHD and behavioural problems from time spent in woodland versus urban and/or indoor school settings (Roe and Aspinall 2011b; van den Berg and van den Berg 2011).

Autism spectrum disorder (ASD): The risk of autism in childhood may be reduced in neighbourhoods with greater proximity to green space (as captured by tree canopy coverage) and lower road density (Wu and Jackson 2017). Another cross-sectional study from the United States explored the effects of proximity to green space and 'grey' space (defined as impervious surfaces such as tarmac) on anxiety outcomes in youth with autism spectrum disorder (ASD) as compared to typically developing children. This study showed different effects between the two groups, with proximity to green space (as measured by tree canopy) *increasing* the risk of anxiety in children with autism but not for typically developing children (Larson et al. 2018). This points to different – and potentially more complex – relationships with green space for youth with autism. Current evidence, though limited, suggests that engagement with the natural environment may benefit children on the autistic spectrum.

In summary, the potential for nature settings to help manage the symptom severity of specific mental health disorders is promising; there is also some evidence to suggest that people with severe mental health problems may gain more from nature exposure and interaction than those in 'good' mental health (Roe and Aspinall 2011a). But the evidence is weak: there have still been only a few randomized controlled trials (RCTs); most are qualitative studies with small sample sizes, lacking replicability across experimental designs and measures and having a limited urban (and international) focus. We must advance this research to generate a more robust evidence base that can direct rehabilitation strategies and guide mental health policy.

Green cities help boost cognitive health

Several studies have shown positive benefits between nature settings and attentional capacity (for a systematic review, see Ohly et al. 2016). Exposure to nature is also associated with improved working memory (by up to 20 per cent), executive functioning and self-regulation (Berman et al. 2012; Berto 2005; Kaplan and Berman 2010), and is often accompanied by improved mood (Berman et al. 2012). The power of nature on brain activity has been shown by several studies using functional magnetic resonance imaging (MRI) scans and electroencephalograms (EEG). MRI scanning has shown that when viewing urban scenes without nature, blood flow to the amygdala – the 'fight-or-flight' part of the brain – increases, suggesting our brains view cities as hostile environments (Kim et al. 2010). Natural scenes, by contrast, light up the anterior cingulate and the insula, areas of the brain associated with empathy and altruism. Several mobile EEG (electroencephalography) studies have identified the neural signatures of different urban settings, showing how walking in urban green areas as compared to busy, noisy streets activates different areas of the cerebral cortex, with increases in alpha activity (relaxation states) and decreases in beta activity (attentional demands) (Neale et al. 2019); these benefits have been shown across ages, from young people to older adults.

Nature exposure seems to have positive effects on children's cognitive functioning (Wells 2000), impulsivity (Taylor, Kuo and Sullivan 2002), and memory and attentiveness in school (Dadvand et al. 2015). Access to an outdoor nature classroom – or 'nature schooling' – is also associated with improved cognitive recall in children (Hamilton 2017) and adolescents (Fägerstam and Blom 2013), richer language use (Waite, Evans and Rogers 2013), more spontaneous thought and creative peer collaboration (Waite and Davis 2007), and improved behaviour in children at risk of exclusion from school (Roe and Aspinall 2011b) (see below for further impacts on child behaviour). Likely environmental factors affecting these outcomes include reduced pollution (noise and air) and reduced heat stress, operating through urban greening in the vicinity of schools and the neighbourhood environment.

A novel longitudinal cohort study in Scotland, UK, has shown associations between increased park provision as a child and better cognitive ageing in adulthood (Cherrie et al. 2018). This is an important finding, showing how exposure to nature as a child may have long-term effects on cognitive functioning into adulthood and later life. It suggests a need for good – and equitable – park provision throughout life, especially in childhood.

Some evidence has shown the benefits of nature-based therapy for the emotional and social wellbeing of people with dementia, although this evidence is still quite limited (for a systematic review, see Lakhani et al. 2019). Most of the evidence relates to residents in care homes, half of whom – on average – have some form of dementia or cognitive impairment. The benefits seem to be associated with improvements in both mood and agitation. In addition, there may be a role for urban green space and gardens in supporting the mental health of caregivers of people with dementia, given that carers themselves are at increased risk of mental health problems. As yet, there is no evidence to show any improvements to cognitive functioning from time spent in urban green space amongst people with dementia or those with cognitive impairment living in the community.

Green cities improve social cohesion

The mental health and wellbeing benefits of social engagement are described in detail in the Neighbourly City chapter, and social contact is one postulated pathway that may help explain how contact with urban green space enhances mental wellbeing. People interact in green spaces on an impromptu social basis (e.g. whilst walking the dog) or via organized social and sports events in a local park (e.g. a picnic or ball game). However, the relationships between urban green space and social wellbeing are complex, and the evidence is limited. Two Dutch studies have shown associations between streetscape greenery and perceived social cohesion (de Vries et al. 2013) and between green space quantity and perceived loneliness and social support (Maas et al. 2009). Other studies have found associations between green space and subjectively reported stress and social wellbeing (Ward Thompson, Aspinall and Roe 2014). Though not showing direct associations, all of these studies indicate that social cohesion may mediate the relationship between urban green space and health outcomes (see Figure 2.1).

The impact of social encounters (impromptu or otherwise) on psychological restoration has not been studied directly in the field, nor has the possible spread of benefits that might derive from dyad (paired) or collective restoration amongst groups of people experiencing individual restoration (Hartig et al. 2013). It is likely that green space facilitates a stronger sense of place attachment, and that this, in turn, may strengthen the sense of community in a neighbourhood. An Iranian study has shown a direct relationship between the amount of time spent in green space and increased social contact in adolescents, as measured by the number of close friends (Dadvand et al. 2019). Elsewhere, studies have shown that the presence of front gardens on a street can significantly increase social interactions within a neighbourhood (Roe and Ward Thompson 2011). In a community experiencing flooding from sea level rise, the presence of urban green space improved social networks, thus offering greater potential resilience to 'at risk' communities (Marín et al. 2015). In an increasingly polarized society, urban parks and squares may also contribute to a sense of civic pride and serve as places where anyone, regardless of income, can meet, debate and publicize their causes. Exposure to nature has also been shown to enhance feelings of generosity and acts of altruism (for a review, see Goldy and Piff 2019). These studies suggest that urban green spaces may act in the collective good as sites of 'civic promise' (Amin 2006: 1020). However, evidence showing the protective effects on social health from such interactions with urban green space is sparse.

Modifiers of impact

Demographic and socioeconomic factors: Age, gender, race, income, education, occupation and culture all play a significant role in modifying the impact of the natural environment on health outcomes. A number of studies have shown mental health benefits of green space exposure for specific sub-population groups, including women (Roe et al. 2013), ethnic minorities (Roe, Aspinall and Ward Thompson 2016), ethnic minority children (McEachan et al. 2018) and older people (Pun, Manjourides and Suh 2018), who typically spend more time in the neighbourhood environment than working-age adults. But there are inconsistencies in the findings, and we cannot assume uniform mental health benefits across particular sub-groups. A few studies have shown that race and ethnicity do moderate relationships between green space and health outcomes in the UK (McEachan et al. 2018; Roe et al. 2016), whereas others have shown that they do not (Roberts et al. 2019). Again, perceptions of urban green space are significant moderating variables and are associated with underutilization of parks, for example, amongst Hispanic populations in the United States (Das, Fan and French 2017). We must continue to explore access to urban green spaces amongst marginalized groups, and future research should consider potential demographic modifiers.

Cultural modifiers: Urban green space and its mental health benefits have largely been conceptualized from a Western perspective. Understanding how different socio-cultural values, traditions and perceptions impact green space meaning, usage and benefits (combined with different conceptualizations of mental health) is crucial in developing culturally sensitive design and policy strategies, including for low-, middle- and high-income countries. Research on this topic from Africa, the Middle East and Asia is critically scarce (du Toit et al. 2018; Lindley et al. 2018), and policymakers in these places may lack locally relevant evidence on which to build urban design, recreational and health policies. A few studies have shown the importance of local contextual differences in green–health relationships. In the Mongolian city of Ulaanbaatar, access to green space was not associated with mental health outcomes; poverty and safety concerns (e.g. crime rates and compliance with societal rules) were stronger predictors (Shagdarsuren, Nakamura and McCay 2017). Other studies, whilst not explicitly exploring health outcomes, have identified distinct cultural differences in user perceptions and usage of green space in Turkey (Özgüner 2011) and Ethiopia (Girma, Terefe and Pauleit 2019). There is a need to recognize the different cultural contexts that may modify green–health relationships whilst also broadening the international context for this research.

Health equity: Evidence has shown that nature may help reduce the gap in health inequity between the rich and the poor; green space seems to have a stronger relationship with mental health outcomes for people living in poorer neighbourhoods (White et al. 2019). However, these neighbourhoods typically have fewer urban parks, which are often of poor quality, poorly maintained and underutilized (CABE 2010). Gentrification further widens such divisions. The High Line in New York City is an oft-cited example of 'eco-gentrification' that greens poor neighbourhoods but, rather than democratizing public space, typically drives property prices up and forces low-income residents out. This gentrification is almost never the intention, but without some form of housing protection for low-income residents, it is almost inevitable. Cities such as Paris and Berlin have managed this process more effectively. For instance, the parks movement in Paris in the 1980s – owing to its sweeping scale – delivered impacts across the city in poor and wealthy neighbourhoods alike. The gentrification argument, however, cannot be used to dissuade against landscape urbanism or rehabilitation of poor neighbourhoods; exemplar models of inclusive planning exist – such as Gleisdreieck Park (a former railway) in Berlin, which was designed with community input and rent controls in place – and offer an alternative vision.

In summary, whilst evidence is growing, it is unclear precisely what characteristics of green space (e.g. accessibility, usage patterns, aesthetic and biodiversity quality) are beneficial to mental health. In addition, it is unclear how different contextual factors affect the relationship between urban green space and mental health. Advancing this research is particularly urgent in low- and middle-income countries owing to the pressure on open space from development associated with rapid urbanization in Asia and Africa, for example.

Design approaches for a green city

Eight key characteristics of green space should be considered when designing a green city with a view to delivering benefits for mental health and wellbeing, but as noted in Chapter 1, these operate within a larger whole with other interdependent factors:

1. **Amount of space:** The amount of nearby green space is the physical characteristic most strongly associated with benefits for mental health outcomes (for a systematic review, see Houlden et al. 2018). But exactly 'how much' green space (i.e. what percentage of land-use cover) makes a difference to mental health is not known. Studies have found effects with higher quantities of green space (43 per cent and above, Roe et al. 2013), but also for lower quantities (28 per cent threshold, Helbich et al. 2018). Other studies report that it is the individual perception of the amount of green space that matters to subjective wellbeing (Ward Thompson, Aspinall and Roe 2014), suggesting that cities consult with local communities on what is 'sufficient' versus 'not enough'.

2. **Accessibility:** Restrictions on movement in many cities during the Covid-19 pandemic and 'stay-at-home' control measures have underlined the importance of neighbourhood access to local green space. Access is measured objectively either as the distance from home to the nearest public green space (as the crow flies), using buffer zones around postcodes (e.g. at 100 m, 500 m and 1 km), or subjectively via self-report measures (e.g. perceived amount of time taken to get to a local green space). Several studies have found associations between these access metrics and mental health outcomes (Bos et al. 2016; Houlden et al. 2018; Triguero-Mas et al. 2015), though the associations are limited. These have led to various standards for access being implemented by some countries (e.g. Natural England's Accessible Natural Greenspace Standard (ANGSt)). Cities should aim to create new areas of green space whilst also improving access to – and the quality of – existing green space, with provision ideally within five to ten minutes' walking distance (or within 300 m) from home.

3. **Type:** A wide range of types of green space are associated with positive mental health outcomes, ranging from street trees, city parks and pocket parks to urban forests and wilder city nature settings. For instance, one longitudinal Swedish study classified green space around residents' homes into five types and identified that 'serene' nature (i.e. quiet, audible nature, with bird sounds etc.) was most strongly associated with improved mental health in women over time (Van den

Bosch et al. 2015). Only one study has identified relationships between specific land cover types and mental health: in Australia, tree cover (of at least 30 per cent) was associated with less psychological distress than other forms of urban greening like grass (Astell-Burt and Feng 2019), suggesting more complex vegetation typologies can help improve mental health outcomes. These studies are in their infancy but suggest that type of green space warrants further investigation, and that urban tree canopy may be a preferred option for mental health benefits.

4. **Views:** Increasing visual access to nature in the city has important implications for mental health outcomes; this might be viewing nature from a window (e.g. views of an inner courtyard or tree-lined avenue) in a residential or workplace context (Gilchrist, Brown and Montarzino 2015; Pretty et al. 2005; Vemuri et al. 2011), but the evidence of how this affects mental health outcomes is not yet conclusive (Houlden et al. 2018). Randomized controlled trials (RCTs) are an excellent method for understanding cause–effect relationships. In Philadelphia, an RCT found that being able to see 'green' (fenced-off) vacant lots was significantly more likely to improve mental wellbeing, reducing feelings of depression and worthlessness, than either unkempt or tidy non-green vacant lots (South et al. 2018). This study suggests that simply viewing nature – as opposed to being physically present (or active) in it – is important for mental health. This type of study needs replication in other cultural contexts and for groups with restricted mobility who typically spend more time at home, such as older people, or people with cognitive or physical impairments. Views of nature for those in confinement play a role in mental health – for instance, during pandemics like Covid-19 – including for people who are self-isolating or in quarantine at home, residing in care homes, or in hospitals recovering from illness.

5. **Quality perceptions**: Not all green space delivers equal health benefits. Individual perceptions of quality, aesthetics and personal safety – which are also related to the management and 'tidiness' (or 'tameness') of green space – are strong determinants of usage patterns, which, in turn, predict mental health outcomes. This is also tied to inequities in park usage since low-income neighbourhoods often have poorer-quality green space, which may also become the setting for crime and other anti-social activity (Groff and McCord 2012). In a review, Calogiuri and Chroni (2014) concluded that the perceived quality of green space (including safety and aesthetics) is essential to increasing physical activity. Understanding perceptions of quality within a local community – and social and cultural variations – is therefore vital prior to creating, or making changes in, urban green space.

6. **Biodiversity quality:** Urban green space that is 'rich' in biodiversity has been linked to increases in psychological wellbeing. A UK study of twelve urban parks found that psychological wellbeing was associated with indicators of biodiversity (i.e. plant and animal species richness), irrespective of age, gender or ethnicity (Wood et al. 2018). There is some evidence to suggest that tree canopy is particularly supportive of biodiversity (Astell-Burt and Feng 2019), which lends more support to arguments for trees over other types of green space. Whilst further research is needed to replicate findings, we suggest that urban planning should enhance ecological diversity in urban green areas to improve mental health outcomes and support planetary health.

7. **Climate and seasonality:** The effect of climate/seasonality (e.g. extreme heat, cold, rainfall, snow) on usage patterns of green space is unclear, but efforts to encourage year-round usage of green space should be facilitated by providing shelters, outdoor heating options in winter (infrared heaters) and cooling mist systems in hot climates (see Chapter 3).

8. **Increasing the amount of time in green space:** Research suggests that people who spend at least two hours per week in nature have better wellbeing than people who spend no time in nature (White et al. 2019). This study also suggests that how the total time outdoors is attained (whether in one long stretch or several short visits) does not affect the outcome, but that the greater the weekly 'dose' of nature exposure, the greater the benefit (up to about five hours for mental wellbeing). Further replication is needed to confirm these patterns, but, informed by this evidence, cities should help facilitate increased usage of green space (e.g. by facilitating guided walking programmes or a 'green-prescribing' health policy).

Green prescribing for mental health problems

Given the strong evidence for 'green health', some doctors, policymakers and service providers are interested in 'green prescriptions' to help patients with mental disorders like depression and anxiety manage their symptoms. Set within the context of 'new models of care' and social-prescribing trends, these initiatives are gaining ground in such countries as the UK, the United States and Japan. Social prescribing is a process by which patients are connected to sources of support and activities within their local community that offer non-medical options to work in tandem with medical interventions. These types of referral programmes have the potential to address many of the factors that perpetuate mental health problems, such as the need for social interaction, as well as, in the context of 'green prescriptions', nature interactions that can provide stress relief and improve mood. Green-prescribing programmes in England (e.g. www.adoseofnature.net) have reported significant improvements in subjective wellbeing, including 'green exercise' programmes (walking in green spaces), nature skills/creative arts and tree planting. The evidence is slowly growing in this area; we need to better understand how we can maximize uptake of and adherence to these programmes as well as what works for whom and in what circumstances.

Green city examples

Paris's Isles of Coolness, France

Just over 9.5 per cent of Paris is given over to parks and green space – the lowest proportion of any European city (by comparison, London has 33 per cent, Vienna, 45 per cent). Paris has pioneered innovation in urban park development, from Parc de Buttes Chaumont (1867) to the radical new parks programme instigated under Mitterrand's *grand projets* in the 1980s (including Parc de La Villette, Parc Andre Citroen, Parc du Bercy and Le Promenade Plantee, the original elevated 3-m long 'high line' on disused train tracks) to its present-day vision for a sustainable, environmentally resilient city. Paris has long been held as an exemplar in its egalitarian vision for public parks, delivering high-quality parks in deprived areas (e.g. Parc de Belleville, Parc Georges-Brassens), which owe their success, in part, to participatory design and engagement with the local communities, who are fiercely proud and protective of their local parks.

That vision continues to the current day, with bold plans to make Paris an exemplar of urban resilience. Designed to tackle Paris's heat-island effect, an innovative programme called *Illots de Fraicehur* (Isles of Coolness) is converting tides of concrete and tarmacadam spaces in the city into cooling green spaces to provide relief from summer heat stress. This includes a widescale greening of forty schoolyards under the Oasis programme (Figure 2.3). The first of the public Isles of Coolness opened in 2018 at the forecourt to Station F (thirteenth arrondissement), at the *plages* (beaches) on the River Seine (between Pont Neuf and Pont au Change) and at the Gare de Lyon. The plan is to ultimately connect these islands and offer a smartphone app to inform residents where these cooler spots can be found. This is to be accompanied by converting car lanes into green boulevards, with some 200,000 new trees and around 500 acres of new green roofs. Surprisingly, however, evidence from Paris on the health benefits of such strategies is sparse compared to other European cities.

FIGURE 2.3 Oasis schoolyard project, Paris, France. Source: Ville de Paris.

Moscow's Krymskaya Embankment, Russia

A former abandoned riverside embankment – on the Moskva River – was transformed into an all-season linear park as part of an intensive urban revitalization programme in Moscow, catalysed by the awarding of the 2018 FIFA World Cup to Russia in 2010, the appointment of Sergei Sobjain as mayor and collaboration with US urban designers (including Diller Scofidio + Renfro, designers of New York City's High Line) (see Figure 2.4). Running 1 km alongside the river, the park includes a Fountain Square facing a

FIGURE 2.4 Riverside Embankment, Moscow, Russia. Source: Martin Knöll, TU Darmstadt.

modernist contemporary art hall, a series of artist-designed pavilions (providing cafés, bike rentals, craft and design shops), a series of small 'green hillocks' that offer year-round recreational opportunities (walking and resting in summer, sledding/skiing in winter), plus hard-engineered 'hills' (for cycling, skateboarding, parkour) and creative night-time illumination. The park connects with an 8-km long green pedestrian/cycling route along the Moskva River linking the Pushkinskaya, Andreevskaya and Vorobyovskaya embankments. It is one of many new urban design interventions that have transformed Moscow over the last ten years; other examples include Zaryadye Park, the first public park to be opened in Moscow in fifty years, transforming a 13-acre derelict site and emulating Soviet landscape typologies (steppe, forest, wetland and tundra). These developments represent a turnaround in thinking about the role of public space in Moscow, embracing a new 'softer' urbanism in contrast to typically austere Soviet architecture. The shift in mindset is quite dramatic and was articulated by Anna Kamyshan, a Ukrainian architect working in the city: 'It's not really [a] simple thing to do in post-Soviet country because [before this park, public space was] not even [a] word' (Zacks 2018). Whether these new public 'green' domains will contribute to the democratization of Russia's public life remains to be seen, but for now, they are improving the quality of everyday life in the city.

Design principles for a green city

General principles

- Maximize use of green space across the city, including both direct exposure (such as park use) and indirect exposure (such as green space experienced en route to work or via a view).
- Maximize green space in close proximity to all homes.
- Maximize accessibility to green space.
- Maximize investment for children, youth and older people.

Neighbourhood scale (see Figure 2.5)
Integrate:

- Front porches and front gardens
- Green roofs and walls
- Street trees
- Connected walkable and bikeable corridors (e.g. canals, green city trails)
- Pocket parks (within a five-minute walk from home)
- Larger urban parks (within a fifteen-minute walk from home)
- Accessible transport to immersive nature (e.g. a forest)

City scale (see Figure 2.6)
Integrate:

- Internal atria/courtyards with natural features
- Views of green space from workplace
- Green roofs and walls
- Street trees
- 'Fresh air' squares/pocket parks within a short walk from workplace
- Connected walkable and bikeable corridors to and from work

Accessibility to green space

- Connect pocket green spaces with green streets to create a series of interconnecting green spaces across the city.
- Open up schoolyards, school/university recreational sports fields and courts to the public.
- Use lighting (ideally solar-powered) to keep parks and sports spaces open late and safe for walking.
- Choose robust green space facilities available in all kinds of weather – cool in summer, with heat for winter.
- Provide plenty of seating and (well-maintained) public toilets in public parks for the less mobile, seniors and children.
- Provide facilities for outdoor recreational activities in parks (e.g. yoga, tai chi, Nordic walking).
- Use mobile apps to identify local and city green space resources for a community.

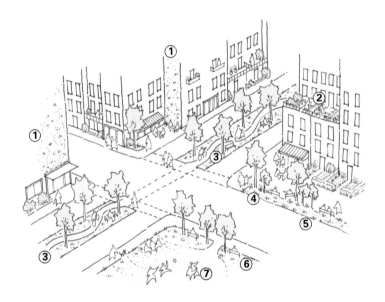

1 green wall
2 green roofs + gardens
3 linear park
4 street trees
5 green edges
6 green space seating
7 pocket park

FIGURE 2.5 The Green City: Neighbourhood Scale.

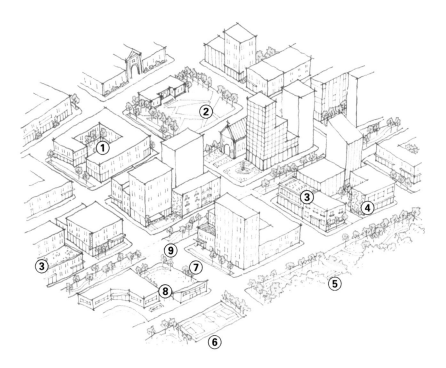

1 green courtyard
2 large downtown park
3 green roof
4 green wall
5 large park
6 shared playing field
7 green edges
8 pocket park
9 linear park

FIGURE 2.6 The Green City: City Scale.

3

The blue city

Highlights

- Scientific evidence shows that exposure to urban water settings (blue space) can help improve mental wellbeing; the benefits include increased subjective wellbeing, a reduced risk of depression and stress alleviation.
- The most common type of blue space explored in the research is coasts.
- 'Blue care' – therapeutic interventions using blue space – can assist in the management of mental health disorders such as PTSD and enhance social relationships.
- Access to water may be particularly important for emotional wellbeing in children and older people.
- The evidence is limited to only a small number of scientific studies. However, evidence informed practice (EIP) might consider the existing evidence to explore how access to blue space in our cities can be improved.
- Whilst water is one of the most important aesthetic qualities in the urban landscape, water engineering is expensive. Greener, 'soft-engineered' water management solutions (swales, berms, retention ponds, reed beds) offer several benefits in terms of cost, water management and health gains.
- Maintenance of urban water features is critical if their potential to assist psychological wellbeing is to be realized.

Key concept definitions

Blue space: Outdoor environments – either natural or manmade – that prominently feature water and are accessible to people either proximally (being in, on or near water) or distally/virtually (being able to see, hear or otherwise sense water) (Grellier et al. 2017). These include coasts, rivers, lakes and engineered water features such as canals and urban fountains.

Blue care: A therapeutic nature-based intervention using blue space.

Heat-island effect: The phenomenon of increased temperatures in urban areas compared to nearby rural areas, associated with human activity and how surfaces absorb and hold heat.

What is the blue city?

The power of water to move us emotionally has long been recognized by poets and artists, articulating what we all intuitively feel about moving water – be it the sea, a river or a fountain – and the unique magic and wonder it harbours. We play in it, swim in it and are hypnotized by the flux and flow of water as it moves across terrain, slope and surface. The potential healing power of water has been harnessed for centuries, from the thalassic therapies of ancient Egypt, Italy and Greece to the brisk sea-bathing tactics used to treat a range of nineteenth-century maladies, from heat stroke to melancholy. Taking in the sea air and ocean views was a critical part of the treatment and was perceived as good for rest and rejuvenation. Coastal and inland spas sprung up around the world, and at its height, there were some 200 'water cure' facilities in the United States alone (see Foley et al. 2019 for further documentation on the use of water as a curative agent across the centuries). Today, hydrotherapy is still used to support recovery from physical injury and as a means of pain relief. But the application of 'blue care' for psychological wellbeing and physical health had been somewhat forgotten until the recent emergence of research endeavours exploring 'blue health' (the health benefits of access to our coasts, rivers and canals), led by several European research groups. This chapter considers the mental health benefits associated with urban blue space across a range of geographical contexts, from coastal cities to inland cities, alongside urban sustainability strategies such as water-sensitive urban design (WSUD) that help manage flooding and promote resilient cities. By 'urban blue space', we mean any environment which fosters human interactions with water: from walking along a canal tow path, interacting with the sparkle and flow of a city water fountain, or passive visual contact from a window or even through virtual reality.

Scientific evidence showing positive effects of urban blue space on psychological wellbeing is still emerging, compared to the more established field of research on 'green health' (see Chapter 2), which shows that contact with urban green space supports a wealth of mental health benefits, including recovery from mental fatigue and stress alleviation. Urban blue space is, more often than not, a hybrid landscape accompanied by green space and has therefore largely been considered under the umbrella of green space. Whilst it is evident there is overlap – interactions with blue space offer a range of physical, mental and social health benefits much akin to green space – blue space arguably offers alternative experiences and a different type of sensory experience and can deliver different benefits and outcomes (Haeffner et al. 2017).

Blue space provides alternative opportunities for physical activity (e.g. swimming, canoeing, sailing); it offers different multisensory experiences, including sonic appeal (fast-moving water; calm, still waters), visual contact with different types of flora and fauna (fish, dragonflies), haptic opportunities (e.g. dipping a finger or toe in water; full-body immersion) and olfactory sensations (healthy and unhealthy water smells). As yet, we do not fully understand the complexity and nuanced differences in how our interactions with blue space compare to those with green space, the differences in impact of varied water typologies and conditions (frozen, flowing, roar, trickle, static, stagnant etc.), or coastal versus inland experiences of water. What is known, however, is that contact with blue space elicits mental health outcomes similar to those associated with green space. Taking a walk along a downtown waterfront, for example, can improve stress regulation (Roe et al. 2019). Viewing images of the sea in a virtual reality environment can reduce the pain experienced at the dentist (Tanja-Dijkstra et al. 2018). In this chapter, we address why water settings have this positive effect on us, citing research from around the world to show how access to water can sustain our psychological wellbeing. We also suggest that – despite limitations – the evidence presented here can help inform policy to increase access to water for mental health outcomes.

Theory

There are three key pathways through which blue space operates to bring positive mental health outcomes (Figure 3.1).

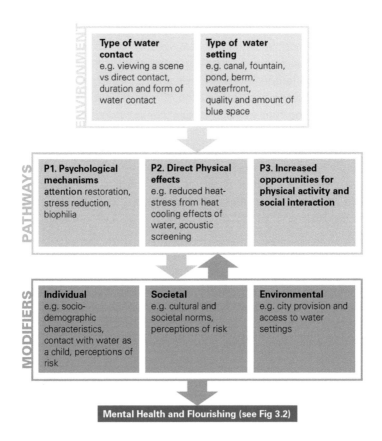

FIGURE 3.1 Effects of blue urban design on mental health and wellbeing.

The first pathway is the direct impact of the water experience on mental health. The way in which exposure to blue space may exert mental health benefits is closely aligned to our understanding of how nature exerts these effects via green space (see Chapter 2). It is posited that contact with water augments and therefore enhances the theoretical attention restoration, stress reduction and biophilic impact of green space (see Chapter 2, page 20). This augmented impact may be associated with water settings being more biodiverse and supporting a richer range of species, a predictor of restorative experiences (Wood et al. 2018). Our levels of fascination, curiosity and engagement (three important triggers of restorative experiences; see Chapter 1) are arguably higher when interacting with moving water (e.g. crashing waves, dramatic waterfalls) than, say, for a static green scene.

The second pathway by which blue space can support mental health is through physical contact with water. One example of this is by reducing heat stress in hot climates via mitigating heat-island effects with cooling water. Extreme heat has an adverse effect on mental health and can make people less mobile, less energetic, more agitated or listless. People may become less productive, and cognitive tasks (such as working memory) can be significantly impaired through heat stress (Hancock and Vasmatzidis 2003). Sleep is also affected (Okamoto-Mizuno and Mizuno 2012), which, in turn, is linked to cognitive difficulties, particularly for older people. People with a pre-existing mental illness are at greater risk of mortality from heat stress (Bouchama et al. 2007), including from suicide (Page, Hajat and Kovats 2007). Extreme heat is associated with increased aggression and violence; interpersonal and intergroup conflict increases between approximately 4 and 10 per cent for each standard deviation in temperature rise (Hsiang, Burke and Miguel 2013). Water can provide a cooling function that mitigates heat stress.

The third pathway by which blue space affects mental health is indirect, by providing settings in which activities that support mental health and wellbeing can take place. For instance, urban blue space provides settings for impromptu or organized social encounters (see the Inclusive City and Neighbourly City chapters), physical activity (such as swimming, kayaking, walking along a canal; the Active City chapter) and play (the Playable City chapter). Notably, blue space offers greater scope for more intense exercise (swimming, kayaking etc.); we may walk farther to negotiate a water body and its bridging points, increasing levels of physical activity.

There is some limited evidence to suggest our experience of blue space varies across the life span. Our experiences of water as a child may modify the effect of blue space on our health as an adult; our subsequent memories of blue space may be stronger owing to a direct physical interaction with water; in turn, stronger (and happier) memories may predispose us to more intense restorative experiences of contact with water as an adult. Whilst water play provides valuable opportunities for child creativity and development, children may be excluded from such activity owing to parental fears around the safety risk (e.g. of unprotected edges of canals and ponds). Some research shows lower blue space usage amongst households with children (Haeffner et al. 2017), and Pitt (2019) suggests that parental 'hydrophobia' causes parents to be more guarded and vigilant with a child in a blue setting. Whilst child safety is paramount, parents need to better understand the benefits of contact with water for child development and emotional wellbeing when weighing any associated risk.

Older adults seem to have distinctly therapeutic relationships with water settings (Finlay et al. 2015). Research has shown that access to blue space for older people constitutes a symbolic connection with the past that can support psychological wellbeing later in life (Coleman and Kerns 2015); these water settings have been shown to support seniors in crafting a sense of a present and future self during ageing. Vicarious engagement with water (experienced in the imagination or through secondhand engagement) and watching ocean waves roll in and out offer a means of coping with day-to-day challenges in older age, including the process of loss and grief. In this way, blue spaces act as a resource to assist independent living and coping resources. This suggests that exposure to blue spaces as a child and the place memory of blue spaces may be particularly important for wellbeing later in life.

Finally, our planet's health and our emotional health are intimately interconnected. To be mentally healthy, it is posited, we need to be ecologically attuned to our environment (Capaldi, Dopko and Zelenski 2014). Being aware of the impact of environmental degradation in our cities and its effect on mental health outcomes is vital to the dialogue on urbanization and mental health.

The impact on mental health

The scientific evidence for the blue city's effects on mental health and wellbeing is still emerging. When health outcomes are measured as part of blue city projects, they are often an afterthought rather than a key driver for catalysing urban change. Whilst it is important to advance our knowledge of health and blue space relationships using robust scientific approaches, the evidence does point to significant opportunity for blue space to act as a mental health resource, supporting emotional health as well as resilience from heat stress and climate change. Gascon et al. (2015) carried out the first (and so far only) systematic review of evidence on the health benefits of blue space, identifying thirty-six quantitative studies, of which just twelve identified the potential benefits for mental health of living near or deliberately visiting blue space. Much of the research meeting the stringent requirements of the review is from a European or Australasian coastal context, and very little of the research found any associations between blue space and specific mental health problems. There has also been one scoping review of urban, freshwater blue space (Völker and Kistemann 2011), as well as one systematic review of 'blue care' interventions focusing on the benefits of therapeutic interventions in blue space (Britton et al. 2020). The findings are summarized below and in Figure 3.2.

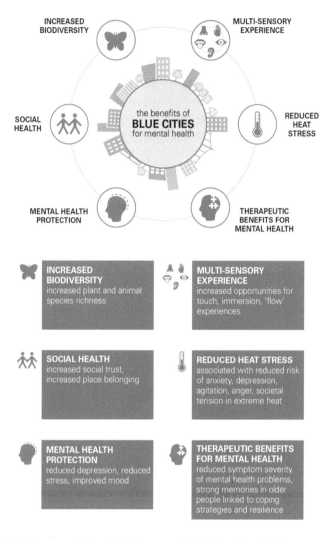

FIGURE 3.2 Benefits of blue cities for mental health and wellbeing.

Blue cities may reduce the risk of depression and improve mood

Very few studies have identified the relationship between depression and exposure to urban blue space. Gascon et al. (2015) found only four studies that have identified associations between blue space and reduced risk of depression (Alcock et al. 2015; Triguero-Mas et al. 2015; White et al. 2013a, 2013b), with one further study (Gascon et al. 2018) showing associations with green space but not with blue space. Subsequent to this review, a study from

Hong Kong, carried out predominantly in older adults, found associations between intentional visits to blue space for recreation and reduced risk of depression, combined with higher odds of subjective wellbeing (Garrett et al. 2019a). Views of blue space, by comparison, showed no association with depression (although the authors did find an association between visual contact with blue space and improved general health). Contrary to the Hong Kong study, a study in older adults in Ireland found that visual contact with sea views was linked to reduced odds of depression, with a stronger association for visual contact than for physical proximity to coastal blue space (Dempsey et al. 2018). In New Zealand, higher visual contact with blue space (oceanic and freshwater) within a 15-km buffer from home was associated with reduced psychological distress in adults and adolescents (Nutsford et al. 2016). Collectively, these studies suggest that both age and cultural factors may modify the effects of blue space on health.

In terms of mood, Gascon et al. (2015) identified several studies reporting improved mood (including happiness) from contact with blue space across a range of ages and settings. Using a smartphone app, adults reported feeling happier in marine and coastal areas as well as freshwater, wetlands and flood plains, as compared to being in any other type of urban or rural setting (MacKerron and Mourato 2013). In children (aged 11–16), increasing exposure to water bodies (ocean, lakes, rivers, streams) was associated with better emotional wellbeing (Huynh et al. 2013). In children (aged 7–10), time spent on the beach was associated with reduced emotional problems and greater pro-social behaviour, as reported by parents (Amoly et al. 2014). Access to an urban waterfront was associated with improved mood, including hedonic tone and energetic vigour (Roe et al. 2019).

Blue cities can reduce stress

There are very few studies exploring real-time stress responses to exposure to urban blue space. Roe et al. (2019) showed that a short walk along a downtown waterfront in West Palm Beach, Florida, improved psycho-physiological stress as measured by heart rate variability (the beat-to-beat interval variability of heart rate) and perceived stress levels. Furthermore, a temporary tactical urban intervention along the waterfront designed to increase comfort levels significantly improved self-reported stress and reduced physiological stress as measured by heart rate variability. The intervention directly engaged participants' sense of escape and their levels of fascination with the blue environment (achieved via historical imagery of the sea) and improved the waterfront's comfort level by offering shade and seating. This unique experiment showed how real-time stress responses to blue environments can be improved by relatively simple and low-cost interventions.

Blue cities can support social health

Only two studies to date have found relationships between access to water and social health. One study identified improved social wellbeing (as measured by social support) but found that results were inconclusive (Triguero-Mas et al. 2015). Another study exploring coastal waterfronts found significant positive change on social wellbeing indicators (including social trust and sense of belonging) from walking along a downtown waterfront designed with short-term seating, shade and interaction opportunities, as compared to an exposed and empty section of the waterfront (Roe et al. 2019). Although the evidence is currently very limited, access to canals and waterways arguably affords significant opportunities for social connections, either impromptu – from, say, walking the dog – or from organized sports activities (canoeing, rowing) or recreational activities (barge festivals, barge music events). Any activity that encourages people to engage with a water setting (e.g. through connecting with the industrial heritage of a city) will also likely generate social connections and cohesion (see the Sheffield example below).

Modifiers of impact

Water is one of the most important aesthetic attributes of the landscape (Kaplan and Kaplan 1989). But not all blue space is equally 'blue' or beneficial to health. If blue space is not cared for or well maintained, the potential for restorative health outcomes is reduced. Water may become stagnant (and smell) or heavily littered and have negative health impacts. Pools of standing water, for example, are breeding grounds for mosquitos in certain climates, increasing the risk of such mosquito-borne diseases as yellow fever, malaria, West Nile virus and Zika virus.

The variance in water quality – its perceived colour and clarity – means that not all blue space is inherently therapeutic. High-quality water is essential for any immersive water-based activities and is aesthetically preferred. When water is tainted a muddy brown or yellow, it has less restorative potential (Smith, Croker and McFarlane 1995).

Water, like green space, can give rise to thoughts associated with foreboding – flood risk/fear of drowning – as well as ambiguity and negative associations that cannot always be termed therapeutic (Pitt 2018). This is particularly pronounced for communities living with the threat of sea level rise and increasing flood risk. Our relationship with water may therefore be 'unhealthy' if associated with certain contexts and negative associations/memories.

Design approaches for a blue city

There has of late been a move towards regenerative blue urban design – a turning back towards city waterfronts and riverways as vital civic and economic arteries, with a role in promoting mental health that is not always fully acknowledged or leveraged. One of the advantages of blue urban design is that it brings instant aesthetic improvement and restorative potential to a city, unlike green space interventions, which need time to mature. One downside can of course be the cost of the development and maintenance of highly engineered structures. Given that urban blue space development can also contribute to gentrification and rising property prices (see the Inclusive City chapter), ensuring inclusive access and controlling rents in blue space zones are important in protecting vulnerable populations.

Opportunities for integration of blue space into urban planning and design will, more than any other feature of the Restorative City, be influenced by the existing geography.

Coastal cities

Research into the mental health benefits of blue cities has largely concentrated on coastal settings. Living within 1 km (0.6 miles) of the coast – and to a lesser extent, within 5 km (3.1 miles) – has been associated with better general and mental health (Garrett et al. 2019a). The frequency of a coastal visit is also a possible factor, as is the duration of the visit and the activity intensity (Garrett et al. 2019b). This suggests improving access to city waterfronts, regenerating coastal towns and providing transit options to the coast may offer mental health benefits. But what if you live in a land-locked country or state?

Inland waterways

The benefits to mental health of rivers, lakes, canals and even city fountains are less well publicized. For years, cities have overlooked their riverfronts; former hubs of economic activity, many city riverfronts have become neglected in the post-industrial era – forgotten, blighted eyesores. The 1980s heralded a regenerative urban 'blue' design programme, with cities turning towards their rivers to spark economic and civic regeneration; Bilbao, Valencia and Seoul are just a few examples of cities that have remade themselves along their respective rivers (see the Seoul example below). Riverside views and access to water now command some of the highest property prices in a city, in turn creating a new problem of inequitable access. Ensuring the revitalization of our inland urban riverways delivers societal and health benefits for all and is discussed further below and in the Inclusive City chapter.

Designing therapeutic blue space

The concept of 'therapeutic blue space' has emerged over the last two decades, building upon Gesler's original conceptualization of a therapeutic landscape as one in which 'the physical and built environments, social conditions and human perceptions combine to produce an atmosphere which is conducive to healing' (Gesler 1996: 96). This has been explored mainly from the perspective of historic places of healing, such as Epidauros in Greece (Gesler 1993), Lourdes in France (Gesler 1996), or sacred wells (Foley 2010) and springs (Burmil, Daniel and Hetherington 1999). Research on current-day 'blue care' therapeutic interventions has been slow to grow and leans strongly towards qualitative methodological approaches in small samples. Thus, the evidence is growing slowly, and health and recreational policy, in turn, is slow to respond. Britton et al. (2020) synthesized evidence from thirty-three studies using 'blue care' interventions (including beach activities, swimming, sailing, fishing, canoeing) facilitated by outdoor educators and healthcare providers, and targeting individuals with specific mental health problems (including PTSD, addiction, depression and cognitive disabilities) as well as people with physical disabilities and injuries. Most of the interventions took place in coastal locations and in the developed world (Europe, United States, Canada, Australasia). Overall, positive effects were found for mental health and social wellbeing in the short term, but results were inconsistent and mixed across studies. The authors identified that the studies took very different approaches to study design and methodology. Since most studies involved group facilitation exercises, separating out the social dynamics from the environmental variables in the experiment (e.g. a grey built environment versus a blue setting) is a challenge in this type of research. Research by Bell et al. (2015) has shown the complexities of studying blue space interactions and health outcomes, highlighting the multiple and nuanced ways in which people engage, experience, recall and interpret coastal settings and their scope to offer different restorative experiences at different stages in life.

Blue space, heat stress and mental health

The number of people exposed to increased heat stress in cities is rising, exacerbated by urban heat islands and rising temperatures. Since cities around

FIGURE 3.3 Cooling water mister, Shanghai Expo Park, China. Source: Jiapeng Sheng.

the world are expected to warm by 2°C by 2050, the impact on shaping human relationships could be quite substantive. Cooling our cities with water is an age-old tool urban designers are returning to in mitigating these problems; the fourteenth-century gardens of the Alhambra, in Granada, for instance, housed courtyards with pools and fountains, stimulating water evaporation and cooling the dry, hot air of Spanish summers. A new prototype of 'heat-proof cities' is emerging that applies similar tactics in the form of pools, fountains, sprinklers and misting systems to cool outdoor spaces (Figure 3.3). One of the world's top 'furnace' cities, Chongqing, China, is experimenting with water misters at bus stops using chilled water to cool the air as well as waiting passengers (Oldfield 2018). Elsewhere in the city, water is central to the design of new projects, including the Fengming Mountain Park (designed by Martha Shwartz in 2014), which uses a variety of water effects such as channels, pools, streams and jets to assist with cooling; elsewhere in China, dry-wet hybrid parks are being used (Jing 2019).

Leveraging the sustainability and economic drivers of blue space development

Much of the resurgence in blue urban design has been catalysed by sustainability and economic drivers, rather than a preoccupation with health outcomes. The Besos riverside regeneration project in Barcelona, for example, was primarily undertaken to increase habitat biodiversity, but indirectly has also improved visitor health and wellbeing. Researchers captured data on physical activity in almost 1,000 park users, developing and applying a new instrument, the Blue Active Tool, to estimate health and health-related economic benefits associated with this physical activity (Vert et al. 2019). The results estimated that urban riverside activity could avert 11.1 disability-adjusted life years (DALYs), a measure used by epidemiologists to quantify disease burden, expressed as the number of years lost to illness, disability or premature death. These health benefits were translated into a health-related economic cost reduction of €23.4 million per year. The largest health and health-related economic benefits were related to the increased number of people cycling and walking along the riverside. The benefits of riverside exposure were associated with a decreased risk of death; there was no explicit association found with a specific chronic disease, but the study did indicate particular benefits for dementia. The trend towards riverside revitalization continues globally; the urban riverside regeneration project in Los Angeles, for example, will transform 11 miles (of a 48-mile river) running through some of the city's poorest neighbourhoods. Whilst this promises to bring economic regeneration and opportunities for active living (cycling, walking) to these communities, at the same time gentrification, displacement and homelessness are projected.

Inclusive blue environments

Healthy urban blue space is not distributed equitably, and this affects mental health (see the Inclusive City chapter). First, there are global socio-spatial inequities in the distribution of 'healthy' waters and opportunities to enjoy them, both between and within countries (e.g. by race, ethnicity, age) (Foley et al. 2019). Warming climates, droughts and human mismanagement mean some bodies of water are drying up and vanishing in various parts of the world, leaving large regions with water insecurity, increased poverty, loss of habitat for birds and fish, and a sense of eco-anxiety or psychologic discomfort caused by environmental degradation, referred to as 'solistalgia'.

Nor is access to urban blue space always equitable within a city. Some people are excluded from existing urban blue space. For example, in the United

States, African American people were historically restricted from visiting coastal areas by segregationist policies in certain states, including Florida, Virginia and Connecticut; racist housing policy meant many African American communities were concentrated in the interior of a city (Connolly 2014), further restricting their access to the coast. Today, these policies may no longer exist, but Black and Hispanic Americans still visit water settings less frequently than White or Asian Americans for a variety of reasons, including proximity/transportation factors as well as racial/discrimination issues (Leeworthy 2001; Wolch and Zhang 2004). A study in London found that this disparity of access was prominent in young women from Black and ethnic minority backgrounds, often unable to access and enjoy the outdoors (including water settings) in the same way as men of the same ethnicity due to cultural norms and gender restrictions (CABE 2010; see the Inclusive City chapter).

There are also economic barriers to blue space access. Much blue space is privately owned or the privilege of an elite few, such as yachting marinas, privately owned beaches and swimming pools. Water locations, as discussed above, command high property prices, which socially exclude and push out the disadvantaged.

Research on inequities in access to blue space owing to race, cultural norms and socioeconomic status is still limited. We need to better understand the distribution of 'healthy' and 'unhealthy' blue space in relation to people's diverse characteristics and mental health outcomes, as well as the cultural differences that affect how water settings are perceived, accessed and used by different types of people.

Blue city examples

Bradford's water access for all, UK

Bradford, a multi-cultural city of many faiths and ethnicities, helped catalyse regeneration of the city via an ambitious water park, the largest water feature in any UK city, designed for people of all ages, genders, social classes and ethnicities. To date, there is one qualitative evaluation of the park's success (Barker, Manning and Sirriyeh 2014), but no quantifiable evaluation in terms of health and wellbeing outcomes or promoting inclusivity (the qualitative report suggests girls from Black and minority ethnic (BME) groups do not visit owing to mobility restrictions). The Bradford water park brings a highly sophisticated water feature into the heart of the city (providing a daily cycle from a low-lying mist at dawn to an underwater light show at dusk) and offers the population (many of whom would not have access to back gardens or to a car to easily

FIGURE 3.4 Water park offering a daily cycle of water and lighting theatrics, Bradford, UK. Source: Born in Bradford.

reach a coastal or inland water setting) an opportunity to interact with water (Figure 3.4). But the £24 million investment has been criticized in a region experiencing extreme poverty; a health benefit and health economic analysis (as was done for the Barcelona river park) could help justify these types of investments in deprived multi-cultural cities, help address equity concerns and show the benefits of inclusive city water access.

Sheffield's blue urban regeneration, UK

Sheffield, in the North of England, is an example of how blue space – in the form of engineered water systems – can be brought together in an integrated system to spark city regeneration. Sheffield suffered from urban degeneration some fifty years ago owing to closure of the iron and steel industries, and the decline of the city centre was further exacerbated by a large shopping centre built outside town in 1990. An urban regeneration project called The Heart of the City (2004–16) integrated a series of water fountains with new squares and gardens to reinvigorate the centre, catalysing economic activity and making walking about the city a happier and more enjoyable experience. The water design capitalizes on the city's skill in steel manufacturing to craft a series of water features symbolic of Sheffield's industrial past. The water

FIGURE 3.5 Sheaf Square, incorporating *Cutting Edge*, a stainless-steel sculpture and waterfall, Sheffield, UK. Source: Jan Woudstra, University of Sheffield.

theme is announced at the city's major arrival point, the train station, featuring a linear water feature that masks the sound of the adjacent traffic (see Figure 3.5) and ensures that the arrival experience is welcoming and memorable. Water continues into the heart of the city, cascading throughout the Peace Gardens, the Winter Gardens and Millennium Square. Any health benefits have yet to be quantified.

Middelfart, Jutland and others leverage rainwater management systems for health, Denmark

Under a major climate adaptation project called Climate Jump, Schulze + Grassov designed a flagship urban waterway utilizing exposed channels to capture rainwater on the streets of Danish towns (see example in Middelfart, Figure 3.6). The developed system increases the street's capacity for handling and retaining large amounts of rainwater during times of extreme precipitation. The project added a 'softer' layer to the street by incorporating plantings along the water channels (perennials and grasses), which, combined with seating, transformed the atmosphere of the street, inviting people to linger, enjoy the water and be sociable. In this way, water is used as a resource to improve the quality of life of a town, whilst turning its back on conventional hard-

FIGURE 3.6 Waterway in Middelfart, Denmark. Source: Schulze + Grassov.

water infrastructure solutions, such as sewer expansion, and transforming communities into resilient neighbourhoods.

Schulze + Grassov are advancing new street typologies for stormwater capture that combine hard- and soft-engineered systems for the capture, diversion, infiltration, cleansing and retention of stormwater. These include rain gardens and constructed 'mobility pyramids' that act as bioswales and ponds during periods of high rainfall, whilst offering seating, performances and play at other (dry) times of the year.

Seoul's Cheonggyecheon River Park, South Korea

The Cheonggyecheon River Park project (2005), an ambitious attempt at stream recovery, transformed a traffic-choked elevated freeway into a habitat-rich, 3.6-mile-long linear parkway (Figure 3.7). The original stream that had flowed through the city was (like many city streams) channelled through a concrete culvert in the 1950s. The restoration process boosted local biodiversity and catalysed economic development, although the need to pump water from the

FIGURE 3.7 Cheonggyecheon River Park, Seoul, South Korea. Source: Sunggun Park.

larger Han River, rather than using natural restoration processes and recycled water, has drawn criticism that the project is not sustainable and has displaced local market traders. Despite these criticisms (Marshall 2016), the project has increased opportunities for active living, helped reduce the urban heat-island effect, added to the downtown quality of life and helped humanize what was an industrial eyesore. It has also served as a model for uncovering other cities' buried streams, including the Los Angeles River restoration project. Any health benefits have yet to be quantified.

Design principles for a blue city

General principles

- Maintain both residential visibility and public access to waterfronts and other aquatic settings, particularly those within easy reach of home.
- Provide all children with an opportunity to experience safe water play within easy reach of home.
- Allow opportunities to walk/cycle/socialize alongside waterways as well as engage in water sports activities (e.g. kayaking, paddling).
- Consider hybrid parks/water features that support sports/social activities in dry weather and capture water to prevent flooding.
- Control rents in areas undergoing regenerative blue urban transformation.
- Social and health impact analysis, combined with economic analysis, could help ameliorate some of the concerns about equitable access to blue space and help identify the health gains (and any losses) under such scenarios.

Neighbourhood scale (see Figure 3.8)

- Water play for children and teens
- Attractive plantings and seating alongside water features
- Interconnected trails linked to urban waterways and green corridors
- Hybrid parks that turn into ponds and can host sports/social gatherings in dry weather
- Climate adaptation systems to support cooling/surface water management, such as rain gardens; street stormwater drainage systems that transform streets into mini-waterways (grass swales, open gutters); stormwater retention ponds; greywater recycling for irrigation

City scale (see Figure 3.9)

- Water fountains to mitigate noise pollution
- Urban water walls capturing the cycle of water (ice/mist/fog walls)
- Riverside parks
- Flexible waterfront spaces to facilitate markets, festivals and other events
- Canalside trails linked to city green corridors
- Climate-efficient 'sponge' city designs, such as dry-wet hybrid parks
- Heat-proof city design, such as cooling street and park sprinklers/ misters
- Floating islands for biodiversity and recreation

1 water wall
2 rooftop rain garden
3 sustainable street drainage systems
4 hybrid water feature
5 blue edges
6 stormwater retention pond
7 rainwater swale
8 natural water features
9 linear park

FIGURE 3.8 The Blue City: Neighbourhood Scale.

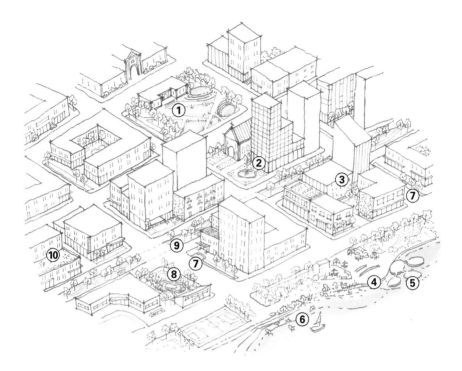

1 hybrid water square
2 water feature
3 water wall
4 urban waterfront edge
5 waterfront park engagement
6 access to water activities
7 blue edges
8 retention pond
9 linear park with sustainable street drainage system
10 rain garden

FIGURE 3.9 The Blue City: City Scale.

4

The sensory city

Highlights

- Scientific evidence is increasingly demonstrating that the senses can be harnessed within urban design and planning to exert positive impacts on mental health and wellbeing.
- Reducing unpleasant noise can improve mental health, particularly in terms of sleep quality; but there are also possibilities for designing positive soundscapes and sonic refuges.
- Visual complexity may hold one key to reducing depression through urban design.
- Smell may be harnessed to evoke feelings of place and belongingness.
- Ensuring access to affordable, tasty and healthy foodscapes in every urban neighbourhood helps reduce obesity, which, in turn, can help reduce depression, improve adherence to medicine regimens and reduce the life expectancy gap between people with and without mental health problems.
- Accessing and promoting food popular with certain countries and cultures offers not just nutrition-related benefits but also the opportunity to build social capital.
- Planners and designers should seize opportunities to integrate salutogenic sensory design and reduce exposure to unpleasant sensations.

Key concept definitions

Sensation: The process by which we receive information from our surroundings through the physical senses, including sight, smell, taste, touch and sound.

Perception: The unconscious process of capturing, organizing and interpreting the sensations we receive in order to understand our surroundings.

Cognition: The conscious process whereby the brain processes perceptions along with knowledge and experience and uses this to form opinions, ideas, beliefs and decisions.

Salutogenic soundscape/smellscape: An acoustic or olfactory environment that supports good health and wellbeing, including by reducing stress.

What is the sensory city?

Urban design tends to privilege only one sense, vision, but we experience our world through our five senses. Finnish architect Juhani Pallasmaa (2014) has criticized the architectural (and modern human) assumption that sight takes precedence over the other senses. He argues that the senses combine to create what he considers a multisensory sixth sense that is greater than the sum of its parts, defined as atmosphere or ambience. The sensation of atmosphere brings together sound, sight, smell, touch and taste. It also incorporates numerous other components like orientation, stability, scale, continuity, gravity, time and even memory. This is also known as 'simultaneous perception' (Hiss 1991). This sensory experience combines to give each individual an instant, intuitive grasp of a place. There is significant interest in use of the senses within design in the urban built environment, though much of the research about how to leverage this effect to promote mental health is still at an early stage. Certainly, urban design can determine whether a place is light or shady, create pleasant odours, influence the frequency of sounds, even affect the temperature; materials used may be pleasant to the touch. The challenge is to bring together these different senses to create something bigger than the sum of its parts – in other words, an atmosphere. Palassmaa notes that 'atmosphere' in itself is not a single entity. Rather, in addition to the atmosphere created by the environment, there are, for instance, cultural, social, workplace and interpersonal atmospheres. He argues that only when the complexity of sensations is interpreted together can we understand how a person really *senses* a place.

Attention to all five senses (plus ambience) has the potential to offer new ways of thinking about the planning and design of a city – and particularly so when designing a city to promote good mental health and wellbeing. Each of our senses impacts our mental health, whether it is frustration, anxiety and sleep disruption from a noisy street; a sense of visual engagement experienced when looking at plant life in a city park; the feeling of home and belongingness from a simple aroma; the touch of a tree's bark; or the conviviality of a social group sharing their food. There has been substantial research on the impact of sound on urban mental health, and some on the impact of sight. Globally, smell, touch and taste have been studied far less. This is not universally the case of course: looking to countries like Japan, there is evidence of what happens to our mental health and wellbeing when senses are considered in the round and environment experiences are designed to maximize their potential. It would be a mistake to assume that urban design can be interpreted from an objective position. Any impact of urban design is predicated on people's senses: it is these senses that, together, deliver a person's subjective reality that forms their experience of being in a place. In this chapter, we will explore the current evidence and the opportunities for urban design and planning to intentionally harness the health-related aspects of the sensory city.

Theory

Sensation is the mechanical process through which our body receives and registers information from our surroundings; perception is the participatory, reciprocal aspect of sensation whereby the brain organizes and interprets sensations in order to understand our surroundings. Cognition is the third stage, whereby the brain combines perceptions with our knowledge and experience to turn them into information. This process enables people to form opinions, ideas, beliefs and decisions and to recall memories of place. There are three key pathways through which sensory experience within urban design operates to bring positive mental health outcomes (Figure 4.1).

The first pathway by which the sensory experience affects mental health and wellbeing is through evolutionary psychology. Significant changes in how we live have affected how humans sense, perceive and interpret their surroundings. American philosopher and ecologist David Abram (1997) describes the sensuous relationship between indigenous cultures and their surroundings and contrasts this with the more binary, text-based interpretation of the city many people experience in the urban realm. By prioritizing sight and sound above the other senses, he argues that our senses are muted, our relationship with the landscapes in which we live has been fractured, we have become isolated from our surroundings and we are less able to interact with landscapes that give us cultural coherence. Abram argues that more attention to all senses may help resolve that psychological fracture and make us feel more connected to people and place (Abram 1997; Bingley 2003).

The concept of evolutionary preference reflections in urban design is further supported by the 'savanna hypothesis'. This considers that human aesthetic preferences are finely tuned to our evolution in the African savanna, including discomfort with wide-open spaces (and completely enclosed ones) and an appreciation of natural features (including possibly experiencing anxiety related to connotations of drought when foliage is not present) (Orians 1986). Similarly,

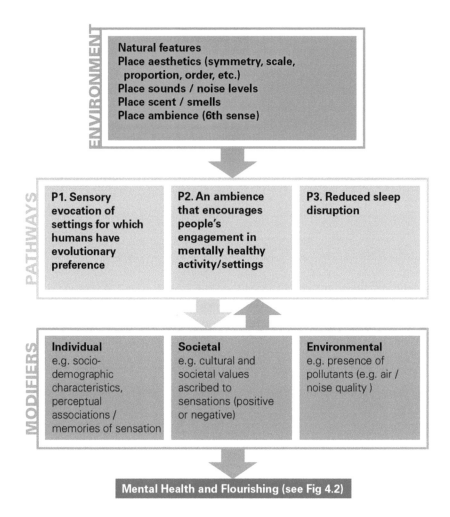

FIGURE 4.1 Effects of sensory urban design on mental health and wellbeing.

today, the sensory evocation of a positive mental state is frequently (though certainly not exclusively) associated with sensations elicited by nature, largely through the process of attention restoration (see the Green City chapter). For example, a study of perceived restorative soundscapes rated rural sounds as most restorative, but also rated an urban park soundscape as more restorative than a general urban environment soundscape (Payne 2013).

This concept fits with theories of aesthetic design associated with a successful urban environment. Moughtin (1992) recommended the importance of symmetry, scale, proportion, order, unity, balance, rhythm, contrast and harmony, whilst Gehl (1996) expanded the list to include the size, shape and connections between objects in the urban environment. Rapoport

(1990) added visual complexity and high levels of enclosure; Nasar (1994) and Nia and Atun (2015) endorsed variation. Many of these recommendations reflect the human preference for natural landscapes, including fractal patterns (patterns that repeat at different scales, creating order from visual complexity, such as the branching of a tree). Research has found that fractals with so-called mid-range complexity (measured as Fractal Dimension, or D = 1.3–1.5) are most likely to reduce stress; this tends to include natural sights like trees, clouds and mountains (Taylor and Spehar 2016).

Conversely, from an evolutionary perspective, certain sensations can evoke anxiety and distress. For instance, unwanted, uncontrollable and unpredictable sound was once an indicator of potential danger, such as a predator approaching; such noise can evoke a similar alarm reflex today. Urban noise, 'invented' during the Industrial Revolution, has led to human-made sound being of sufficient volume and duration to create a state of chronic alarm, with mental and physical health impacts (Basner et al. 2014; Hughes and Jones 2003); humans rarely fully habituate to urban noise (Basner et al. 2011).

The second pathway by which the sensory experience affects mental health is indirect, by providing an ambience that encourages or deters activities that support mental health and wellbeing. Sensations significantly affect how people experience a place and how they use and move through space, including their experience of the conviviality of that place. We are less keen to socialize, play or engage in physical activity in places where we experience unpleasant noise, sights, smells, tastes, touch sensations and ambience; and being associated with such places, such as living next to a sewage plant, also affects our self-esteem. A place with pleasant sensations will be more attractive – and the more feelings of belongingness that sensations evoke, the more positive a person's experience of that place is likely to be. All of this is a challenge for design because senses are generally a subjective spectrum, imbued with personal meaning by factors like familiarity, novelty, upkeep of a place, historical significance and a person's sense of attachment to that place. For example, smell is processed in the same part of the brain as emotions and, for most people, is uniquely evocative of memories and feelings (Billot et al. 2017); smell may account for up to three-quarters of people's feelings about a place (Lindstrom 2005).

Perhaps the most impactful pathway through which the sensory experience affects mental health is the support or disruption of sleep (Basner and McGuire 2018). Sleep is essential for mental health and wellbeing. Good sleep quality reduces the risk of developing mental health problems and supports recovery; sleep continuity disorders are a feature of most mental illnesses. Nocturnal external noise and other sensations that disrupt sleep are therefore an important pathway for developing and sustaining mental health problems. Research in Montreal found that 12.4 per cent of the population had their sleep disturbed by outdoor environmental noise over the course of a month, including by road, rail and air traffic; mechanical sounds; and neighbourhood noise (Perron et al. 2016; Vianna et al. 2015). A systematic review found that the clearest impact is from traffic noise, which affects both objectively measured sleep and subjectively assessed sleep, including sleep quality, problems falling asleep and nocturnal awakenings (Basner and McGuire 2018). Stansfeld and Matheson (2003) considered that objective sleep disturbance is likely to occur if there are more than fifty noise events per night with a maximum level of 50 dBA indoors (A-weighted decibels, the loudness of sound in air as perceived by humans).

The impact on mental health

Let us now consider each of the senses in isolation and the impact of their perception on mental health in urban settings (Figure 4.2).

FIGURE 4.2 The benefits of sensory cities for mental health and wellbeing.

Sounds can affect mood, stress and cognitive function

Classified as a pollutant by the World Health Organization, noise is generally considered a negative feature of the urban soundscape, and chronic exposure can lead to health problems (Basner et al. 2011). There is extensive research about links between noise and physical disorders like cardiovascular disease (Munzel et al. 2018) and type 2 diabetes (Dzhambov 2015). More recently, evidence is emerging that noise also affects mental health.

Noise in general can aggravate mood symptoms such as anxiety, stress and anger. One study in Porto, Portugal found 41.7 per cent of people experienced annoyance caused by urban noise; the more exposure, the greater the degree of annoyance (Vianna et al. 2015). Moderate but persistent traffic noise is linked to symptoms of depression (Orban, McDonald and Sutcliffe 2015), and sudden loud noises such as beeping horns in heavy traffic can trigger auditory reflexes that move people from tranquillity into a state of high alert, which can contribute to chronic stress over time (Pheasant et al. 2010).

Noise stress can also affect cognitive function, specifically attention, working memory and episodic recall (Wright et al. 2014). For children, there is growing evidence of associations between noise and hyperactivity, memory and reading comprehension (Stansfeld and Clark 2015). For older adults, there is growing evidence of links between noise and cognitive decline (Paul et al. 2019).

Reduced noise annoyance consistently results in significantly better self-reported health (Aletta et al. 2018). This is not to say that silence is the desirable state. Sound has been used effectively to mask noise, such as water being used to mask urban traffic noise (Jeon, Lee and You 2012). And studies consistently show that the acoustic environment has opportunities to enhance people's mental state – in particular, that 'pleasant' soundscapes aid in stress recovery (Aletta et al. 2018). The most restorative acoustic characteristics seem to be freshness, calmness and temporal variation; for instance, a natural stream or waves may be a more restorative acoustic experience than a fountain or waterfall (Hong and Jeon 2013). And whilst the natural sounds of birdsong may intuitively seem restorative, not all bird sounds are created equal: quiet, familiar, complex songs, such as those from the greenfinch, are considered more restorative than loud calls, such as those from the magpie (Ratcliffe et al. 2018). Restorative sound sources are not confined to nature. A soundscape study by Quercia, Aiello and Schifanella (2017) found that certain household noises (showers, toilet flushing) and noises from places of worship (such as bells ringing) were associated with feelings of trust, and a study of soundscapes in urban parks favoured the happy sounds of people (Payne 2010). Each city has its own acoustic profile, and sounds can also evoke feelings of belongingness and home.

Sights can reduce depression and affect mood

As cities have developed over the years, street-level facades have undergone a transition in visual complexity. Small, occupied, fine-grain facades and features of nature give personality and diversity to the street view, occupying people's brains with the need to process varied and complex information from the external world. The new urban form has developed in ways that do not always reflect human visual preferences. Configuration in the urban realm tends to include monotonous facades and landscapes (such as blank walls that extend for city blocks, mass homogeneous housing projects or uniform office building typologies that extend for blocks). A visually monotonous street view activates several processes that can be detrimental to mental health (Ellard 2017):

- Lower levels of interest and pleasure and increased dwelling and rumination on pessimistic internal thoughts, contributing to the risk of depression and anxiety
- Boredom, associated with stress, and risky behaviours, particularly addiction
- Opportunities for social interaction limited by reducing people's interest in interacting with their environment

For people with dementia, monotonous architecture and street planning create an additional challenge: the loss of visual environmental navigation cues. Varied shapes, features, colours and contrasts in building form and architecture create navigational landmarks that are particularly important for people with dementia (see the Inclusive City chapter). Fragmented landscapes where objects are visually discordant (Nia and Atun 2015), or visual pollution, such as unattractive advertising (Jaśkiewicz 2015), can create a cluttered perception that may lead to further confusion.

The perception of light and colour also affects mental health. Lighting can facilitate human activity; it can also increase visual acuity, add playful elements to the cityscape, and enhance both perceived and actual safety of a place.

Colour can aid navigation and wayfinding (in turn, supporting wellbeing by fostering sense of control and efficacy; see the Active City chapter), yet it is rarely used as an organizational urban planning tool. Jean-Philippe Lenclos (1999) first put forward the concept of 'colour geography', capturing how different geographical locations have a unique chromatic character and foster different aesthetic tastes as a result. The concept of an urban colourscape suggests that the elements of a city can be united by a cohesive colour plan that sets out the basic colour of buildings and other objects, including urban advertisements, public buses, post boxes etc. A rare and little-known example of intentional city colour planning is the city of Turin, Italy, which devised a co-ordinated chromatic system for the city in the 1800s that has been re-instated in recent years, discussed later in this chapter. Whilst there is no evaluative evidence of the system's ability to support mental wellbeing, anecdotal evidence suggests it certainly helps orientate the visitor, stimulates the senses and resonates in the imagination long after visiting. Whilst there is a danger that urban colour planning is too prescriptive/regulatory (and interferes with the creative expression and necessary transformations of a city), more research is needed to show how urban colourscape planning can support a city's public image, assist wayfinding, and foster place identity and belonging.

Colours are known to evoke spontaneous emotional reactions affecting mood and stress, but rigorous scientific research on the specific impact of colours on mental health is in its infancy – and is not without controversy, given the complexities of individual colour perception and personal and cultural associations. Some environmental psychology research points to oranges and yellows as being associated with optimism, greens with peacefulness, greys with sadness and blues with feelings of safety, but there are many confounding factors (Hanada 2018).

Smells can be a risk factor for mood disorders and affect recovery

A 'smellscape' can be defined as the totality of the olfactory landscape, accommodating both episodic (foregrounded or time limited) and involuntary (background) odours (Henshaw 2014; Porteous 1990). It is difficult to understand the full impact of smells, as they have different connotations for different people. Smell has the capacity to evoke both pleasure and disgust; it is also linked with self-esteem and belongingness.

Urban smells are typically identified formally via complaints, and so tend to be classified as a negative environmental feature. Smells identified in this way derive from sources like sewage, abattoirs and tanneries, and are associated with perceptions of unhealthy environments (Quercia et al. 2016). The rate of complaints has increased in line with cities bringing industry closer to residential and commercial centres in pursuit of mixed land use. Often these 'unpleasant' smells occur in places associated with disadvantage and disorder, stigmatizing a neighbourhood and affecting the self-esteem of its residents.

This approach is limiting from an urban planning perspective. Since people have the ability to perceive 1 trillion smells, opportunities to leverage positive experiences abound. Attempts have been made to map olfactory 'pleasantness'. Xiao, Tate and Kang (2018) identified aspects of smell that seem to be most associated with pleasantness: cleanliness, appropriateness to the location, naturalness, freshness, healthiness, familiarity, calmness, intensity and purity, with personal indicators including personal preference, memories and habituation. In general, smells of nature and food seem the most likely to evoke positive feelings and perceptions (Quercia et al. 2016).

People's sense of smell is often affected when they have mental health problems; in particular, there is evidence that depression can reduce people's sense of smell; conversely, depressed people who also have a poor sense of smell may experience more severe symptoms (Kohli et al. 2016). Schizophrenia and some types of dementia are also associated with a poor sense of smell. Finally, smellscapes have also been noted to influence the therapeutic environment for people with mental health problems, affecting people's engagement and willingness to engage in certain environments (Gorman 2017).

Touch can reduce depression and anxiety

Haptic experience creates feelings of self-awareness and connection to people and place (Bingley 2003). This has been studied in terms of interpersonal physical touch and, to an extent, in certain settings with clear haptic elements, such as swimming and lying on a beach. The haptic experience of cities is a newer field with many interesting possibilities.

Mechanosensory stimulation is integral to human development (Ardiel and Rankin 2010). Touch is one of the most important senses to help us understand the world, and just as our ancestors used touch to navigate the forest, we rely on tactile sensations to move around the city. Tactile urban design includes the haptic sensation of contact with skin: exploring objects in terms of their texture, consistency, form and movements. It also includes the wider experiences of temperature, wind movement and other physical sensations. Design factors that evoke touch sensation can vary from a cobbled street that slows people down and causes them to spend more time in the environment to a wind tunnel that deters people's use of a street.

Tactile design approaches can also support mental health. In particular, physical activity is a key moderator of mental health (see the Active City chapter). Ground-feel can facilitate movement: for instance, by reducing slipping risk or by installing textured ground that identifies crossings for people with visual impairment; it also plays a role in people's motivation to walk, run and cycle. With a desire to 'get away from the tarmac' and move on ground with more complex consistency, surfaces can be designed to actively encourage physical activity (Brown 2017). Textural immersion like this can create pleasurable somatic sensations, a sense of connection to place, a sense of playfulness and feelings of empowerment. It has also been proposed that moving on textured ground may support mood regulation by providing the tactile version of avoiding monotonous visual fields to reduce the risk of negative ruminations (Brown 2017).

Tactile experience – along with increases in access to nature, physical activity and social interaction – is considered part of the reason gardening and urban farming activity are associated with reduced depression, anxiety and psychological distress, and increased mindfulness, quality of life and sense of community (Soga et al. 2017). Touch has also been studied in the context of museum science. The findings of this research indicate that engaging haptically with objects and surroundings not only helps connect people to their environment but can also relieve stress and even promote wellbeing (Howes 2014).

Tastes can support physical health of people with mental health problems and contribute to feelings of belongingness

There are two components of taste in the urban design context that are relevant to mental health: flavoursome food/access to nutrition and food as an indicator of cultural identity and belongingness.

It is particularly important for people with mental health problems to have access to nutritious foods because of the link to their reduced life expectancy compared to the general population, a discrepancy of ten to twenty years for people with major mental illness (Chesney et al. 2014). Less than 5 per cent of these deaths are from suicide; people with mental illness are far more likely to die of heart disease and metabolic diseases like diabetes, linked in part to obesity and poor diet (John et al. 2018).

Often, people with mental health problems are at higher risk of obesity than the general population. This link works in two directions: obesity can increase the risk of developing mental health problems by reducing quality of life, self-esteem and social interactions and by disrupting sleep through sleep apnoea. Obesity increases the risk of a person's developing depression by 55 per cent;

conversely, having depression increases the risk of developing obesity by 58 per cent, with a dose–response gradient (Luppino et al. 2010). Dietary improvements can reduce symptoms of depression (Firth et al. 2019). Conversely, having mental health problems increases the risk of developing obesity. The symptoms of many mental illnesses may affect people's ability to eat healthily and exercise regularly. And several anti-psychotic medications used to treat disorders like schizophrenia and bipolar affective disorder have a side effect of weight gain, which can lead to people choosing to discontinue medication, leading to relapse of symptoms and other problems (Kolotkin et al. 2012).

Specific food consumption may also affect mental health: higher intake of foods with saturated fat, refined carbohydrates and processed food products are associated with poorer mental health for young people (O'Neil et al. 2014); low intake of fats and high intake of vitamins and minerals help prevent some types of dementia (Engelhart et al. 2002). Local access to healthy, affordable, nutritious food has the potential to reduce obesity and increase diet quality. Living in places without such access, known as 'food deserts', reduces people's consumption of healthy foods like fruits and vegetables (Diaz-Roux et al. 1999). Food insecurity is also a form of stress in itself, increasingly prevalent in low-income neighbourhoods as grocery stores move out of the city centre (see the Inclusive City chapter). Urban design should include consideration of people's access to healthy food in terms of shops and markets.

In terms of food as an indicator of cultural identity and belongingness, urban residents being able to buy and grow foods associated with particular cultures can contribute to a sense of belongingness, place identity and home. One example is the migrant experience of taste (and smell) of foods common to people's home culture in creating a sense of diasporic identity, reducing feelings of dislocation, and increasing feelings of comfort and stability; the 'taste of home' also provides economic opportunity to migrants (Rhys-Taylor 2013). There is particular evidence of this for people of minority ethnicities with dementia, who experience improvements in wellbeing, mood and feelings of belongingess by reinforcing their cultural identity through access to traditional foods (Hanssen and Kuven 2016).

The places where cultural or place-specific foods can be purchased, such as urban markets, have additional value as bumping places to meet neighbours with similar cultural backgrounds or interests (see the Neighbourly City chapter), and also create talking points with neighbours who may be less familiar with these foods, thus growing social capital, the potential for facilitating transcultural exchange, and a convivial metropolitan multi-culture (Gilroy 2005) through which dialogue can occur. In addition to places to purchase food, community gardens for minority ethnic groups and refugees have proved helpful for growing culturally specific foods and building social cohesion.

The sixth sense: ambience and affective atmosphere

There is no one objective way to describe the evocative concept of ambience and affective atmosphere, which bring together all the senses, plus other inputs, to create a sensory background that evokes a pre-conscious reflex that determines how a person experiences a place at a particular moment in time. Some helpful definitions:

> An ambiance can be provisionally defined as a space-time qualified from a sensory perspective. It appears as an alternative to bridge the sensitive, the spatial and the social domains.
>
> (Thibaud 2011: 203)

> Possibly the most effective way of grasping the idea of an affective atmosphere is … to think of it as a propensity: a pull or a charge that might emerge in a particular space, which might (or might not) generate particular events and actions, feelings and emotions.
>
> (Bissell 2010: 273)

It has been argued that ambience and affective atmosphere both play a role in urban mental health in the following ways:

- Multi-sensorial input, including the physical, the sensorial and the atmospheric, contributes to sensorial overload, hypervigilance and attention disorders; this may theoretically play a role in disorders like schizophrenia (Winz 2018).
- Transition between different ambiences and atmospheres, and constantly having to adapt between the pleasant and the abrasive as people move around the city, may cause feelings of dissonance and disconnection (Winz 2018).
- A convivial ambience facilitates pleasant, impromptu social connections that engender feelings of belongingness in diverse populations (Thombre and Kapshe 2020).

Modifiers of impact

Sensory design is challenging because of the subjective nature of the sensory experience. A significant part of how people perceive and interpret sensory inputs is based on their perceptual memories and exposure to a particular sound/smell, particularly in childhood. People's experience is also modified by the societal value (positive or negative) ascribed to certain sensations, such as what constitutes a 'bad smell'. The quality of the environment also modifies people's perceptual capabilities (e.g. levels of air and noise pollution), as do people's individual physical and cognitive variations.

Design approaches for a sensory city

There is clearly opportunity within urban planning and design to promote good mental health and wellbeing, and to support recovery and resilience through intentional design of the urban sensescape, leveraging senses individually and in combination. Much of this opportunity is yet to be fully realized. Research is still emerging about how best to harness the senses in urban design to promote mental health. Our understanding of this field is growing every year, with three main design approaches:

- Leveraging positive emotions, connotations and other impacts evoked by senses to deliver a salutogenic sensescape
- Reducing distress by removing or reducing people's exposure to sensations commonly deemed to be unpleasant
- Overcoming the negative psychological impacts of monotony with sensory diversity and visually engaging, cohesive urban landscapes (in turn, facilitating fascination, an integral component of restorative wellbeing; see Chapter 1)

Sensory experience is rarely confined to one modality; rather, the senses should be considered together. However, for practical reasons, they will be considered separately here.

Sound: reducing unwanted noise and increasing access to restorative soundscapes

Sound offers one of the greatest urban design opportunities within the sensory landscape to support mental health. Understanding the qualities of the sonic environment, the sources of sound and the needs of the people who experience the space enables the sound environment to be designed with mental health in mind.

The research is clear that whilst certain soundscapes have the potential to be restorative, urban noise has negative impacts on people's mental health, particularly traffic sounds and sudden, startling sounds. Effects range from concentration at school and work to sleep quality to enjoyment of the public realm. Urban design should therefore prioritize two sonic landscape design approaches: increasing salutogenic soundscapes and measuring and reducing exposure to unwanted urban noise.

Salutogenic soundscapes

Designed soundscapes that seek to deliver stress reduction should make use of nature-based sounds that indicate freshness and calmness and include temporal variation, such as animals and birds, wind in the trees, and choosing a burbling creek over a monotonous-sounding fountain (Payne 2013). Parks, atria and other places that use such nature-based sounds to promote tranquility over ambient urban noise, alongside noise abatement or other control measures to eliminate unwanted sounds, or psycho-acoustic measures used to mask or divert attention from them with more 'tranquil' sounds can be characterized as sonic refuges. Soundscapes that seek to instill feelings of trust and belongingness should also enable the transmission of sounds from homes and places of worship (Quercia et al. 2017) and sounds of happy people, such as children playing in a park (Payne 2010).

Noise management

- Elimination: Where possible, good urban planning and design should remove traffic and other sources of noise or else separate pedestrians from noise – for instance, using two-tiered streets and pedestrian precincts. This can be challenging when mixed zoning brings residential, commercial and industrial uses together, or when new roads are routed through poorer areas (see the Inclusive City chapter).
- Reduction: This may include reducing traffic density and speed around residences, public spaces and pedestrian and cycle routes; avoiding all-glass buildings in urban canyons; and considering quiet-pavement road-surfacing technology (Ohiduzzaman et al. 2016).
- Blocking: Barrier walls and vegetation can help reduce noise (Echevarria 2016).
- Masking: Nature sounds can help mask urban traffic noise (Jeon, Lee and You 2012).

Smell: harnessing the smellscape to create belongingness

Although reactions to odour are particularly subjective, smells can affect feelings of stress, stigma within a neighbourhood and how people use the public realm. Factors such as frequency, intensity, duration and location of smells (Nicell 2009) and urban design should prioritize two approaches: increasing the opportunity for salutogenic smellscapes and reducing unpleasant smells (Ministry for the Environment 2016).

Salutogenic smellscapes

There has been growing interest in understanding and designing the urban 'smellscape', distinctive to neighbourhoods and cities. In 2001, the Ministry of the Environment in Japan designated 100 sites associated with 'best' fragrance across the country to draw people's attention to pleasant, distinctive local smells. These range from fields of lavender to seaweed shops to the smell of barbequed meat at a particular station (*Japan Times* 2001). Smells associated with certain neighbourhoods at certain times of the year can be used to create a sense of place and belongingness. In the urban realm, people seem to react particularly positively to smells that evoke cleanliness, appropriateness to the location, naturalness, freshness, healthiness, familiarity, calmness, intensity and purity, particularly nature and pleasant food smells (Xiao, Tait and Kang 2018); care should be taken not to mask such smells with less-pleasant smells (such as traffic pollution).

Reducing unpleasant smells

Producers of unpleasant smells should adjust their processes to reduce their production as much as possible and to confine such smells to their own sites. In addition, separation distances can provide a buffer between the source of a smell and the people who may be affected. This is largely achieved through zoning for industry and by gradation of zones from heavy industry to light industry through to residential areas. It is preferable to eliminate or separate than to mask unpleasant smells.

Sight: leveraging the visible cityscape

As one of the senses most closely associated with urban design, the visual impact of a city can significantly affect people's mental wellbeing. Designing places that are visually pleasing encourages people to use those places; as described earlier, this may include attention to symmetry, scale, proportion, order, unity, balance, rhythm, contrast harmony, creating feelings of enclosure, and connections between objects in the urban environment, as well as visual engagement and fascination.

There are some specific visual interventions particularly associated with mental health and wellbeing.

Reducing monotony and increasing legibility

Visual engagement and fascination with the urban landscape promote psychological wellbeing (see Chapter 1). Urbanist Jan Gehl (2011) has recommended that to keep people's minds sufficiently engaged to prevent ruminations and boredom, the average walker, moving at a rate of about 5 km/hour, should encounter an interesting new sight once every five seconds. Natural features are one way to meet this need: attention restoration theory (see the Green City chapter) works by drawing people to look at complexity, which includes nature, fine-grain shopfronts (multiple small units), fractal-associated nature, and other engaging people-scale sights, such as public art.

Complexity in urban design also contributes to urban legibility, enabling people to efficiently and safely navigate their city. This is particularly important for people with sensory and cognitive challenges. For instance (as described in detail in the Inclusive City chapter), people with dementia are at risk of loneliness, isolation, mood problems and cognitive decline when they cannot independently navigate within their neighbourhood. Easily recognizable buildings with clear functions, historical or civic buildings, distinct structures like clock towers or permanent public art, places of activity like parks and squares, practical features like bus shelters, and natural features like trees or flower beds are all helpful (Mitchell and Burton 2006); monotonous and ubiquitous structures are less helpful.

Improving safety through urban lighting design

Crime Prevention Through Environmental Design (CPTED) has two objectives (Cozens et al. 2005). First, lighting human activity empowers people to use the city and access its restorative benefits twenty-four hours a day; and secondly, lighting design can enhance safety and reduce crime. A New York City study found that bright lighting in a neighbourhood resulted in a 36 per cent reduction in outdoor crime at night (Chalfin et al. 2019). The CPTED approach recommends the use of LED lighting to improve quality of light, create even illumination, increase acuity and reduce shadowing and high contrast, enhancing overall visibility. It also helps address criticisms of urban lighting for energy use and light pollution; access to a dark night sky supports circadian rhythms, gives people a sense of themselves and facilitates pro-social activities like stargazing.

Public art and creative design

Public art and other creative features, including creative lighting, can produce a sense of place, providing focal points in the city and encouraging playful social engagement and sensory interaction. Graffiti and murals in appropriate places can foster personal expression and visual stimulation, further contributing curiosity, fascination and engagement with place (see the Playable City chapter).

Touch: nudging people to use restorative environments through haptic experience

Tactile factors can be used to modulate people's use of space to encourage activities that promote mental health, like spending time in nature, engaging in physical activity or socializing; for instance, using cobbled streets or managing wind intensity to reduce pace and encourage lingering, or creating textured running and cycling routes. It is also likely that there are tactile benefits to mental health of biophilic design (see the Green City chapter). Theoretically, more natural, touchable materials like wood may have a salutogenic effect, but more research is needed (Gillis and Gatersleben 2015). The impact of the Covid-19 pandemic on raising people's awareness of fomites (surfaces that may carry infection) could affect people's willingness to engage in hand-touch; hand-washing facilities may become in greater demand where such engagement opportunities are used.

Taste: maintaining health and evoking belongingness

Access to flavoursome, nutritious food

Under- and over-nutrition can interact with various mental health problems. Urban designers can help enhance people's nutrition by reducing the risk of food deserts and by designing neighbourhoods with convenient and prominent access to and availability and affordability of healthy foods. Approaches can include supermarkets, local grocery stores, food markets,

FIGURE 4.3 The Saanjihi Programme, West Midlands, UK. Source: Black Environment Network.

food trucks and urban farming and allotments events like food festivals may also be helpful.

Harnessing restorative benefits of cultural identity and place belongingness associated with food

Markets that sell foods popular with certain countries and cultures not only increase availability of affordable, fresh, healthy and culturally appropriate foods, but also help maintain people's sense of identity and belongingness. Such venues should be easily accessible and provide bumping places and settings to facilitate social interaction and grow social capital within the communities that use them. Other opportunities include community gardens that appeal to diverse groups (Figure 4.3).

Combined sensory design

Urban design approaches that seek to engage all senses often have a basis in nature. The benefits and approaches of natural settings are described in the

Green City and Blue City chapters. Here, we consider the sensory benefits of nature immersion. This is perhaps most famously described in the context of 'forest bathing', where all-senses nature immersion is associated with improved mood and reduced anxiety (Hansen et al. 2017). These benefits can be captured in urban design.

In particular, sensory gardens, where all elements are designed for appealing sensory stimulation in all sensory domains, are already used as a therapeutic approach for children with special educational needs and older people with dementia. However, they can contribute to all users' mental health, and whilst typically associated with schools, healthcare facilities and nursing homes (Gonzalez and Kirkevold 2015), they can be extended to the wider public realm. Opportunities include gardening, urban farming and park design; for instance, Hussein (2014) has recommended plants with diverse but balanced colours, sounds, textures and smells; running water; and sensory pathways that offer accessible circulation through the space.

Sensory city examples

Derry/Londonderry's Foyle Reeds for suicide prevention and wellbeing, Northern Ireland

The bridge over the River Foyle connecting Derry/Londonderry had developed negative connotations for being a site increasingly used for planned suicides. The city sought to develop a barrier to reduce this risk that would not reinforce feelings of imprisonment for mentally vulnerable people on the bridge. To compound this challenge, public psychological distress associated with the

FIGURES 4.4A AND B The Foyle Reeds lit up at night and controlled through an app, Derry/Londonderry, Northern Ireland. Source: Our Future Foyle, HHCD, Urban Scale Interventions.

location had created negative feelings about the place, reducing people's willingness to engage in health opportunities of the nearby riverside development. Public art with lighting was used to address both these challenges. The Foyle Reeds comprises 12,000 aluminium LED-embedded 'reeds' along the bridge (Figure 4.4). These create an architectural barrier to prevent suicides, harness salutatory opportunities by evoking nature and the local setting, increase safety by providing lighting, and offer a playable component by enabling the public to change the colour and intensity of the lights on special occasions. This installation has changed perceptions of the bridge to create a new landmark with positive connotations (Spencer and Alwani 2018).

Tokyo's use of blue light to prevent suicide at train stations, Japan

Japan is a leader in exploring the use of blue light to reduce suicidal ideation (Figure 4.5). Blue light is the sharp daylight of mid-day, the visible light ranging from 380 to 500 nanometres. Train companies in Tokyo have installed blue LED lights on station platforms as well as blue translucent roofing. A meta-analysis

FIGURE 4.5 The use of blue light in a Japanese station to deter suicide. Source: Jan Moren.

has found that this approach has the potential to reduce suicides (and also possibly increase safety more generally), though the size of the impact is not yet clear (Barker et al. 2017). The mechanism of action is speculated to be the association of the colour blue with calmness and nature; other potential mechanisms are colour associations with the police or even a simple disruption in predicted visual colour perception. Or it may simply be that blue light helps maintain our circadian rhythms, in turn helping us sleep and thus maintain good cognitive health.

Turin, an example of urban colour planning, Italy

Whilst many cities are demarcated by colour (New York City by its yellow cabs, London by its red buses), this is mostly accidental. Turin is one of the few examples of colour planning on an urban scale. In the 1800s, Turin's Council of Builders devised a co-ordinated chromatic system for the city's major processional routes, commencing at the city's natural arrival point – the train station – and culminating in the main square, the Piazza Castello. The major routes were interconnected with a network of smaller streets, for which secondary and varied colour sequences were developed, using around eighty different colours. Weakened by war with France, Turin was anxious to improve its public image; colour was seen as a way to create a new public image, and bolster city morale. Warm pink and reddish hues were used to demark the piazzas, designed to encourage visitors to linger, whilst cooler blues and yellows were used on interconnecting streets, encouraging pedestrians to move more quickly through the space. The facades of key city landmarks, such as the Royal Palace, were painted in warmer hues, which – glowing brightly in the Italian sunshine – would attract people to them. Over the intervening centuries, the colours weathered and the scheme collapsed; the urban facades were subjected to the indiscriminate and widespread use of 'Turin yellow'. In the 1980s, Brino and Rosso (1980) revived the scheme, in part to resurrect the city's public image after its decline owing to an economic recession. To avoid the authoritarian prescription of colour throughout the entire city, only a small central area of Turin is now rigorously controlled by colour (see Figure 4.6). This gives the city an underlying unity and cohesion, aids orientation in the city centre and adds vitality to the sensation of experiencing – and remembering – a city.

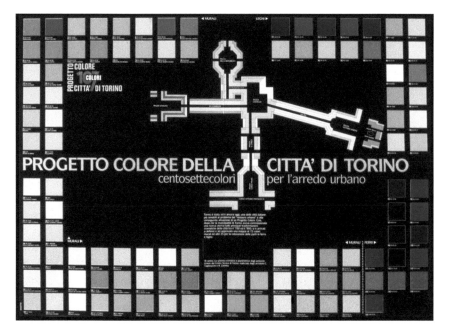

FIGURE 4.6 The 107-colour palette of Turin, Italy, and the schematic chromatic map of the axes of the historic city centre. Source: Germano Tagliasacchi and Riccardo Zanetta, architects of the chromatic plan for Turin.

Design principles for a sensory city

As well as separating design principles into general principles, neighbourhood scale (Figure 4.7) and city scale (Figure 4.8), it is more helpful to approach the sensory city in terms of two design objectives.

Seize opportunities to include salutogenic sensory design with evidence of promoting mental health and wellbeing

- Use nature-based 'tranquil' sounds to create 'sonic refuges', and use gentle sounds from homes, schools and places of worship to instill belongingness.
- Position public spaces to take advantage of smells appropriate to the location that are clean, natural, fresh and familiar, particularly nature and pleasant food smells.

- Use symmetry, scale, proportion, order, unity, balance, rhythm, contrast harmony and colour to increase aesthetic pleasantness, wayfinding and local character.
- Use fine-grain shopfronts, natural features, buildings with visually clear purpose and other structures of visual interest, including public art, to increase diversity, reduce monotony and encourage fascination in the landscape; avoid featureless expanses.
- Use LED lighting at night to increase people's use of the city and to improve safety.
- Use textural variation, including nature-based textures, underfoot and in structures' composition to encourage healthy use of spaces.
- Ensure that all neighbourhoods have convenient access to nutritious foods with a diversity of stores, outdoor markets and food trucks catering to different tastes, as well as access to urban farming and allotments.
- Design markets to incorporate bumping places and opportunities for social interaction.
- Provide space for food festivals and cultural celebrations that involve food.
- Apply the principles of sensory garden design more widely to increase multisensory engagement and immersion in parks and other public spaces.

Reduce exposure to unpleasant sensations by decreasing production and transmission

- Reduce people's exposure to unpleasant sensory output, particularly near residences, public spaces and pedestrian/cycling routes.
- Reduce traffic density by investing in pedestrian and cycling infrastructure and in green public transport to reduce unpleasant sights, sounds, smells and atmosphere associated with traffic.
- Reduce traffic noise by reducing traffic locations, speed, density and noise transmission (e.g. speed bumps/platforms, gateway infrastructure for low-speed zones and natural traffic-calming features such as humpback bridges and winding roads) and by using quiet-pavement road-surfacing technology.

- Mask traffic noise with barrier walls, berms, trees, sound-masking facades and water.
- Focus on reducing rather than masking unpleasant smells through industrial odour-management processes, zoning and other separation-distance buffer approaches.

1 mural
2 bakery
3 water wall
4 varied facades
5 linear park
6 rooftop garden
7 speed bumps for traffic control
8 fine-grain storefronts
9 food market
10 community garden
11 sensory garden
12 gently flowing water
13 textured pathways

the senses

sight
sound
taste
smell
touch
atmosphere

FIGURE 4.7 The Sensory City: Neighbourhood Scale.

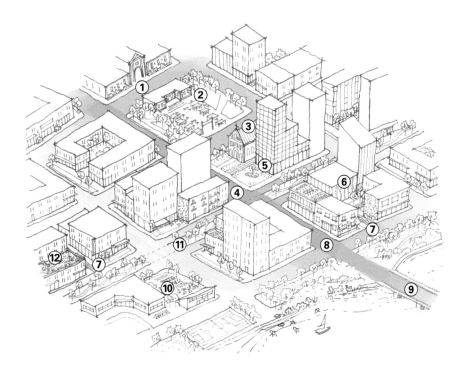

1 buildings with visual interest 👁
2 food market + festival ✋ 👅 🌸 ⚙
3 church bells 👂 ⚙
4 colour organization for wayfinding
5 water feature 👂 👁
6 water wall 👂 👁
7 pedestrian surface texture ✋
8 connecting artery from downtown to waterfront ⚙
9 bridge light installation 👁 ⚙
10 community garden ✋ 👅 🌸
11 linear park ✋ 👁 🌸 👂 ⚙
12 sensory garden ✋ 👁 🌸

the senses
sight 👁
sound 👂
taste 👅
smell 🌸
touch ✋
atmosphere ⚙

FIGURE 4.8 The Sensory City: City Scale.

5

The neighbourly city

Highlights

- People who have strong networks of supportive social relationships are less likely to develop mental health problems and more likely to recover from them.
- Social isolation and loneliness increase the risk of mental health problems like depression, anxiety and suicidal thoughts.
- Housing can be designed to promote positive, natural social interaction and networks across all ages, mixed incomes and all ethnicities.
- Parks and urban green space facilitate social interaction and foster place belonging, altruism and greater perceptions of trust in a neighbourhood.
- Local amenities, parks and mixed-use, walkable neighbourhoods with fine-grain storefronts and avoiding 'boring' featureless walls foster social capital.
- Volunteering improves mental health and wellbeing and should be harnessed by urban design, in terms of both community involvement/co-design and designing places where neighbourhood volunteering can take place.
- Investment in public spaces associated with facilities that people use regularly and in bumping places where people can regularly meet and linger on an impromptu basis, such as a dog-walking park, can enhance neighbourliness and reduce mental health problems.
- Depending on cultural norms, different people need different types of public and semi-private space to facilitate positive social interactions, and design should reflect this.

- Urban spatial attributes that support conviviality include human scale, accessibility, aesthetics and engaging surroundings, and comfort and safety.
- The Covid-19 pandemic affected mental health by reducing people's ability to benefit from neighbourly potential in urban spaces.

Key concept definitions

Belonging-in-place: Connections to people in a place, plus connections to places themselves, over time create active participation in the social life of that place.

Community: A social unit comprising a group of people with a shared location; interests; or other social, religious, ethnic or other backgrounds or attributes, leading to commonality of social norms, values, customs and/or identity.

Conviviality: In this context, a quality of public space that encourages human interaction and liveliness, a mingling of people in the course of their everyday lives to form transient connections that make them feel happier and part of a bigger 'whole'.

Loneliness: A subjective, unpleasant and distressing feeling due to a discrepancy between a person's desired and achieved volume and/or quality of social relationships.

Neighbourliness: The quality and quantity of relationships, support, reciprocity and trust with respect to people who live nearby.

Social isolation: An objective state where a person has a low level of contact with normal social networks, including community involvement and communications with family, friends or acquaintances.

Social capital: The quantity and quality of formal and informal social networks, relationships, cooperation, interactions, civic participation, reciprocity and trust in others.

Social cohesion: The extent to which people in society are boun d together and integrated and share common values.

What is the neighbourly city?

Social relationships and connections have long been recognized as a key determinant of individual and community mental health (Bagnall et al. 2017; Kawachi and Berkman 2001). Regular social interaction builds people's self-esteem, self-confidence and empathy; increases their feelings of support and belongingness in a community; helps people cope with life's challenges; and mitigates feelings of loneliness, anxiety and isolation. Social interaction can also improve brain function, particularly memory and intellectual performance. Conversely, loneliness and poor social connectivity increase people's risk of depression, anxiety and suicidal thoughts (Beutel et al. 2017; Cruwys et al. 2014).

And yet the urban environment itself is a risk factor for loneliness and social disconnection. Studies tell us that whilst at least one in ten working-age adults report feelings of loneliness (Beutel et al. 2017), that figure increases to nearly half of people living in cities (Wilson and Moulton 2010). The urban phenomenon of feeling alone in a crowd can be socially isolating (Bennett, Gualtieri and Kazmierczyk 2018). Urban design that promotes natural, positive social interaction therefore has the potential to help prevent mental health problems and to support recovery.

There are many reasons that city life predisposes people to loneliness. City residents seeking to build new social networks encounter several challenges, perhaps most famously, and still relevantly, described in the seminal 1938 work *Urbanism as a Way of Life*, by Louis Wirth, summarized below:

First is migration, the biggest driver of urbanization. At least 3 million people migrate to cities every week (UN Habitat 2009), with an extra 2.5 billion predicted by 2050, largely in Africa and Asia (UN DESA 2018). In doing so, these people leave at least part of their social support networks behind. They need to build new networks in their new city, often having to start from scratch without the benefit of local connections based on family, longevity and shared religious/cultural values. City residents are often less homogeneous than in people's place of origin. With divergent social norms and values, it can be challenging for city residents to identify social affinity (a reason some migrants find themselves living, at least for a period, in so-called 'ethnic enclaves'; see the Inclusive City chapter).

Migrants are not the only ones seeking to build and re-build social networks. Because cities are transitory places, urban social networks tend to be unstable, with high turnover rates. This can lead to superficial social connections and social networks that are not tied to place. Even for people who have lived in a city for a long time, established social networks can rapidly disintegrate when key members of those networks change jobs and/or move out of the city or even to the far reaches of a metropolis.

People who live in cities may also be less integrated with their communities. They often do not own their homes, they are more likely to live in single-person households and less likely to have an established family unit, they are less likely to participate in ritual dimensions of religion (Nikkhah et al. 2015), and they are more susceptible to significant social mobility in both directions.

All of these factors make it particularly difficult to sustain solidarity of local social groups and membership of community organizations.

Another challenge is social overload. The typical city resident will encounter thousands of strangers every week, which reduces social cohesion and contributes to overload in three main ways: by reducing the likelihood of encountering the same people regularly, which would foster social relationships; by increasing the potential stress associated with the prospect of having to socially interact with an overwhelming number of people; and by reducing the likelihood of being observed by an acquaintance, which increases the risk of anti-social behaviour, including criminality in the city.

Finally, the geographical separation of home, work and other amenities means that city residents may have less time to invest in local social networks, in particular due to work commitments and commute time and when transport is inefficient (see the Active City and Inclusive City chapters).

Feeling socially supported increases people's mental health resilience and has the potential to reduce rates of mental health problems. Developing urban planning and design solutions that foster positive social interactions and increase people's mental health resilience is a key contributor to public health. In particular, there is the opportunity to modify through design and planning the extent to which a place is 'neighbourly' – reducing social isolation; facilitating the development and sustaining of social networks and subcultures; and increasing social cohesion, conviviality and feelings of local belongingness, where people from all walks of life can come together and enjoy public space.

Theory

There are three key pathways through which the neighbourly city can affect mental health and wellbeing (Figure 5.1).

The first pathway is through social capital. Positive, natural social interactions help people develop the social networks and social support that strengthen mental health resilience, reducing the risk of developing mental health problems and supporting recovery (Ehsan and De Silva 2015). This happens through the development of individual and community conviviality and neighbourliness that create 'social capital' – how people participate and cooperate in relationships, community and civic networks, membership organizations and other associations that link them together. This in turn contributes to local civic identity, including trust, values, reciprocity and norms of cooperation, attitudes, altruism, information and responsibilities within a community (Putnam 1993). Three main components of social capital have been found to particularly affect mental health: social integration, quality of relationships and social networks

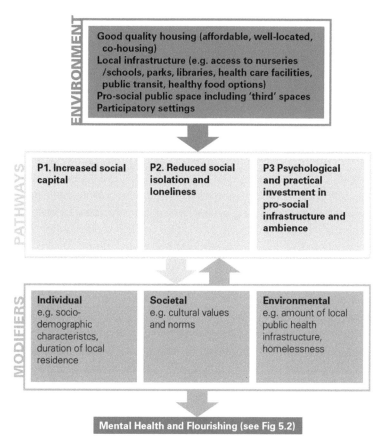

FIGURE 5.1 The effects of neighbourly design on mental health and wellbeing.

(Umberson and Montez 2010). Social capital includes having networks within a group or community, as well as networks that span social groups, social class, race, religion and other diverse characteristics.

Conversely, the second pathway is the role of neighbourliness in preventing social isolation and loneliness. Loneliness is associated not only with earlier death (Rico-Uribe et al. 2018) but also with a wide range of mental health problems, including depression (Holvast et al. 2015; Meltzer et al. 2013), psychosis (Badcock et al. 2015) and suicide (Joiner 2009). Loneliness can also inhibit recovery and affect mental health outcomes, particularly following depression (Leigh-Hunt et al. 2017; Wang et al. 2018a).

Loneliness occurs when insufficient socially integrative relationships and close, confiding relationships lead to feelings of not belonging and exclusion (see the Inclusive City chapter). It has been defined as a negative emotional state that occurs when there is 'a discrepancy between the desired and achieved patterns of social interaction' (Peplau and Perlman 1982).

The third pathway is the indirect impact of how 'neighbourly' a place is (Buonfino and Hilder 2006) on people's access to settings that support mental health, such as nature (see the Green City and Blue City chapters), inclusivity (the Inclusive City chapter), physical activity (the Active City chapter), play (the Playable City chapter), and convivial public spaces that foster living well together and encourage impromptu human interaction amongst friends and strangers.

More 'neighbourly' neighbourhoods tend to have two features: (1) a significant proportion of people who remain living in the same neighbourhood over time, including intergenerational longevity, and (2) a significant population who are invested in using amenities within their immediate residential environment rather than going elsewhere in the city to work and socialize; this allegiance applies particularly to children and older people who have less impetus to travel beyond the immediate neighbourhood (Garin et al. 2014). These 'neighbourly' neighbourhoods attract investment in local infrastructure (e.g. high proportions of families attract nurseries, schools, parks, libraries), which in turn create bumping and meeting places where neighbours not only regularly encounter each other, but also have reason to interact in positive ways. Access to good-quality, affordable homes attracts the longevity, neighbourhood attachment and neighbourhood investment that help embed social activity and community life, thus growing social relationships.

Less 'neighbourly' neighbourhoods, on the other hand, tend to suffer from lower levels of financial and psychological investment (Buonfino and Hilder 2006). They often have fairly transitory, predominantly working-age populations, including people newly arrived in the city who may not yet have had the opportunity to develop social networks or may have language or cultural barriers that impede informal social interaction with their neighbours. These residents may be living only temporarily in the neighbourhood, until they establish themselves and settle somewhere more long term.

Such neighbourhoods are often characterized by lower socioeconomic status (see the Inclusive City chapter). Neighbourhood investment is often low: there may be evidence of crime, litter and disorder; air and noise pollution may deter lingering outdoors (see the Sensory City chapter); and there may be less pro-social infrastructure in situ. Crime reduces people's feelings of personal safety and security in a neighbourhood and affects their trust and pride in that place. Experiencing or witnessing crime is independently associated with developing mental health problems (Clark et al. 2006). Litter is a manifestation of neighbourhood disorder – creating an impression of a neighbourhood that is not safe, valued or cared for – and of a tolerance of disorder and lack of oversight that reduces feelings of both safety and pride in a place. Good maintenance of an area is a key factor that encourages positive social interaction (Dempsey et al. 2014).

The impact on mental health

Of all the restorative design interventions described in this book, some of the most compelling concern neighbourly design. The research consistently demonstrates that a neighbourly city that achieves good social cohesion, trust and robust social networks for its citizens can promote and support their mental health. Neighbourliness in the form of social capital and positive social interaction affects mental health, from depression and anxiety to cognitive function (Figure 5.2).

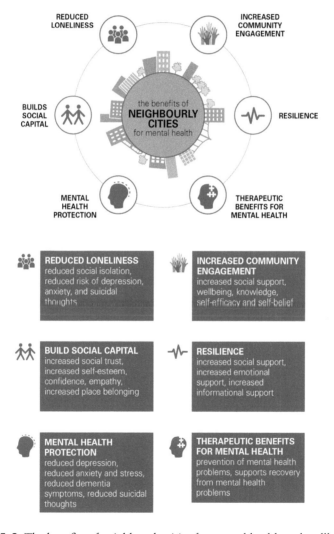

FIGURE 5.2 The benefits of neighbourly cities for mental health and wellbeing.

Neighbourly cities reduce depression

A huge number of studies demonstrate a strong link between depression and social capital, social interaction, belongingness and neighbourhood social cohesion (Cohen-Cline et al. 2018; Leigh-Hunt et al. 2017; Santini et al. 2015). People with chronic depression tend to have smaller social networks than people without mental health problems (Visentini et al. 2018), and living alone is more highly associated with depression when the perceived 'social quality' of the neighbourhood is low (Stahl et al. 2017). Good social support and social networks have been found to be the main protective factors. In particular, high-quality relationships that deliver emotional support and diverse social networks are helpful in reducing the risk of mental health problems; there is also increasing interest in the positive impact of the psychological sense of belonging to a community. An interesting study from China found that the key factors reducing the risk of depression are improving neighbourhood-level reciprocity and social group membership (Wang et al. 2018b).

Neighbourly cities reduce anxiety

There are links between having poor social networks (including neighbourhood traffic noise and perceived lack of safety mediating neighbourhood social interactions) and developing anxiety disorders (Generaal et al. 2019; Teo et al. 2013).

Neighbourly cities may protect against psychosis

The risk of developing schizophrenia is increased in neighbourhoods with high levels of social exclusion, social fragmentation and racial discrimination (Heinz et al. 2013).

Neighbourly cities can help reduce symptoms of dementia

Loneliness and low social participation are both associated with an increased risk of dementia (Kuiper et al. 2015). Older people who do not experience social isolation and feelings of disconnection are half as likely to experience rapid cognitive decline in multiple functional domains (Mitchell and Burton 2006).

Neighbourly cities reduce suicide

Loneliness and a poor sense of belonging to a community are associated with both increased thoughts of suicide and suicide attempts (Hatcher and Stubbersfield 2013).

Modifiers of impact

Certain groups are at particular risk of both developing mental health problems and missing out on the protective factors of urban design that could confer neighbourly benefits on their mental health:

- **Age:** People aged sixteen to twenty-four and older people share a similar, elevated risk of loneliness (Lasgaard, Friis and Shevlin 2016). For young people, this may be associated with having recently moved away from home or relying predominantly on digital communication rather than socializing in person with friends, family, neighbours and even colleagues. Meanwhile, as our populations age, an increasing number of older people live alone and become socially isolated, lonely and at increased risk of developing mental health problems, particularly depression (Courtin and Knapp 2015). Part of the explanation seems to be a narrowing of social networks and geographical sphere, related to physical and cognitive limitations.
- **Immigration:** The majority of the world's migrants move to cities, for reasons ranging from economic to asylum; many drivers of immigration (like unemployment or exposure to trauma) are themselves risk factors for developing mental health problems and involve migrants leaving their social networks behind. These people often need new social networks, which they must develop whilst potentially feeling overwhelmed and overloaded by the increased stimulation in the city or being marginalized from community activities due to barriers like language and fear of discrimination or victimization.
- **Homelessness:** There is a complex relationship between homelessness and mental health problems whereby one may precipitate the other. A study in Melbourne found that 15 per cent of homeless people had mental health problems prior to becoming homeless, and a further 16 per cent had developed a mental illness since experiencing homelessness (Johnson and Chamberlain

2011). People become homeless for many reasons, many of which, again, are also risk factors for developing mental health problems. Homelessness itself is a risk factor, associated with people experiencing rejection, stigmatization and dehumanization. Part of this is lack of belongingness within a neighbourhood, including restrictions on people's use of public space, whether those be rules and policing associated with public-private spaces; hostile or defensive architecture, such as the 'anti-homeless spikes' used to prevent people from resting in certain areas (Petty 2016; see the Inclusive City chapter); or lack of safe shelters and local access to water and facilities to meet people's hygiene needs.

Design approaches for a neighbourly city

A neighbourly city helps people come together, build social networks, develop social capital, participate in community life and feel a sense of neighbourhood belongingness (Bagnall et al. 2017). Such social connections build mental health resilience, reducing people's risk of developing mental disorders and supporting their recovery. Urban design for a neighbourly city is not simply about increasing social exposure; social connections should be natural and chosen, not overwhelming. This can be achieved in the design of homes and their environs, and also by extending out into the neighbourhoods and bringing the community into the design process (Osborne 2016).

Housing

The physical, social and psychological attributes of the housing environment have significant impacts on mental health (Shaw 2004), which contribute to the restorative aspects of neighbourliness: the likelihood of people developing relationships with their neighbours, feeling welcome, feeling safe and feeling that they belong. Social capital, social networks and social cohesion can all be modulated by housing design. Research has found that people's perception of their neighbourhood's social climate alone significantly affects their mental wellbeing (Wright and Kloos 2007). Key modifying factors include:

Availability/affordability: Housing insecurity and debt affect mental health. The definition of homelessness has evolved beyond whether a person has a roof over their head. Having a home means having rooms in which to sleep and socialize, access to bathroom and kitchen, privacy and safety, and security of tenure. This means that homelessness includes not only rough sleepers but also people moving around temporary accommodations (from emergency hostels to couch surfing), those living in very overcrowded homes, and those living in housing of inadequate quality or safety or in homes with short tenure, contributing to a transitory population (Brackertz, Wilkinson and Davison 2018) and affecting personal and neighbourhood mental wellbeing. For example, the negative effects on mental health associated with social housing increase with each home transition people make (Bentley et al. 2018).

Available homes at an affordable cost (generally considered to be less than a third of gross household income) help reduce homelessness and enable the development of people's security, social capital, social networks and social cohesion in a neighbourhood. This often may involve investment in affordable housing (homes that are available often below market price, usually aimed to ensure that low-to-medium-income households spend no more than a third of their gross household income on housing). This includes good availability of social housing, also known as welfare housing. Social housing usually comprises rental homes provided/managed by the government or non-governmental organizations for people who cannot access accommodation on the private market.

Adequacy: Availability of housing is not in itself adequate to protect mental health and wellbeing. For instance, people who live in social housing are more likely to have worse mental health and more psychological distress than those occupying other tenures, likely associated with inadequate quality, disadvantageous location, stigmatizing effects, safety concerns and lack of neighbourhood investment (Bentley et al. 2018). Poor indoor air quality, high lead levels in paint, dampness, high noise levels, presence of pests and overcrowding have also been associated with depression, anxiety and stress (Krieger and Higgins 2002; Srinivasan, O'Fallon and Dearry 2003).

Location: The quality of the neighbourhood in which people's housing is located impacts neighbourliness and thus mental health and wellbeing. This includes people's access to services, facilities, transport, jobs, education and places suitable for socializing, including natural features. Housing should be co-located or easily accessible to wider social and health infrastructure, including social, recreational, commercial, health and educational facilities, as well as economic opportunities. This helps create social cohesion. Isolating housing without these features can result in mental health problems at the individual and community level, whilst prioritizing them can create social hubs within the community. Older adults living in low-amenity and moderate-amenity neighbourhoods are more likely to experience symptoms of depression compared to people living in high-amenity neighbourhoods (Gillespie et al. 2017). In Tokyo, these are conceived as Daily Activity Areas and form part of the city's policy for long-term care. The aim is for all key services and amenities to be available within a thirty-minute walk of older people's homes (Baba 2017). This may include a 'healthy street' which contains health-related and other key amenities on a street designed for accessibility and safety (see the Active City chapter). The principles are widely applicable: living in walkable neighbourhoods rich in amenities affords people the opportunity to bump into each other, to develop relationships with local service providers, and therefore to reduce social isolation. If people need to travel (particularly by car) to access amenities, the mental health benefits of the neighbourly city are squandered.

Stigma: Stigma flows in different ways in housing. People with mental health problems may experience stigma and discrimination in trying to secure housing. And some people also experience socioeconomic stigma in two main manifestations. First, living in a neighbourhood considered to be of low quality, including visible disorder and the presence of significant noise or unpleasant smells, inhibits lingering, sociability and neighbourliness, and affects self-esteem (see the Sensory City and Inclusive City chapters). Secondly, when people of different socioeconomic status live in the same neighbourhood, they may still experience segregation by design, such as 'poor doors' (where people who own their homes are physically and psychologically separated from those in receipt of social housing, even within the same building development).

Cohousing: The association between marriage and mental health varies by culture, but research suggests being happily married seems to promote good mental health and wellbeing. This effect is largely attributed to social support associated with cohabitation (Bierman et al. 2006; Horn et al. 2013). Shared facilities like kitchens, gardens, laundry rooms and recreational areas can foster meaningful social relationships.

There has been an evolution, particularly in high-income countries, towards living in individual or single-family homes; but now, increasingly, the trend is moving away from this towards cohabitation. This is driven by diverse reasons, including romantic, economic, social, filial and, increasingly, in pursuit of a philosophy of communal living. Many instances of communal living are multi-generational, which can have both negative and positive impacts on mental health. Multi-generational living is more common for people who are related, and its impact may depend on its perceived desirability. In some cultures, multi-generational living can be a desirable social norm; whilst some people – especially when thrown together unwillingly due to financial problems, relationship dissolution or housing crises – may feel unhappy, frustrated or ashamed to be living with their parents or grandparents. Multi-generational living can reduce people's autonomy, increase the risk of interpersonal conflict at home and increase the likelihood of experiencing overcrowding. The impact of multi-generational living on mental health is therefore complex, but overall tends to increase healthy people's social capital and wellbeing – and even their life span (Muennig 2017). These benefits are not restricted to people who are related to each other. Unrelated cohabitation is traditionally most common for students (such as a university hall of residence) and older people (such as sheltered housing or nursing homes), but cohousing has become of interest between these groups (see the city examples of Deventer and Zurich below).

Housing design for social opportunity: The design of housing impacts potential sociability. For instance, urban high-rise living can affect people's relationship with place. High-rises are often associated with fewer instances of friendly interactions with neighbours compared with those living in low-rise homes for people of all ages; dark lifts/stairwells and communal space near entryways associated with safety concerns deter social engagement (Barros et al. 2019). The effect of high-rise living on reducing social interaction is pronounced for children who lack a safe play area near the level of their home – parents may be deterred by safety concerns from sending their children unsupervised to playparks at significant vertical distance (Lai and Rios 2017). People living in high-rises may be more likely to experience stigma, further challenging their mental health (Barros et al. 2019). The Happy City's Happy Homes Toolkit draws out key recommendations for increasing neighbourliness through housing design for multi-family houses (Lai and Rios 2017). The toolkit identifies key design features, including attractive, accessible communal spaces, that encourage diverse residents to spend time together: clustering homes into groups to achieve socially manageable numbers of neighbours, reflecting residents' cultural identity to improve their belongingness, supporting long-term residents, and enabling walkability to increase bumping points and social opportunities.

Privacy to enable sociability: The need to balance privacy and social interaction is important. Having the opportunity for solitary time, with people being able to exert personal control to regulate their social interactions with others in their environment, enables people to choose to socialize, which can enhance the quality of their interactions (Evans 2003). Design that distinguishes public and private space by using creative demarcations and configurations of space, from nooks to porches to positioning of plants, can help clarify the difference between public and private space. This approach has also been taken to increase safety by enhancing features like territoriality and natural surveillance (Newman 1976).

Beyond housing

Social settings within the wider neighbourhood: The design of a neighbourhood impacts upon its conviviality and the extent to which it facilitates social interaction for good mental health. Positive, natural social interactions in communal/public places can increase people's sense of belonging, reduce stress and have restorative effects.

Public space design is particularly important for promoting socialization by causing people to pause and engage with their surroundings, and by creating temporary bonds as a result of shared spatial experience, for instance by stopping to watch a street performer in a city square. Dines and Cattell (2006) identified prerequisites for social interaction in public spaces, particularly for bringing together diverse urban populations to socialize in a natural way: people are familiar with the space, it is in regular use, it remains in use for similar purposes over time, and facilities within or nearby give purpose to the space and enhance its social vitality. This includes social spaces next to places of worship, schools, libraries and other such regularly visited amenities.

Thombre and Kapshe (2020) brought together the extensive research on designing for conviviality to conceptualize the characteristics of public space that contribute to conviviality in three distinct categories. First, availability of public space for convivial activities such as eating and drinking, people watching, play, participating in cultural activities, and bumping places. Second, people need to perceive a public space as convivial (defined as convivial perception by the authors); that is, it has to feel safe and comfortable, be easily accessible, and promote positive mood (joy, relaxation, delight, excitement), and can be interpreted (consciously or unconsciously) as a place in which one belongs, and/or has special meaning via positive memories/personal associations/ symbolism of a place. Third, built form and spatial attributes that support conviviality, such as human scale, accessibility, aesthetics, and engaging surroundings. Also mixed land use, because people are more likely to engage in convivial activity as an adjunct to more necessary activity (Gehl 1987). In this model, conviviality of a place is not binary but may vary depending on, for instance, time of day, or when the place plays host to convivial occasions like festivals.

Other pro-social design factors include:

- Bumping places where people routinely encounter each other on an impromptu basis; for instance, at a farmers' market or at a dog park. Enhancing safety, comfort and attractiveness of these spaces can increase opportunity and inclination to stop and chat.

- Intermediate-complexity surfaces and permeable facades, such as fine-grain storefronts with windows and doorways along the street rather than uniform concrete walls, can alleviate boredom and negative ruminations and make people more attentive and engaged, encouraging lingering and sociability (Ellard 2015).
- Participatory elements suitable for different age groups and interests, such as benches aligned for conversation, chess tables, outdoor gyms, gardening opportunities and spaces for community altruism/volunteering (see below).
- Flexible accommodation that facilitates cooperative community activity like street markets and public celebrations, including shared space with multiple uses. For instance, in Hong Kong, groups of older people meet daily on university plazas to engage in group tai chi or chi qigong before the students arrive; and on weekends, thousands of home workers convene and socialize in plazas belonging to closed offices.
- Climate-sensitive design that relieves heat stress, offers shade and protects from heavy rain, depending on the needs of the location.
- Good stewardship of meeting places: public space investment in marginal places can promote sociability. If a public place is run-down, has evidence of crime or disorder and feels unsafe, people tend to avoid it and experience reduced feelings of belongingness and pride in their neighbourhood. This can engender discord between neighbours, particularly if certain groups of people are blamed for the disorder, or if people without other places to socialize, such as homeless people, unemployed people, street drinkers and teenagers, are felt to dominate the space and intimidate other users (Madanipour 2004).
- Shared services: the sharing economy, which includes bikeshare, car-sharing schemes and other types of neighbourhood sharing, creates feelings of trust, reciprocity and belonging in a digital neighbourhood with physical neighbourhood manifestations, augmenting the community belongingness benefits of existing shared services such as libraries (Celata et al. 2017).
- Design for safety to promote people's willingness to linger and socialize, including sufficient space to enable social interaction whilst maintaining physical distance.

Pro-social places incorporate places of assembly, market and ritual; these accessible places, where people can spend time without spending money, are also sometimes called third spaces and provide the opportunity to foster a sense of local community. Parks, water and other natural features within the urban realm (see the Green City and Blue City chapters) offer particular public space design opportunities for people to convene or meet on an impromptu basis. Design opportunities for restorative social interaction also extend to so-called hard spaces, such as streets and markets. Examples of both include a park next to a school, a street opposite a mosque, a temple courtyard and a market that has a communal purpose that attracts people regularly but also enables lingering and wandering.

An interesting example of a potential pro-social space is Hong Kong's 'sitting-out area' concept – small, unused nooks between building developments that are usually paved, with benches and vegetation installed (Figure 5.3). They seek to maximize use of space; however, design and location are critical to their success. Some are connected to thoroughfares and are designed with shade, greenery and benches that promote rest and conversation; others are in 'left over, residual areas … so they are not well-connected or well-appointed', and 'there's a lot of concrete … benches in a row' that can inhibit conversation and afford little protection from the sun and rain (McCay and Lai 2018).

FIGURE 5.3 A sitting-out space in central Hong Kong. Source: Leung Hoi Shuen.

The 'pet factor'

As well as providing companionship and supporting mental wellbeing, pets can be an important catalyst for both spontaneous social interactions and local friendships, helping build social networks. This works by naturally convening people regularly at bumping points (such as parks where dogs exercise), providing both an icebreaker and a commonality to instigate conversation and precipitate friendship. In particular (but not exclusively), people with dogs are about five times more likely than non-pet owners to speak to people they do not otherwise know in their neighbourhoods; for almost half, this leads to some type of social support, like providing advice and emotional support or looking after one another's pets (Wood et al. 2015). It is worth considering pro-pet policies in both residences and public places and using pro-social design for pet owners' infrastructure and routes to maximize mental health benefits.

Participatory settings within the neighbourhood

Extensive research has demonstrated that volunteering is associated with better mental health, life satisfaction, self-esteem and happiness. Volunteering reduces depressive symptoms and psychological distress and improves quality of life by supporting better physical health (Yeung et al. 2018). Volunteering improves people's mental health and wellbeing by building social integration, social networks, social capital and the experience of gratitude, combined with increasing feelings of self-worth and a sense of mattering and life meaningfulness. The effects can be cumulative with multiple volunteering activities and are greatest when the volunteering activity helps others in need: altruistic, intergenerational volunteering has more longevity; self-preoccupation counteracts the positive effects of volunteering. Urban design can promote volunteering in two main ways:

First, by establishing pro-volunteer spaces in the public realm. These can range from community gardening spaces to hospitals, care homes and other settings within the neighbourhood where volunteering may be appropriate, as well as public spaces suitable for bringing people together (e.g. for games or festivals).

Secondly, the process of urban design itself can increase volunteering through participative design, decision making and bottom-up development of spaces. Community involvement in collaborative city making is a central theme of the child-friendly city movement, the dementia-friendly city movement, the hackable city movement (where new media technologies are used to change urban institutions and infrastructures in the public interest), and the place-making and place-keeping movements. In all of these, a primary tenet is that the community is expert in what it needs and designing an inclusive place is a group effort (see the Inclusive City chapter); the process is also a neighbourly, pro-social mental health intervention in its own right. Community engagement can improve people's social support, wellbeing, knowledge, self-efficacy and self-belief (NICE 2016). In particular, community engagement and co-design in the development of projects with a health focus have been found to improve housing, safety, community empowerment, social capital and social cohesion (Milton et al. 2011), all of which benefit mental health. By providing residents with opportunities to influence decisions about their neighbourhood, community engagement builds their confidence to exert control over their circumstances whilst also facilitating regular contact between neighbours, including those of diverse ages, ethnicities, socioeconomic status etc.

The positive impact of community engagement in urban design on mental health is strongest when residents are genuinely empowered to affect the end result; conversely, when this proves not to be the case (e.g. by deploying a simple consultation), the participants' mental health may be negatively affected (Attree et al. 2011).

Conversely, there is a risk that community participation may expose or ignite neighbourhood discord. This is most commonly seen with the NIMBY ('not in my back yard') phenomenon, whereby groups of neighbours develop social capital by uniting to oppose developments they consider undesirable, such as mental health facilities or shelters for homeless people. Doing so may encourage discrimination against certain community members.

To avoid this, community involvement in urban design projects should ideally be more proactive than reactive. An interesting example is Japan's *machizukuri* – a technique whereby citizens play a key role in improving and governing their neighbourhoods. Machizukuri is characterized by neighbourhood-based volunteer organizations that incrementally encourage public and private land developers to voluntarily respect the wishes of the community and create new civic spaces, increasing greenery and reducing pollution in a neighbourhood (Sorensen et al. 2009).

Beyond the neighbourhood: transit design

Feelings of entrapment can lead to tension and social discord and limit access to opportunities that promote mental health and wellbeing. Urban planning should prioritize and facilitate legible connections to and between potential hubs and gathering places. Walkable, bikeable cities for all provide opportunities for social interaction; plus, efficient transit can reduce commutes, freeing up more time for people to spend with friends, family and neighbours. In terms of road design, separating pedestrians from cars as much as possible facilitates more social interaction, and avoiding splitting neighbourhoods with large roads is an important investment in social cohesion and social equity (see the Active City and Inclusive City chapters).

Neighbourly city examples

Deventer's intergenerational housing model, the Netherlands

In Deventer, a small city in the Netherlands, there are problems with availability, cost and quality of experience for both student campus housing and long-term-care facilities for older people. Frustrated with the noisiness of his accommodation, one student famously approached Residential and Care Centre Humanitas – and a new housing model was developed. Six university students moved into the Humanitas facility to live rent-free in the care home with 160 older people; their payment was in the form of social return on investment against loneliness for the older residents through intergenerational social interaction. The students participate in at least thirty hours of activities each month – celebrating birthdays; teaching the older residents how to use social media; watching sports together; and other interactions that emphasize togetherness, diversification of conversation, strengthening of relationships, and no 'us' versus 'them' (all residential units are designed for all levels of frailty). The Care Centre also invites non-residential community members: a group of children with autism has put up a train set in the basement; the Centre hosts clubs; the garden is open to the public; a local photographer exhibits work; and people struggling in the neighbouring community are offered free temporary support. In this way, the Care Centre has shifted from social isolation to social wellbeing and community integration, becoming an intergenerational anchor institution within the city (Arentshorst et al. 2019).

Zurich's cooperative housing, Switzerland

Zurich has a long history of *Wohnbaugenossenschaft* (cooperative housing). One of its more famed developments is Kalkbreite, completed in 2014 (Figure 5.4). Kalkbreite prioritizes residents' mental and social wellbeing, focusing on the social fabric of the neighbourhood and embodying the principles of citizen-led development. The residents co-designed this housing development in partnership with local authorities. Like other co-ops, land is leased by the city at affordable rates. The communal ownership and pooling of finances mean that the residents can innovate in how they want to live together; they

FIGURE 5.4 Kalkbreite housing development, Zurich, Switzerland. Source: Singh Simran.

have chosen to prioritize social and civic inclusion and harmony. This includes a shared commitment to protecting the environment, manifesting, for instance, in choosing to invest in bike parking and transit links instead of car-parking facilities. The Kalkbreite development provides collective living for 250 people, with flexible residential units suitable for nuclear families and extended households, as well as shared communal space; some units have access only to communal kitchens. The units also foster socioeconomic inclusion: most of the apartments are used by middle-income occupants, but a portion is available to and reserved for higher- and lower-income occupants. These approaches aim to meet residents' changing needs and demographics over time. Alongside these residences are facilities like a public park as well as work, commercial and entertainment spaces (e.g. a cinema), all atop a tram depot.

Design principles for a neighbourly city

General principles

- Design should be human-scale and human-centred.
- Meaningful neighbourhood participation should be part of planning and design projects (see the Inclusive City chapter for details).
- Ensure good stewardship and maintenance to attract people to linger and use places.

Neighbourhood scale (see Figure 5.5)

- Provide adequate, available homes, co-located and/or easily accessible to wider social infrastructure and diverse amenities, including recreational, educational and economic.
- Design housing that integrates social infrastructure, including opportunities for communal and multi-generational living, as well as appealing communal spaces that attract and facilitate appropriate interactions for different age groups.
- Use design to demarcate private and public space for privacy, safety and positive social interaction.
- Co-locate public social spaces with facilities such as schools or religious buildings to give purpose to the space, harness regular use and familiarity, and enhance social vitality.
- Create bumping places for people to encounter one another in attractive, safe, informal settings, including streets, squares, parks, play areas, village halls and community centres.
- Provide fine-grain, permeable facades such as storefronts that are lively and engaging (avoid monotonous, uniform blocks).
- Provide pet and animal amenities and infrastructure that promote social interaction, such as dog parks, bird hides and wildlife spots.
- Invest in third spaces that are welcoming to all, require no money to be spent and facilitate lingering and meeting, including libraries, churches, community gardens and the opening of semi-private spaces for public use.
- Incorporate participatory features suitable for all ages, including flexible settings for cooperative community activities such as benches for chat and seated views, facilities for exercise and games, and places that can host celebratory events and various types of volunteering.

City scale (See Figure 5.6)

- Ensure accessibility that is inclusive of different abilities and needs (see the Inclusive City chapter).
- Avoid hostile architecture and rules that exclude certain people; prioritize inclusive facilities, for example, facilities that meet homeless people's safety and hygiene needs (see the Inclusive City chapter).
- Design walkable and bikeable cities that include pedestrianized areas, well-maintained pavements, traffic-calming measures, street

benches, public toilet facilities, bicycle parking, shared transport services such as bikeshare and good lighting and signposting.

- Allow for flexibility in use of space, such as temporary pedestrianization, or space sharing whereby one location can be used for different purposes, such as a university plaza for use by a neighbourhood exercise club in the mornings and for use as a farmers' market on weekends.
- Design parks and other public spaces to include physical infrastructure that facilitates social interaction, such as seating, separate areas and features that provide comfort, interest and engagement.
- Create ludic spaces for flexible, playful opportunities that inspire social engagement.
- Provide safe shelters and access to water and facilities to meet homeless people's safety and hygiene needs.

1 community hub
2 fine-grain storefronts
3 housing with communal space
4 housing with public/private spaces: porches + balconies
5 roof gardens for residents
6 seating for social interaction
7 community garden
8 pedestrian connections

FIGURE 5.5 The Neighbourly City: Neighbourhood Scale.

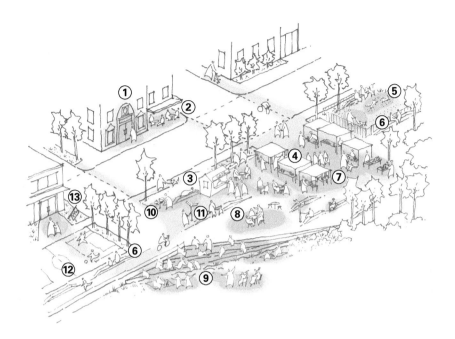

1 place of worship
2 community cafe
3 pop-up cafe
4 flexible space for city festival days
5 dog park
6 bench seating for social interaction or reflection
7 farmers market
8 seating for eating + socializing
9 gathering space
10 public amenities: drinking water
11 public amenities: charging station
12 shared sports field
13 school

FIGURE 5.6 The Neighbourly City: City Features.

6

The active city

Highlights

- An active city integrates physical activity into everyday urban life and designs urban spaces to enable mobility for all citizens.
- Urban design strategies for active living are almost entirely driven by physical health motives in order to reduce the risk of chronic health conditions. But physical health is inter-related to mental, social and cognitive wellbeing; 'whole' health active living strategies are needed.
- The mental health benefits of active cities include a reduced risk of depression and anxiety and improved stress regulation.
- Being active supports brain health and memory functioning and plays a significant role in healthy ageing and healthy child development.
- The characteristics of an active city include mixed-use communities, multi-modal (or 'comfortable') streets, street connectivity, subsidized and integrated public transit, and street trees and urban greening.
- Place aesthetics (e.g. architectural variation, visual delight) in the streetscape increase people's curiosity and motivation to walk/cycle.
- The spatial design of a city – and how stimulating and engaging it is – determines how easily citizens can navigate through it, in turn impacting brain functioning and wellbeing.
- There is a need for novel ways to increase opportunities for regular physical activity in the everyday environment, including using underutilized public infrastructure (e.g. vacant parking lots) for parklets and pop-ups, bikeshare schemes, all-age mobility opportunities, and paying more attention to mood of place and the psychological experience of walking and other modes of active travel.

Key concept definitions

Active living: A lifestyle that integrates physical activity into everyday routines, including walking to work or school, using public transit etc. An active city integrates opportunities for active living into urban design.

Active travel: Modes of transport that incorporate physical activity, such as walking, jogging, cycling, skateboarding, rollerblading and electric scooters.

Cognitive function: A set of mental processes responsible for learning and understanding (Donnelly et al. 2016).

Brain health: The development and preservation of optimal brain integrity and neural network functioning for a given age (Gorelick et al. 2017).

Mixed-use development: Blending a diverse mix of uses and activities (residential, commercial, cultural, institutional, entertainment) in close proximity to where people live and work, also referred to as 'live-work' space.

Multi-modal street: Offering safe, attractive and convenient travel by foot, by cycle, or on public transit, as well as in motorized vehicles; also referred to as a 'comfortable' street.

Street connectivity: Street network connections with short block lengths and many intersections that provide direct routes between destinations.

What is the active city?

We know that active cities deliver a host of benefits that support flourishing cities. These include economic benefits (increased land value, increased footfall, retail profitability, more jobs), safety benefits (injury prevention), environmental benefits (reduced air and noise pollution) and social benefits (social capital and cohesion) (Sallis et al. 2015). Designing a city that promotes physical activity is also widely acknowledged to be good for our physical health. National and global public health movements now seek to increase physical activity through the design of 'active cities'. The physical health benefits of active cities include a reduction in the risk of chronic diseases, including obesity, cardiovascular disease, stroke, cancer, diabetes and respiratory disease (Booth, Roberts and Laye 2011).

Less attention has been paid to the myriad of mental, social and cognitive wellbeing benefits of active cities, including reduced depression and improved brain functioning from exercise, increased opportunities for social connection and community building, and psychological restoration through street and place aesthetics.

Because the research identifying the health benefits of an active city is skewed towards identifying physical health outcomes, improved safety, environmental impacts (e.g. reduced air/noise pollution) and economic outcomes, urban design interventions are also skewed towards these findings (e.g. favouring traffic calming) rather than taking a more integrative approach that also considers how other attributes of place (e.g. aesthetics) motivate travel behaviours. Consequently, active cities are underutilized in urban design interventions for mental health.

International health guidelines now recommend at least 150 minutes of moderate-intensity aerobic exercise per week and 60 minutes of physical activity per day (WHO 2011). But around the globe, increasingly sedentary behaviours (including driving, sitting at length) mean very few individuals reach these targets. In the United States, for example, only a quarter of adults and children meet these criteria (Blackwell and Clarke 2018); in the UK, only 17 per cent of older men and 13 per cent of older women meet recommended activity guidelines (Age UK 2011).

Making exercise part of the everyday routine – so it simply ensues from the right environment – and encouraging people to be active through small goals (like walking to a local shop) are arguably a better public health strategy than lofty targets that seem unattainable for many. It has been suggested that simple strategies – and starting small – can deliver significant health benefits over time ('We Are Undefeatable', www.weareundefeatable.co.uk, is one example of a campaign encouraging small steps for people living with long-term health conditions). Some estimates suggest that urban design strategies can also make a significant difference, helping facilitate up to ninety minutes a week of physical activity (Sallis et al. 2016). Moving through city streets – walking, running, cycling – is free and is also how we most naturally move around. Making our cities safer, more pleasant and more convenient to navigate is therefore a worthwhile infrastructure investment and public health priority.

In this chapter, we document how mobility affects emotional, social and cognitive wellbeing. Next, we identify the specific urban design characteristics that support active living across the age span, drawing on a well-established literature. Finally, we conclude that since so few people currently meet national physical activity targets, there is a need to think much more about the quality of experience for active travel and for innovative approaches that include opportunities for intergenerational physical activity. As in previous chapters, we draw on systematic and/or umbrella reviews of the research evidence where possible.

Theory

Both leisure- and transport-related physical activity positively affect mental health. There are four key pathways through which urban planning and design to increase physical activity is believed to deliver positive mental health and wellbeing outcomes (Figure 6.1).

The first pathway is the neurobiological mechanism, which proposes a direct effect of regular physical activity on brain health, or cognitive function, including memory and attention. In terms of memory, physical activity is believed to

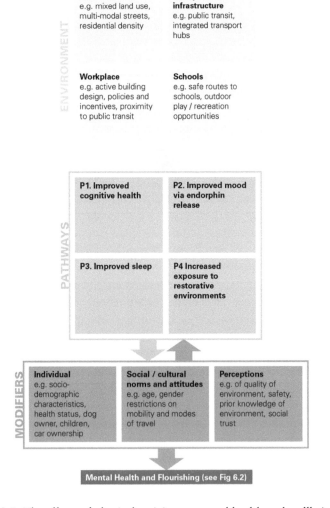

FIGURE 6.1 The effects of physical activity on mental health and wellbeing.

enhance certain brain chemicals (including brain-derived neurotrophic factor, insulin-like growth factor and vascular endothelial growth factor) and increase the volume of the hippocampus, a key part of the brain's memory network involved with spatial memory (memories of place), episodic memory (personal memories of specific events) and semantic memory (objective knowledge of the world and facts) (Erickson et al. 2011). This change in hippocampal volume may, in turn, lead to improvements in cognitive functioning. There appear to be cognitive health benefits from physical activity for all ages, including pre-adolescents (Pesce et al. 2009) and young adults (Stroth et al. 2009). But there seem to be particular benefits from physical activity for middle-aged people (Hörder et al. 2018; Rovio et al. 2005; Won et al. 2019), including reducing the risk of dementia (Smith et al. 2013), even with light exercise (Spartano et al. 2019). In terms of attentional capacity, moving through a city delivers exposures to busy urban spaces, which increases beta brain waves, associated with directed attention; moving through green spaces (e.g. parks) increases alpha waves, associated with relaxation and reduced attentional demands (Neale et al. 2019). See Macpherson et al. (2017) for a detailed review of the role of exercise in brain health.

The second pathway is the direct effect of physical activity on mood and stress resilience. Participating in physical activity is believed to cause the release of endorphins (the brain chemicals dopamine, noradrenaline and serotonin), which can produce feelings of euphoria. The research is unclear whether this temporary feel-good effect would have any longer-term impact on mental health and wellbeing. It is more likely that physical activity positively affects the perception of self by engendering social interaction (relatedness), mastery in the physical domain (self-efficacy and perceived competence), improvements in self-perceived physical appearance (body image) and feelings of independence (autonomy) (Lubans et al. 2016).

The third pathway is the positive impact of exercise on sleep, which is highly protective of mental health. Physical activity can improve sleep duration, sleep efficiency and sleep onset latency and also reduce sleepiness (Lubans et al. 2016; see the Sensory City chapter), thus improving mental alertness and performance.

The fourth pathway is the indirect impact of physical activity on mental health by leading people to conduct their physical activity in settings that support mental health and wellbeing. For instance, in the course of undertaking physical activity, people may pursue 'green exercise' (e.g. running in a park; see the Green City chapter), use blue space (e.g. cycling by a river; see the Blue City chapter), seek positive sensory immersion (e.g. walking through a food market; the Sensory City chapter), or incorporate play (e.g. climbing in a playground; the Playable City chapter). Such physical activity may also provide an inclusive experience (e.g. accessible bikes; see the Inclusive City chapter) or facilitate social encounters (e.g. a team game; the Neighbourly City chapter).

The impact on mental health

Active cities that facilitate opportunities for regular exercise can provide a wealth of health benefits. The physical health benefits are well documented and are not the focus of this chapter (for a review of physical health benefits, see Panter et al. 2019); these work in synergy with the benefits for mental and social health across the life course (Falck et al. 2019), (Figure 6.2).

FIGURE 6.2 The benefits of active cities for mental health and wellbeing.

Active cities reduce depression, anxiety and stress

Regular walking (and other forms of exercise) is a proven strategy for reducing depression, anxiety and stress (Barbour, Edenfield and Blumenthal 2007; Martinsen 2008; Powers, Asmundson and Smits 2015; Smits et al. 2008), with a meta-analysis of eighty studies showing positive effects regardless of gender, age or health status (North, McCullagh and Tran 1990). There is also good evidence that walking in outdoor settings – particularly in urban green space ('green exercise') – delivers benefits over and above exercise indoors or in more hostile 'grey' urban settings with noise and congestion (Barton and Pretty 2010; Kondo, Jacoby and South 2018). Green exercise in children with ADHD has also been shown to improve such children's symptoms and increase their attentional capacity (Faber, Taylor and Kuo 2009).

Active cities improve the mental wellbeing of children and adolescents

Research exploring the benefits of active cities for children and youth has largely focused on the benefits of walking and/or cycling to school for health outcomes, including physical, emotional, social and cognitive wellbeing (Biddle and Asare 2011; for an integrative review of the literature, see Waygood et al. 2017). Benefits of active travel for both child and youth mental health include reduced depression and anxiety and increased self-esteem (Dale et al. 2019); improved mood and subjective wellbeing (Ramanathan et al. 2014); improved stress regulation (Ramanathan et al. 2014); increased social integration, both parent–child and child–child (Romero 2010); improved cognitive health, including better concentration and improved cognitive ability, working memory and academic achievement (Hillman et al. 2009; Kamijo et al. 2011; Kibbe et al. 2011; Pollard and Lee 2003; Westman et al. 2013); and improved spatial cognition and navigation skills, which increase autonomy (Ahmadi and Taniguchi 2007). But the literature has so far largely ignored the need for autonomous access by youth and children to other desirable destinations that may contribute to wellbeing (including access to cultural events, downtowns, or wilder, farther away 'adventure' spaces). Autonomous travel increases self-control and self-esteem (van Vliet 1983) and is vital to allowing children to access both social and play affordances (see Chapter 1).

The evidence is currently weighted towards activity in primary school children and school programmes; there is much less evidence showing the benefits of active cities for adolescent health and wellbeing. What constitutes an active city for youth has largely been overlooked. Research has shown, from the perspective of teenagers, that an active city should allow for freedom of movement (including the ability to use unusual forms of transit such as skateboards and free running); personal safety; the ability to access a variety of places to meet friends, to play formally and informally, to participate in sports and adventurous activities, to do community work, to shop and access cultural activities in the city; and freedom to gather in public spaces without the presence of anti-loitering deterrents such as 'acne lights' and 'mosquito alarms' (Roe and Roe 2019).

Active cities reduce the risk and symptoms of dementia

Regular exercise appears to help our brains be more resilient to ageing, a concept referred to as brain 'reserve', which can help reduce cognitive decline later in life. An active city, then, is one strategy that can promote healthy brain ageing and potentially help reduce the burden of dementia, the greatest global challenge for public health and social care in the twenty-first century (Livingston et al. 2017).

Active cities support spatial cognition and wayfinding

Knowing where we are going and how to reach a destination is associated with a number of mental health-related factors, including our sense of control, our levels of stress and our personal mastery of an environment. We each have our own 'inner GPS' system implanted in our brain – our stored mental maps of places, or 'cognitive map' – that allows us to effectively navigate through space using various cues and landmarks. This is referred to as the 'imageability' of a city (Lynch 1960). But new GPS technologies are changing how we navigate a city, our travel choices and, in turn, our sense of personal control and mastery. Google Maps (and other smartphone apps) negates the need to scan the city for spatial knowledge that helps formulate a mental map of a route (and image of the city) and may change how we relate to our environment. Currently, little is known about how such technologies change our experience of a city, our long-term spatial memory capabilities and our wellbeing, although early research has shown that use of 'sat nav' (satellite navigation) affects the muscle in the brain associated with navigation, the hippocampus (Javadi et al. 2017).

Active cities improve social wellbeing

Mobility in a city is social activity: the leisurely *passeggiata* taken in an Italian city, for example, which offers opportunities for spontaneous and organized social encounters, increasing social cohesion and strengthening community ties. But robust evidence is limited to only a handful of studies, which show associations between active-living design and increased social benefits. Much of the research points to the effects of specific urban design interventions on increased footfall and numbers of people on streets, not on specific social health outcomes. Multi-modal street design, for example, is associated with increases in pedestrian volume of up to 76 per cent (GDCI 2016). Similarly, road closures/car-free streets bring more people out into a city to partake in civic engagement and the life of the city. Ciclovias (temporary closure of a road to automobiles, allowing access for walkers/runners/cyclists) increases opportunities for social interaction, with one US study showing that it can strengthen perceptions of sense of community (Hipp, Eyler and Kuhlberg 2013). Another study has shown how these types of interventions can also promote quality of life (Gössling et al. 2019).

Access to city parks and green spaces – a key characteristic of the active city – is associated with increased social wellbeing (see the Green City chapter), including decreased feelings of loneliness (Maas et al. 2009), stronger social integration (Kweon, Sullivan and Wiley 1998) and a greater sense of belonging (Ward Thompson et al. 2016). 'Soft' front-garden edges are also linked with greater street activity and neighbourly social interaction (Gehl 1986) and emotional wellbeing (Chalmin-Pui et al. 2019). Walkability and easy access to desirable destinations are significantly associated with increased social cohesion (Mazumdar et al. 2017) and higher perceptions of sense of community (Wood, Frank and Giles-Corti 2010).

Using public transit also improves social opportunities and social satisfaction as compared to private vehicular travel (Besser, Marcus and Frumkin 2008; Christian 2012; Delmelle, Haslauer and Prinz 2013; Mattisson, Håkansson and Jakobsson 2015). Commute time also impacts social outcomes, including levels of social participation and time spent with family (Besser et al. 2008; Mattisson et al. 2015). Better access to public transit – with subsidized travel – can reduce social exclusion and social isolation (Holt-Lunstad, Smith and Layton 2010), particularly for at-risk groups such as older people. For example, entitlement to concession fares for public transportation in London increased community inclusion in youths and older adults (Jones et al. 2013). Use of different transport modes (bicycle, car and public transport) significantly reduces loneliness and supports independent living in older people (van den Berg et al. 2016).

Modifiers of impact

Individual characteristics affect how people engage with the active city, including age, gender, ethnicity, socioeconomic status and health status. So do lifestyle factors, such as whether a person has children, has dogs to walk or owns a car.

People's individual perceptions are also modifiers: their assessment of the quality of the environment, their feelings of safety, prior knowledge of the neighbourhood, social trust and environmental beliefs.

Societal attitudes and cultural norms also play a part, such as gender restrictions on mobility and acceptable forms of transit (e.g. use of bikes by women in some countries) and tolerance of youth preferences for alternative modes of transport, such as skateboarding, roller skating and scooters.

Design approaches for an active city

Over the past decades, 'active living' research has consistently identified certain design and policy characteristics that increase physical activity, although this knowledge is largely restricted to middle-to-upper-income countries. There is a need for further research addressing how these characteristics work together, their success in increasing activity in low-income countries, and the challenges of implementing such features in rapidly growing cities where urban sprawl is advancing.

Spatial characteristics associated with increased active living include residential density (the number of people living and working in an area), mixed-use development (a diverse mix of services and activities), active building design (e.g. the presence of bridges and stairwells), street connectivity (better connections between streets and safe intersections), traffic calming, separated pedestrian and cycle paths, park proximity, street trees and urban greening (Panter et al. 2019; Sallis et al. 2012, 2015, 2016). Active cities provide opportunities for traditional physical activities like running, tennis, swimming etc.; they also integrate opportunities for physical activity into everyday routines, promoting pleasant walking routes, cycling and use of public transport to and from school and work. Public policies associated with promoting active living include providing subsidized public transit and workplace/school physical activity programmes that offer incentives to cycle/walk.

These design approaches should not be implemented in isolation, for two reasons. First, combinations of these characteristics appear to be more effective in promoting physical activity than any single characteristic alone, suggesting that integrated approaches are needed to design active cities

(Sallis et al. 2015). Secondly, the context influences the impact: for instance, whilst residential density may promote physical activity, it may also increase traffic as well as noise and air pollution detrimental to health. Impact will also be modified by a wide diversity of individual and behavioural factors, including social and cultural preferences, whether one has children or a dog, the familiarity of a neighbourhood etc. Key characteristics of the active city include:

Accessibility and street connectivity

Greater street connectivity is consistently associated with active living (Badland, Schofield and Garrett 2008; Hajrasouliha and Yin 2015; Koohsari et al. 2014; Panter et al. 2019). Typically, street connectivity is measured using metrics that capture the physical interconnections between streets. Higher physical connectivity usually means a shorter travel time to a destination. But this metric-based approach fails to take into account the psychological experience whilst walking or how pleasant it is. We might, for example, trade a more pleasant – but longer – walk for a shorter, less pleasant walk. In addition, higher street connectivity may increase traffic volume on residential streets (Handy, Paterson and Butler 2003).

Safe routes

Safe routes for pedestrians and cyclists are segregated from motor vehicles and well lit at night, increase perceptions of personal safety, reduce perceptions of risk of crime, and are consistently associated with increased walkability and cycling (Panter et al. 2019). Safe routes include traffic-calming speed bumps and conveniently-located pedestrian crossings. The Covid-19 pandemic has highlighted a less well-recognized aspect of safety: sufficient space for pedestrians and cyclists to maintain physical distance from one another whilst moving around the city in order to reduce the risk of spreading infection.

Mixed land use

Having a diverse mix of services and activities in close proximity to where people live and work is consistently associated with increased physical activity (Durand et al. 2011; Sallis et al. 2012) and has prompted planning policies for compact development, such as the '20-minute city' model, whereby people can access their work/life needs within a twenty-minute walk, bike ride or public transit ride (currently being trialled in the US city of Portland, Oregon). But mixed land use is difficult to achieve, requiring the collaboration of private investors/real estate developers as well as government agencies. Also, the findings are inconsistent across different geographies and cultures (Sallis et al. 2016).

Residential density

Residential density is typically defined as the number of residences divided by the size of a given area/neighbourhood. But urban density is more complex than just the number of people living in a place. In a mixed-use neighbourhood, residents may be only a small proportion of the total population (i.e. density includes the number of people working there, the number of people passing through etc.), and patterns will rise and fall during work hours and weekends. Also, high residential density is often misinterpreted (particularly by real estate developers) as high-rise living, but building tall does not necessarily increase residential density (in New York City, for example, apartments can be exclusive, large and expensive, reducing population density). High-rise public housing (four storeys or more) has been associated with poorer mental and social health as compared to alternative housing, although there is a lack of high-quality evidence (Barros et al. 2019). Residential density has a complex relationship with health outcomes, with evidence of both positive and detrimental effects. Higher residential density may be associated with more vibrant street life, but higher numbers of people living in close proximity to one another can also increase such stressors as noise and cramped living conditions. Whilst higher residential density is associated with environmental sustainability and economic benefits, it does not alone appear to increase levels of physical activity and may even contribute to higher air pollution and increased safety concerns/injuries (Sallis et al. 2015).

Parks and street trees

Sallis et al. (2015) conducted a systematic review and concluded that, of all urban design features to promote physical activity, the strongest evidence for mental health benefits is the presence of urban green space. Park proximity and the presence of urban greenery/street trees have been consistently associated with increased physical activity (see the Green City chapter). Whilst parks support specific recreational activities (e.g. sports pitches/tennis, play, picnic areas), networks of nearby parks also contribute to vital green 'corridors' that facilitate walking/cycling to key destinations (work, school). These findings are consistent with restorative environment theory and research showing a positive effect of urban green spaces on cognitive overload, and they have implications for how we design to reduce cognitive overload – for instance, ensuring sufficient aids (safe crossings, signage) at busy street intersections – as well as designing green spaces for attentional restoration.

Urban design characteristics for all-age active cities

Given that active cities offer particular mental health benefits for children, young people and older people, there are specific characteristics that facilitate active living for these communities. The characteristics of the outdoor urban environment that improve mobility for children, youth and seniors are well documented (Arup 2017; Tinker and Ginn 2015) and are advocated by the WHO age-friendly city (WHO 2007) and the UNICEF child-friendly city (UNICEF 2018) initiatives, which have considerable synergies. The characteristics, many of which are expanded upon in other chapters, include:

- 'Comfortable', traffic-calmed streets with wide pavements (with smooth surfacing); frequent road crossings and sufficient seating (including informal seating such as sitting walls)
- Accessibility for people with wheels (e.g. strollers/buggies/ wheelchairs/rollators and other walking aids)
- Clearly visible, appropriately positioned and easy-to-read signage
- Sheltered bus stops with comfortable seating and electronic notifications of 'due' times
- Well-maintained public bathrooms and drinking-water fountains
- Public gardens and access to gardening opportunities (e.g. community gardens)
- Local parks, urban green spaces and water settings
- Street trees and shade canopies to avoid heat stress
- Street aesthetic and architectural interest
- Independent mobility options (e.g. free public transit, bike and car share schemes)
- Opportunities for exploration and curiosity
- All-age outdoor gyms and intergenerational playgrounds
- Opportunities for synergistic, playful activity between old and young

The psychological experience of active travel

Our travel choices are motivated not just by the convenience, speed or affordability of getting from A to B, but also by the experience and the associated positive affect (Jensen, Sheller and Wind 2015). Alongside the practical attributes of urban environments, the affective dimensions of space (how relaxing, stressful, safe it feels) have a direct impact on walking and other active travel behaviours, the routes we choose, and our motivation to move through and explore our environment. Our emotional connection to space may shape our health outcomes just as much as, if not more than, the distance (or number of steps) travelled.

Transportation policy for health has focused almost exclusively on increasing physical activity and decreasing driving. Consequently, the dominant urban design approach favours increasing walking and cycling opportunities through traffic-calming measures and 'comfortable' street design. Success is typically measured using metrics that capture travel distance, frequency of trips, and before-and-after pedestrian and cyclist volumes (GDCI 2016). But 'the experience of travel – how daily life shapes mobility – goes beyond distance traveled or number of trips' (Mondschein 2018: 19). The experiential component of travel – the role of street aesthetics, engagement with one's surroundings, sensory stimuli or mood of the street – has been neglected. Arguably, walking (or cycling, skateboarding, scooting) offers a more embodied 'lived' experience of a place than driving. Urban designers and transportation planners have been slow to consider the types of experience that promote walkability, although these questions are beginning to be explored (Bornioli, Pankhurst and Morgan 2018, 2019; Mondschein 2018).

Place aesthetics, perceived 'interestingness' and architectural variation improve the likelihood of people walking or cycling (Panter et al. 2019) and are associated with psychological restoration, improved wellbeing and reduction in perceived levels of stress (Bornioli et al. 2019; Knöll et al. 2019; Lindal and Hartig 2013).

The strongest association between place aesthetics/interestingness and the mental wellbeing benefits of active cities is urban green space. The benefits for psychological wellbeing from walking in green spaces ('green exercise') as compared to busy urban streets (characterized by noise, busyness, traffic etc.) are well established (Barton and Pretty 2010). However, integrating green space is not always practical (and also needs longer-term maintenance). Understanding what types of place aesthetics (e.g. colour, pattern, complexity) can help foster psychological wellbeing through impact on travel behaviours is still in its infancy and is an important area for future research. Several urban walking studies, for instance, have found that walking in historic downtown districts is associated with improved mood (Bornioli et al. 2018) for both healthy adults and those with mental health problems (Roe and Aspinall 2011). This is likely owing to the inherent fascination and level of visual complexity in historic street facades that promote involuntary attention (see the Green City and Sensory City chapters). Mobile phone technologies are now helping researchers capture people's psychological experience of moving around a city, associated with such characteristics as nature, noise levels, safety and sensory stimulation; unsurprisingly, these studies have found that people report feeling happier in natural settings (Bakolis et al. 2018; MacKerron and Mourato 2013). However, happiness is a transitory feeling, and as yet, such techniques have been unable to find convincing correlations with long-term mental health outcomes.

Another tool being pioneered to advance understanding of mobility in relation to mental health outcomes is space syntax. This method originated in architecture and urban design and characterizes and quantifies four spatial properties of the built environment: building density, street connectivity, visibility and predominant type of open space (e.g. park, courtyard, street) (Hillier and Hanson 1989; Hillier, Hanson and Graham 1987). The research has largely focused on showing relationships between walkability, pedestrian volume and street integration rather than psychological wellbeing (Koohsari et al. 2019; Lerman, Rofè and Omer 2014). But these spatial aspects of urban form can also be correlated with mental health data. One study in Darmstadt, Germany, showed that good street connectivity (accessibility and walkability) was significantly related to reduced stress, underlining the importance of walkability connections for mental wellbeing. Visual complexity (higher levels of detail and complexity in a facade) was also significantly associated with reduced stress (Knöll et al. 2019), emphasizing the need for more visually engaging building facades that draw our attention and curiosity. Whilst there is a need to replicate this research in different cities with different urban typologies, the framework is particularly helpful for showing how selected attributes of the built environment affect stress.

It is of course extremely complex to translate research findings from models like space syntax into design interventions that improve street connectivity or introduce new land-use mixes in cities where city form and street layout (and human behaviour) have been fixed for decades. It requires significant vision and leadership, collaborative partnerships, flexibility and the will of a community for change. Below we explore one city where this vision is currently being realized: Barcelona.

Active city example

Barcelona's superblock model, Spain

Barcelona is leading innovation in health urbanism with the implementation of a new 'superblock' model that integrates traffic-calmed areas with new parks,

FIGURE 6.3 Barcelona superblock, Spain. Source: Abigail Chan.

playgrounds and squares to reduce vehicular transport and promote active living (Figure 6.3). No other city in the world has envisioned such a 'grand plan' for urban health (Roberts 2019), with approximately 70 per cent of the city's streets to be devoted to car-free, mixed-use zones. A total of 500 superblocks are envisioned, with 4 superblocks already completed (in the Born, Gracia, Poblenou and Sant Antoni neighbourhoods), 3 in progress (Les Corts, Horta and Hostafrancs), and 10 in the planning stage. The 'idealized' superblock comprises nine square city blocks and has around 6,000 residents, although there is some variation. Streets are prioritized for walking/cycling, with traffic speed restricted to 10 mph; vehicular access is restricted to residents' vehicles and delivery vehicles. Parking is largely underground, and public space is prioritized for parks/squares (with picnic tables), urban greenery, play, sports and open-air concerts. The superblock is envisioned as a social unit, housing a diverse range of ages, ethnicities and socioeconomic strata and increasing opportunities for social contact via new parks and squares. Signage, lighting and the configuration of crosswalks are being creatively designed to nurture a distinctive sense of place for each block. Another key strategy in the superblock model is the siting of the block around an existing facility and destination (or 'attractor'), such as the Sant Antoni market.

The pilot for the project, in the Poblenou neighbourhood, used methods of community engagement and tactical urbanism to test out various design scenarios (i.e. low-cost, short-term changes), which allow urban design interventions to be trialled and adapted and residents' behaviours and responses taken into account prior to making permanent changes.

To date, only predictive health analysis has been carried out, forecasting substantive environmental benefits (reduced air/noise pollution and heat stress), increased levels of physical activity, and reduced mortality rates (in premature deaths, fewer road injuries and reduced heart disease) (Mueller et al. 2020). But evaluation of health outcomes in the real world has yet to be carried out; this evaluation should include mental and social wellbeing indicators alongside those for physical activity. It will also be important to understand how socioeconomically disadvantaged residents benefit from the superblock model (including ethnic minorities) and any barriers to increasing walkability.

Barcelona's vision for 500 superblocks has been described as 'utopian' and subject to the vagaries of the political system and likely changes in political leadership in Catalonia (Roberts 2019). Nor is the model without opposition owing to fears about 'superblock gentrification', rising rents, displacement and clogged traffic in streets in the outer perimeters. Mediation measures for these problems include provision for social housing, rent controls and ambitious plans to re-design the city's entire public transit system, creating an integrated mobility network that will link pedestrian/cycling corridors with bus/metro stops. Addressing the commuter needs of residents living farther out of the city, in adjacent suburbs and towns, is also under consideration (Roberts 2019).

It has been argued that the street design of Barcelona and other European cities lends itself more easily to superblock-type interventions than, say, the United States or rapidly urbanizing cities such as Delhi or Kathmandu. Urban space in the United States has a different spatial make-up and is built primarily for car travel, comprising sprawling suburbs, multiple-lane highways and interstates, and strip malls. But US cities have the advantage of space and the opportunity, therefore, to integrate new infrastructure; tactical urbanism strategies in US cities are demonstrating how multiple-lane highways can be modified to make a city more walkable, play-friendly and social. The spatial argument – as a reason for inaction – would appear to fall flat in light of the success of these interventions.

Design principles for an active city

General principles

- There are several excellent blueprint guidelines for designing active cities, including the *Global Street Design Guide* (GDCI 2016), the Center for Active Design's *Civic Design Guidelines* (2010) and *Designed to Move Active Cities* (2016).
- As an overarching goal, we urge urban designers and architects to be creative about putting the 'active' in the everyday environment – for example, making stairwells and bridges 'events' in their own right – 'attractors' (and more attractive than elevators) to which people are drawn and where they can linger for a while rather than just use as a route to some other place.

Neighbourhood and city scale (see Figures 6.4 and 6.5)

Open space/parks (read in conjunction with the Green City chapter design guidelines)
- Provide pocket parks within a five-minute walk of home, larger parks within a fifteen-minute walk.
- Connect parks to multi-modal streets and other city green spaces.
- Plant street trees and encourage front-garden design and 'soft' street edges.

Mixed-use design
- Provide a diverse mix of facilities within a twenty-minute walk of where people live (residential, schools, commercial, cultural, recreational etc.).
- Provide a mix of economically diverse housing in a community.
- Foster connectivity between facilities via short block lengths with frequent and safe intersections that provide direct routes between destinations.
- Provide mixed-income and multi-unit housing (e.g. shared/intergenerational/supported housing) built around activity centres with shops, services and transport hubs.
- Reorganize city parking (e.g. via underground parking or out-of-town parking lots with integrated public transit).

Street design (see also GDCI 2016)
- Provide multiple modes of transportation (safe, continuous routes for cycling, walking, scooting/skateboarding), with wide sidewalks, cycle lanes, bike parking and safe street crossings.
- Provide good lighting and frequent seating.
- Be creative in the design of details (signage, lighting, curbs, seating) to produce a distinctive sense of place.
- Provide pedestrianized zones around key 'attractors' and daily destinations (e.g. railway stations, markets).
- Design connectors (e.g. bridges and public stairwells) as 'events' to encourage use.
- Make navigation intuitive (e.g. by distinctive landmarks and nodes).
- Limit garage walls facing streets.
- Provide cut-throughs in cul-de-sacs for pedestrian connectivity.

Cycling infrastructure
- Provide clear and comprehensive signage and dedicated bicycle signal lights.

- Design cycle tracks that are separated from pedestrian and vehicular traffic.
- Provide integrated cycleways connected to public transit.
- Provide cycling superhighways for commuting longer distances.
- Include bus/train bike racks.
- Provide bicycle 'parking' and shelters at work and public transit hubs, with water fountains, public lockers, and public showers.
- Foster bikeshare schemes.
- Ensure level crossings.
- Provide lighting over busy highways.
- Provide lighting for tunnels and underpasses.
- Ensure that air pump facilities are available across the city.

Public transit
- Provide easily accessible, regular and integrated public transit to and from destinations.
- Provide public transport that is convenient, affordable, frequent, safe, comfortable and equitably distributed.
- Foster bike/scooter hire/share schemes.

Schools
- Locate schools within walking/cycling distance of homes and provide safe routes to schools (e.g. walking, buses).
- Encourage shared-use agreements to open up school recreational, sports and green space facilities to the wider community on evenings/weekends.

Active design in buildings (see also Center for Active Design 2010)
- Ensure that frontages are open to the street, accessible for all and welcoming, particularly for public facilities (e.g. libraries, health facilities).
- Design stairways as 'events', open and visible at entranceways.
- Connect to green space corridors for walking/cycling to work and for break/lunchtime recreational opportunities.
- Connect to public transportation.
- Subsidize public transit for vulnerable groups (e.g. youth, seniors).
- Illuminate at night to encourage evening/night walking.

Use underutilized infrastructure
- Reorganize parking lots to provide parklets and to prioritize bike parking and provide protected bike storage.
- Use vacant lots for pop-ups, parklets, community gardens, urban farming.

- Reclaim underutilized infrastructure – elevated highways, disused railway lines, disused industrial buildings.

Active living policy and promotion
- Provide information about active transit routes (e.g. green bus and walking maps).
- Encourage employers to offer active transportation incentives and to promote walking meetings and stair use.
- Improve place keeping to minimize crime/vandalism and to nurture a sense of safety and pride in a place.
- Use tactical urbanism to test out various design scenarios on health behaviours prior to making longer-term structural changes.

1 subway
2 bike + pedestrian path
3 safe intersections
4 ride share
5 open active space
6 exercise trail
7 bus stop: shelter + seating
8 bike share
9 bike lane

FIGURE 6.4 The Active City: Neighbourhood Scale.

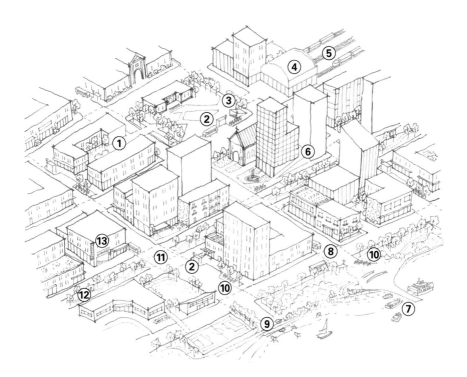

1 pedestrian-only through-block connections
2 bus stop: shelter + seating
3 subway access
4 multi-modal transit hub
5 regional connections
6 active building circulation
7 water transportation: ferry, water taxi
8 connecting artery from transit hub to water
9 bike paths, waterfront connections + activities
10 bike share
11 safe intersections
12 green belt bike path
13 subway access

FIGURE 6.5 The Active City: City Scale.

7

The playable city

Highlights

- Playable cities nurture creativity, learning, self-identity, agency and social interaction.
- Providing opportunities for play is vital for child and adolescent wellbeing, fostering physical, social, cognitive and emotional development; playable cities also offer continued development opportunities for adults.
- All-age, multi-functional open spaces are needed for everyone to enjoy.
- Playful cities encourage people to interact with the city and promote civic engagement.
- A playable city has two main characteristics: pure play contexts (props and contexts designed specifically for play, such as playgrounds) and other playable contexts (not designed for play but in which playful activities can take place).
- The playable city needs to be understood from a broader geographical and cross-cultural perspective.

Key concept definitions

Play: An enjoyable, spontaneous activity undertaken for its own sake.

Playful: A stance or attitude (or character trait); a way of engaging and being in the world (Sicart 2014).

Play affordance: The opportunities – or possibilities – that an environment offers for play relative to the individual; that is, 'what's in it for me' (WIIFM) (Gibson 1979).

Appropriative play: Play that takes over the context in which it exists and is not predetermined by such context (Sicart 2014).

Pure-play context: A context that exists for the pure purpose of play, with no other design function intended.

Play-*able* context: A network of things, people and places that may be appropriated for playful activities, personal expression, performance or civic activism.

What is the playable city?

The idea of a playable city for all ages is not new; historically, cities have always included playful infrastructure for adults (e.g. the Saturnalia of ancient Rome, a winter festival of partying and general revelry; the carnivals of the Middle Ages; and the eighteenth and nineteenth centuries pleasure gardens of Victorian London and New York City). More abstract concepts of a playable city have also abounded; the twentieth-century Situationist movement, for instance, challenged citizens to think more creatively about how to interact with the city and fostered the idea of 'drifting' through unfamiliar streets (the theory of *dérive*), a kind of early twentieth-century urban mind game (Ackermann, Rauscher and Stein 2016).

The idea that play is beneficial to our mental and physical health is not new either. But play has been slow to emerge as an urban design consideration for cities. The United Nations (UN) has achieved much in terms of prioritizing play via the 'child-friendly city' movement, and child-friendly urban design has gained significant momentum around the world; its characteristics – together with evidence of health benefits – are well documented (Arup 2017). But a role for play in building health beyond childhood has largely been ignored. It has traditionally been considered from the perspective of children. Whilst play is crucial for children's physical, social, psychological and cognitive development, the benefits of play for adolescents and adults have received much less attention. Even less attention has been paid to a universal city design for all-age play. It has also traditionally been demarked and designated for specific locations in a city rather than conceptualized as a network of spaces, that is, considered in the context of providing connected spaces (e.g. play trails) for children's play in urban environments. Newly emerging urban movements (such as the Playable City) are challenging both of these assumptions in perceiving the city as one boundless playground for all in which a plethora of creative opportunities lie.

Play is a complex concept to define, and theories regarding what play is and its benefits go back decades (Erikson 1968; Huizinga 1938). Play – in its traditional sense – can be defined as any kind of enjoyable, spontaneous activity undertaken for its own sake (i.e. for pure pleasure) rather than for any end goal (Graham and Burghardt 2010). At its most elemental, play incorporates fun, but it is also a process that incorporates uncertainty, anticipation, challenge, surprise, flexibility and problem solving (UN 2013). Urban design provides for this type of play in the form of age-specific playgrounds, segregated and closed off, typically located in parks, schools and public housing estates.

Play in adult life is less well defined and is generally perceived as less essential, as a frivolity rather than a necessity for wellbeing. But assumptions that play is the opposite of work in adulthood are refuted by theoreticians and empiricists alike (Csikszentmihalyi 2008). Another way of thinking about play is as 'flow' – a state of being in which you are totally engaged and the challenge of a particular activity matches your skill level, so you are neither bored because it is too easy nor anxious because it is too hard (Csikszentmihalyi 2008). Flow, then, captures the essence of adult play: being fully immersed and happy in what you are doing.

The 'purposeless' definition of play (and the division between work and play) has been challenged by Sicart (2014), who has argued that play has a purpose of its own. According to Sicart, play is a way of engaging and expressing our being in the world. Play is critical to our sense of place, our sense of identity and relationship to the world: 'Through play we experience the world, we construct it and we destroy it, and we explore who we are and what we can say' (Sicart 2014). Play is creative, expressive, appropriative, personal and autotelic (Sicart 2016). Play, then, is an important process in shaping flourishing societies (Huizinga 1938), in fostering meaningful lives (Pellis and Pellis 2010) and, in short, a way of 'being in the world' (Sicart 2014). In this respect, play is an important determinant of our mental wellbeing.

Moreover, Sicart and others (e.g. Proyer 2017) distinguish between play (an activity) and playfulness (an attitude or stance towards the world). Playful people possess an ability (or disposition) to transform any context to make it more enjoyable and stimulating. This distinction, Sicart argues, is crucial since it articulates two different ways of thinking about urban design for play (Sicart 2016): play often occurs with objects or in contexts designed specifically for it (e.g. a playground), but playfulness enables the 'play-ification' of objects or situations to allow for appropriative, personal expression. Examples include skateboarding and parkour, both of which appropriate street infrastructure (steps, railings, ledges) beyond the original intentions of the urban designer.

The playable city provides its players with the opportunity to re-imagine or reconstruct their everyday contexts. This can happen in formally designated spaces – for example, a playground that provides props to stimulate play or interactive public art installations that provoke 'players' to interact with space differently (e.g. the outdoor sculpture *Cloud Gate* in Chicago (see Figure 7.4), which, through mirrored reflections, encourages visitors and residents alike to engage with the cityscape and their place within it) – or by players being able to appropriate spaces for play (e.g. parkour or *Pokémon Go*, which, through technology, makes everyday spaces the backdrop of its game, allowing these spaces to take on new meanings for its players (see Knöll and Roe 2016)). Play therefore fosters creative expression and stimulates a connection with the urban environment itself and others within it.

Play can be active but can also be a non-physical activity, a form of mental freedom (e.g. daydreaming, mindless wandering) allowing the individual to escape everyday responsibilities, routines and rules. This requires a context that inspires daydreaming, drifting and contemplation – an *emotional playground* with cues that inspire deep thought. The mood of a place contributes to this process; it offers a sense of being away and of connecting to a whole other world, much like the attributes of a restorative environment.

The playable city is always creating new ways of imagining and experiencing the city (Sicart 2016), providing opportunities for both play and expressions of playfulness for all ages. It is disruptive: the city as a playground challenges the status quo and 'traditional' uses of space to allow for creative expression and connection in our urban environments, which can be alienating and inhuman. The playable city is therefore fundamentally human-centred and liveable; it allows its inhabitants opportunities for fun, creativity, self-expression, spontaneity and social connection. In short, it encourages its inhabitants to be active citizens, appropriating spaces for their own health and wellbeing.

This chapter explores the potential of the playable city – the city as a playground – to support the mental and physical health of its inhabitants. Having defined the playable city and what play is from a life span perspective, we will summarize the evidence of the role of play in supporting mental health before setting out the characteristics of an all-age playable city. As urban populations become increasingly sedentary, we propose that the playable city provides a powerful means to call for creative, stimulating and playful encounters amongst inhabitants, visitors and the urban environment itself to support wellbeing.

Theory

Research exploring the benefits of play for mental and physical health has tended to take a piecemeal, age-specific approach using a traditional definition of play (as a time-limited activity). Play (and playfulness), however, is possible throughout a person's life and is a 'state of being' rather than a defined activity one participates in. Play positively affects mental health for people of all ages. There are five key pathways through which urban planning and design to increase play is believed to deliver positive mental health and wellbeing outcomes (Figure 7.1).

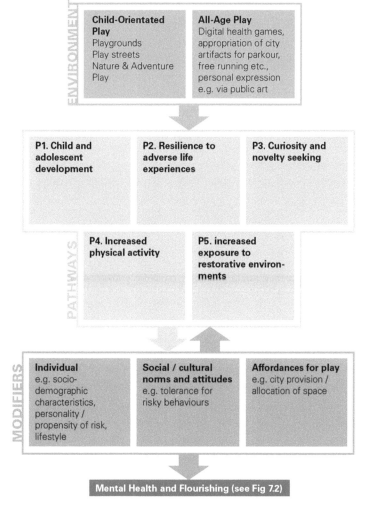

FIGURE 7.1 The effects of playable cities on mental health and wellbeing.

The first pathway through which play supports mental health is by promoting young people's social and emotional development (Berk 2013; Frost 1988; Ginsburg 2007; Shonkoff and Phillips 2000; Tamis-LeMonda et al. 2004). This is why the right of a child (aged 0–18) to play is endorsed in the United Nations Declaration of the Rights of the Child (UN 1989), according play equal importance to nutrition, housing, healthcare and education in healthy child development. From a young age, play helps children develop key social, emotional, physical and cognitive competencies and allows new behaviours and identities to be tested out, a critical component of self-development and growth (Nijhof et al. 2018). Play promotes creativity, imagination, self-confidence and self-efficacy (Lester and Russell 2010) and has been shown to have a central role in the formation and maintenance of friendships (Panksepp 2007). As a protective process, play can also enhance adaptive capabilities and resilience, helping children better manage stress and cope with adverse childhood experiences (Fearn and Howard 2011; Lester and Russell 2010).

The continued importance of play for adolescents has received less attention, but evidence suggests that play provides vital opportunities to test new identities, develop relationships and navigate transitional situations that bridge the gap between childhood and adulthood (for a discussion of the importance of play for adolescent mental health, see Roe and Roe 2019).

Evidence of the benefits of play in adulthood is much more limited; however, there is some evidence that play helps foster continued development in physical, social, cognitive and emotional functions (Graham and Burghardt 2010; Pellis and Pellis 2010; Sutton-Smith 2008, cited in Nijhof et al. 2018). This research has largely been approached from the perspective of adult–child play interactions and/or digital game playing or rehabilitation contexts. Play can offer opportunities throughout the life course for individuals to develop attachments to people and places, as well as nurturing the wider culture of a community (Hart 1978; Lester and Russel 2008, cited in Mahdjoubi and Spencer 2015).

The second pathway is resilience. So-called risky or adventurous outdoor play, in which children are allowed a degree of autonomy in their choice of play, is an important contributor to the development of resilience (Whitebread 2017). In a systematic review, Brussoni et al. (2015) found consistent evidence of the contribution of free play to children's physical and mental health. In adventurous outdoor play, children can challenge themselves, test their limits, express creativity and learn to regulate their emotions (Brussoni et al. 2015). There is evidence that playfulness (as a personality trait) supports stress regulation and adaptive coping strategies, suggesting playfulness may also support resilience in adults (Magnuson and Barnett 2013), with particular evidence for older women (Hutchinson et al. 2008).

The third pathway is nurturing curiosity and novelty seeking, an important determinant of wellbeing (Kashdan and Silvia 2009), contributing to cognitive functioning, mental health and physical health, particularly in older age (Sakaki, Yagi and Murayama 2018). The playable city encourages us to see places differently, to be curious as we navigate our everyday environments and 'take notice' – which can all help catalyse mental wellbeing (NEF 2011). Recent evidence has illustrated the health benefits of public art and interactive art installations – a feature of the playable city – including reducing stress, eliciting awe and curiosity, promoting positive health behaviours and developing a shared identity (Thomas 2017).

The fourth pathway is indirect: incorporating physical activity for people of all ages (Brussoni et al. 2015; see the Active City chapter). The World Health Organization's global strategy on physical activity and health now recognizes a role for play not just for children but also for adults in improving physical activity and health (WHO 2010).

The fifth pathway is the indirect impact of urban play settings (particularly outdoor play) on mental health and wellbeing (see the Green City, Blue City and Sensory City chapters). In particular, a growing body of research shows that daily exposure to natural environments whilst playing has a positive impact on children's sense of wellbeing, fitness levels, resilience, cognitive functioning and motor ability (Gill 2014). And by providing settings for social interactions (see the Neighbourly City chapter) and inclusivity (see the Inclusive City chapter), play can enhance our connection and interaction with the environment and with other people.

Much of the research on the benefits of play has focused on play as an activity that takes place in 'designated' contexts (e.g. a playground or playing a game). Further research is needed to fully understand the potential of the playable city to support mental health.

The impact on mental health

Playable cities can help reduce depression and stress

By promoting good social, emotional, physical and cognitive development throughout the life span, play contributes to mental health resilience and may reduce the risk of developing a wide range of mental health disorders, particularly depression, anxiety and stress (Figure 7.2).

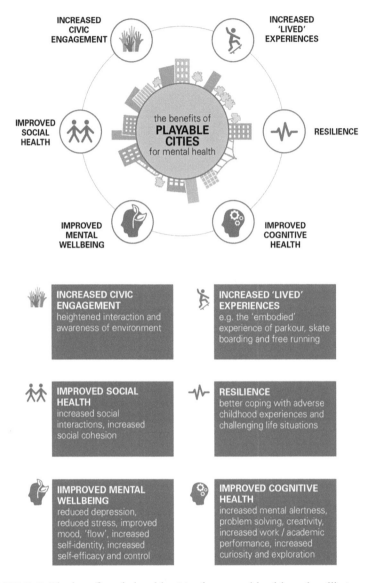

FIGURE 7.2 The benefits of playable cities for mental health and wellbeing.

Playable cities can improve brain function

The improved mental alertness, problem solving and creativity associated with play at all ages contribute to good cognitive function; this may enhance learning in youth and reduce the risk of developing dementia in older people.

Play can reduce the risk of adverse childhood experiences and promote resilience

Play is a well-used therapeutic strategy (targeted mostly at children aged 3–13) to alleviate mild-to-severe psychological and emotional trauma arising from, for example, the loss of a parent, domestic violence, or the trauma of armed conflict and enforced migration. Typically, play therapy is carried out in indoor settings, but outdoor settings – and strategies such as imaginative play in forest settings – have been effective in managing PTSD in children and for adolescents suffering from trauma and behavioural problems such as ADHD (Roe and Aspinall 2011). Whilst research has shown the effectiveness of play therapy for emotional and mental health, a meta-analytic review identified very few studies that used the outdoors as a play context (Jensen, Biesen and Graham 2017).

Modifiers of impact

The opportunities for all-age play depend on the possibilities an environment offers for play (the number of play affordances), as well as a culture's norms, rules and laws, which determine whether those opportunities can be actualized. For example, does a particular society allow – and support – freely chosen play whereby a child (or adult) can decide and control their playful activity following their own instincts, curiosity and imagination? Is risky play by adolescents (e.g. in derelict buildings) tolerated?

Other modifiers include parent/carer perceptions of risks and dangers associated with different types of play – particularly 'free-roaming' play – and cultural norms that may exclude females from appropriating the built environment in the same way that males do.

Individual modifiers include physical and cognitive variations (e.g. in manual dexterity) and personality and risk propensity.

Design approaches for a playable city

Play design in cities takes many forms, including designated playgrounds, school playgrounds, public open spaces, parks, streets and squares offering structured play experiences (i.e. on designated play equipment). Play activities have typically been assigned specific locations in a city, closed off from other forms of human activity.

This is important because the landscape of play has changed dramatically in recent years, with fewer opportunities for outdoor and risky play and the emergence of new digital play technologies. A report written for the UK National Trust, for example, stated that the area where children are allowed to play unsupervised around their homes has shrunk by 90 per cent since the 1970s (Moss 2012). Parental concerns about safety, traffic and pollution, as well as a lack of good-quality natural environments and public open spaces, all limit a child's opportunity to engage in free play. In a study of children's opportunities for free play in the United States, Gray (2011) directly linked the decline of outdoor play with the rise of depression and anxiety in this group. Moreover, the emergence of new digital play technologies and social media has changed the way children play. Whilst there is some evidence that digital activity can decrease anxiety and depression in adolescents and foster social networks, at the same time, excessive screen time is a determinant of sedentary behaviour, which in turn can increase the risk of chronic health diseases (e.g. obesity, diabetes) (Barnett et al. 2018).

Whilst play has been slow to emerge as an urban design principle, new perspectives on playful cities are emerging (Sicart 2016). Some authors have set out 'ludic' urban design interventions (spontaneous and undirected playfulness) based on the ideas of cultural theorist Johan Huizinga (1938) and his idea of *homo ludens* (man, the player). Drawing on twenty-three case studies of ludic urban design interventions, Donoff and Bridgman (2017) set out a typology of urban play categorized by play type (e.g. creative play), design feature (e.g. paths) and implementation style (e.g. temporary, pop-up or seasonal). This is a useful starting point from which to expand ideas on all-age urban design for play but draws on conventional concepts of play as 'activity' rather than 'appropriative play' (i.e. as an attitude or stance, or way of being).

Given these changes and the increasing political concern about children's and young people's mental health, greater investment in the playable city – and the provision of opportunities for structured and unstructured play – is one way to support emotional wellbeing/development and physical activity amongst this group. We argue, later in this chapter, that digital gaming in real-world contexts holds immense potential to deliver benefits for physical health and social and mental wellbeing across all ages.

Using Sicart's (2014) 'ecology of play things and play contexts', we have identified three characteristics of playful urban design: pure-play contexts (i.e. props and contexts designed for play, such as playgrounds), playable contexts (not designed for play but which offer a rich context of play affordances) and contexts that afford appropriative play (where the context of play is non-determined).

Pure-play contexts

- **The playground:** The strongest and most recognizable forms of play in a city are playgrounds; they exist for the pure purpose of play activity (although they may be appropriated for other activity). Manufactured equipment, such as swings, slides, climbing frames, ropes and brightly coloured 'novelty' play structures (e.g. rockets, ships, pyramids), has dominated city playground design for many years. More recently, table tennis, table football and chess in public spaces have provided play infrastructure for all ages. Cultural norms, rules and laws have also governed the design of these spaces, ensuring, for example, that they meet specific safety standards. Whilst the creativity of these bespoke structures has improved over the years, with more adventurous structures emerging, a number of play theorists (Gill 2014; Hart 1978; Louv 2008) have argued for a freer, more spontaneous form of play embracing the wider urban landscape as a means to both improve access to play opportunities for children and offer richer play experiences. This means looking beyond designated playgrounds to utilizing a wider urban network of streets, squares and parks (see also the Green City chapter).

- **Play streets:** One such opportunity for flexible, multi-functional play space is the street. Streets have been identified as the largest single public asset in any city (UN-Habitat 2013), with 'comfortable' or 'liveable' streets providing walkable, active city spaces (see the Active City chapter). 'Play streets' – temporary closure of streets to cars – are one example of how cities are increasing opportunities for safe and accessible play immediately outside a child's front door (Figure 7.3). Often used in under-resourced and/or deprived urban communities, play streets offer a means to address inequities in access to play space in communities without designated playgrounds. They offer moveable apparatus (bikes, inflatables, ball games) and a range of surfaces (e.g. artificial turf, road painting) orientated (mostly) towards younger children. The approach is not new; play streets date back to as early as the 1920s in the United States and the 1930s in the UK, but cities worldwide are now experiencing a resurgence in play streets. As of 2018, there have been some 660 play street interventions in the UK (Umstattd-Meyer et al. 2019). Evaluation of these urban interventions has focused on physical activity outcomes and wider community social outcomes (Umstattd-Meyer et al. 2019). Identified benefits include

FIGURE 7.3 Play street, *Crezco con mi barrio* (I grow with my neighbourhood) urban95 initiative, Bogotá, Colombia. Source: Fundación Casa de la Infancia.

increased social interactions and strengthened community ties (Murray and Devecchi 2016; Umstattd-Meyer et al. 2019; Zieff, Chaudhuri and Musselman 2016), increased levels of physical activity (Cortinez-O'Ryan et al. 2017; D'Haese et al. 2015; Umstattd-Meyer et al. 2019) and reduced gang and drug use (Zieff et al. 2016). Whilst play streets have achieved considerable success in increasing play opportunities for young children and their families, they have been less successful in engaging adolescents (Zieff et al. 2016). There is also a lack of evidence on how streets are used for play in other geographical contexts. For children and youth in low-income countries, the street may be the only open space opportunity for play, exposing children to the risk of uncontrolled traffic or vacant sites that may be polluted. In a systematic review of evidence, Umstattd-Meyer et al. (2019) concluded that the current research on play streets lacks rigour and systematic evaluation, identifying only six studies meeting stringent inclusion criteria and none containing any evaluation of mental health or developmental outcomes in children.

Play-able *city contexts*

Play-*able* spaces are not designed for play but offer a rich context in which play activity can take place. These include interactive public art installations, hybrid spaces for urban digital gaming (i.e. real and virtual worlds), play with water fountains (see the Blue City chapter), pockets of urban green space, and derelict, vacant lots offering affordances for wilder, unstructured play.

- **Interactive art:** Art is defined as interactive when audience behaviour is an integral component of the piece; it springs to life via audience participation, which, in turn, can cause dynamic change in the appearance of the artwork itself. It is through these human interactions that playful activity emerges. A well-known example is Chicago's *Cloud Gate*, a mirrored concave sculpture by Anish Kapoor that was officially dedicated in 2006 (Figure 7.4). Nicknamed 'The Bean', it is set in Millennium Park, which allows users to interact with their images that are reflected from a variety of city perspectives. The viewer can 'sculpt' a multitude of frames, mixing up elements as they wish – the sky, the light, the city skyscrapers,

FIGURE 7.4 *Cloud Gate*, Chicago, United States. Source: Jenny Roe.

other people. It is a highly malleable artwork, which encourages interactivity with the city itself. In this way, play is a means of engaging with the world, helping citizens understand the network of people and of things around them. Cities that encourage interactions with artwork in these ways create a strong foundation for engaging with the city through urban play and building unity through play.

- **Non-defined play contexts:** A number of authors (Gill 2005; Hart 1978; Louv 2008) recommend a freer, more adventurous form of play integrating nature places (e.g. pockets of urban fringe woodland) that offer opportunities for unsupervised and unstructured play. Louv (2008) has argued that detachment from nature is harming children's health, coining the term *nature-deficit disorder* and positing that connection to nature is vital for wellbeing (see the Green City chapter). Gill (2005) and others (e.g. Natural England 2010) have argued for 'free-range' children and teenagers, independently mobile to explore a city without constant adult supervision. This includes access to urban nature and vacant land for exploration. A growing body of research has found that nature-based play has a positive impact on child and adolescent mental wellbeing, fitness levels, resilience, cognitive functioning and motor ability (see Chawla 2015; Gill 2014; Roe and Aspinall 2012). Abandoned buildings and vacant land ('off-grid' spaces) offer children and youth more-adventurous play opportunities, a different set of raw play props (junk, natural materials) and absolute freedom. These unsupervised, off-grid spaces offer opportunities for spontaneous play, discovery and expression that are essential to child and youth autonomy and self-governance. But often children's presence in such places is not legal, and these types of spaces may be unsafe owing to contamination, toxins or rodents. This presents a challenge. City planners/governors need to allow children and youth the freedom to appropriate spaces aside from the environments specifically created for play (i.e. designated playgrounds) and they need to ensure that city spaces are safe and not contaminated. This type of play also requires a society that is tolerant not only of children and adolescents playing unsupervised but also of messier (and riskier) play (Natural England 2010).
- **Urban digital games:** The city is becoming more playable via a wave of digital city-orientated games that operate within a hybrid space, combining human interactions with real-city infrastructure and the virtual world and appropriating smartphone technologies

to build games that interact with city artefacts. This includes games like *Pokémon Go* that (indirectly) encourage physical interaction with the outdoors and social interaction with other players (Knöll and Roe 2016). Examples of games designed with health in mind include the UK's *Beat the Street*, which increases levels of moderate and vigorous activity in players and holds much promise for reducing the risk of obesity in children (Harris 2018). In Germany, *Stadtflucht* (Urban Flight), staged in Frankfurt, has shown promising health outcomes in adolescents (Halblaub and Knöll 2016), see below.

Playful infrastructure

Appropriative play takes over the context in which it exists and cannot be predicted or predetermined by such context – it simply emerges from that context. This includes performance, public art and political activism that may disrupt or dismantle preconceptions of what a city should be and may also prompt civic action. According to Sicart (2016), 'Playful engagement with urban environments [is] a constant mode of resistance and appropriation of cities for their citizens.'

FIGURE 7.5 The Heidelberg Project, Detroit, United States. Source: Deborah Ploski.

- **Playful rebellion:** A famous – and controversial – example of a disruptive playful infrastructure is Detroit's Heidelberg Project, created in the 1980s by African American resident artist Tyree Guyton (Figure 7.5). The project is an outdoor installation created from abandoned everyday objects (toys, stuffed animals, car hoods, shoes, hoovers) found in the McDougall-Hunt neighbourhood on the East Side of Detroit. Stein (2016: 54) has argued that the Heidelberg Project is a prominent example of 'playing in and with the city'; the artist's urban recycling of trash into new artefacts is likened to the process of play, 'a mode of child-like creation unbounded by conventional rules and decorum' (e.g. polka dots are painted on the walls and roofs of buildings) that also references childhood play (with toys and pavement painting). The project spills out beyond any contained 'play' space into the urban fabric, utilizing streets, parking lots and trees, in what Stein calls a form of 'playing' the city; Stein further suggests that the project is an example of an urban form of 'playful politics' that aims to catalyse change by fostering new discourse on post-industrial decay and challenging conceptions of place aesthetics, gentrification and urban renewal. Owing to its messiness – and utilization of trash – the project has been highly controversial and subjected to attacks from city governors and arsonists alike. But, in a new turn, the artist is now dismantling the installation (to allow for travelling exhibits) and envisioning a new future for the neighborhood with Detroit's planning department and the Detroit Land Bank. Empty houses are being purchased to establish new housing and studios for a community of artists, who, in turn, will spark new life into the neighborhood. The project has been called a 'reverse memento mori – an assertion of life' (Miller 2019), fostering urban transformation and healing. It could even be interpreted as a form of urban play therapy helping the city reverse the trauma of post-industrial decline and offering a new and resilient future.
- **Playful appropriation:** Playable cities provide the materials (or artefacts) for playful, creative expression and invite novel appropriation of those attributes. For example, parkour (moving as efficiently as possible from one point to another by using nothing but the human body) has been described by Sébastien Foucan (the founder of free running) as a 'way of life' that brings liberation, freedom of expression and self-confidence as well as physical health benefits and environmental mastery (El-hage 2011). Parkour appropriates and reinterprets urban spaces using city infrastructure as a tool of personal expression (Sicart 2014); the whole city

becomes a parkour playground. Traceurs (participants in parkour and free running) are masters of adaptability, appropriating a variety of urban forms (railings, walls, stairs, benches, bollards) for the purpose of travelling. Parkour is described as a deeply embodied experience in which the city itself becomes a 'canvas for bodily expression' (Sicart 2014). Parkour (and free running) thrives in cities with Brutalist 1960s concrete structures, such as London's Southbank, or cities that have a unique urban form, such as the favelas of Rio de Janeiro. There is an obvious danger in this kind of play, and it thrives best where attitudes are liberal and the rebellious activities of street artists, skateboarders, traceurs and young people – exploring new ways of navigating city space – are tolerated.

New play movements and playable technologies

The Playable City movement has set out a new vision for transforming cities through the application of playable technologies (https://www.playablecity.com). A response to the utilitarian data capture and efficiency of smart cities (data-rich cities), the playable city puts fun and human interaction at the heart of urban design. Three key ideas underpin the movement: first, data is more than a utility for planners. By encouraging playful data interactions amongst citizens, the smart city becomes more human-centred, more transparent, and the data more 'democratized' (i.e. the data is accessed, manipulated and played with by its citizens). Second, that collective action is needed to build healthier cities; play and games encourage people to get involved in their city, to better understand their environment, in turn building agency and increasing the potential for participation. Third, cities can be somewhat grey and artificial: by encouraging playful activities, they become more fun, colourful and liveable (Baggini 2014).

The playable city encourages human interaction by engaging with technology. For example, the fountains at Bradford's City Park (see the Blue City chapter) respond to the movement of people around the space; by experimenting, users of the space can learn how to choreograph the fountains (Baggini 2014). In this way, the urban users of public space become participants in creating the dynamics of the space. Other examples include digital crosswalks and piano stairs in subways that respond to pedestrians' footfall and encourage physical interaction.

As yet, these playable city projects lack robust scientific evaluation. Arguably, they encourage people to be more physically interactive by engaging with the infrastructure. But do they also help build social cohesion and mental wellbeing? The movement is not without its critics, who argue that playable city gadgetry is artificial and infantile (O'Sullivan 2016). Cities rich in inherently curious architecture and street networks arguably offer just as much scope for delight and joy as any playable gadget (see the Sensory City chapter). But playable attributes do bring a new whimsical ambience to the city, encourage civic interactions and fill public spaces with laughter. Robust evaluation of mental wellbeing outcomes, however, remains lacking.

Intergenerational play

Intergenerational play is an emerging field with identified benefits for older people and children alike. Benefits of intergenerational programmes for older people include reduced loneliness, improved cognitive functioning and memory, and improved mobility (Age UK 2018); for children and youth, the benefits include language development, increased social skills and less ageism (United for All Ages 2019). Currently, intergenerational play largely comprises formalized programmes that pair care services for the old and the young (e.g. twinned nurseries and senior care, in-school or after-school programmes) or multi-age community-led programmes (arts, gardening, theatre). (A review of these programmes and their health benefits is included in the Neighbourly City chapter.) By far the most common pairing is between pre-school and senior daycare (44 per cent), with paired programmes between youth and older people much less common (15 per cent) (Generations United and Eisner Foundation 2019). Digital gaming offers one way of connecting youth with older people (e.g. Minecraft events), but these benefits have been evaluated mostly from a within-family perspective (e.g. between grandchild and grandparent or child and parent) and have not been tested in other contexts (e.g. intergenerational gaming outdoors).

Intergenerational playgrounds are emerging in many cities. But their designers rely on manufactured play (or exercise) equipment, offering older people physical activity opportunities, rather than think creatively about where the activity and play needs of young and older people might converge and how that space might be co-created. More opportunities for spontaneous playful interactions outdoors between young and older people are needed. Play streets are one example of an urban intervention that can foster neighbourly multi-age interactions; conventional play equipment (swings, slides) in public spaces, offering opportunities for all-age play, is another. But cities need more multi-age, multi-functional public space that is more equitably distributed and that all ages can enjoy together. We also need to think more creatively about where older and young people's needs converge and how reciprocity and sharing of skills might be fostered. For example, older adults might share their skills in traditional children's games (hopscotch, jump rope, cat's cradle) or their skills in traditional crafts (knitting, crocheting) to assist young people in novel appropriation of the city. Youth might share their skills in digital urban gaming, help capture older people's social histories and promote richer engagement in public space for all.

The playable city: next steps

We have approached the design of the playable city through an all-age lens, arguing that playful urban design is crucial in shaping our interactions and experiences with the world. Drawing on new theories of play (Sicart 2014), we define the playable city as one that offers boundless opportunities for both 'play' (i.e. activity requiring play-related props and designated areas) and 'playfulness' (a playful stance that takes place in a non-defined play context). This includes allowing for appropriative play and full immersion in city space (and the state of flow). The playable city has the potential to foster increased curiosity, engagement with the environment and social connection, as well as provide opportunities for self-expression and creativity in the cityscape – all factors that can contribute to positive emotional wellbeing. Since play operates within cultural norms, rules and laws, we offer a framework for exploring all-age play affordances that acknowledges this context. As yet, the idea of the playable city has not been considered through a geographical lens: how would broader geographical or cross-cultural lenses influence the concept of all-age play affordances? And what will be the legacy of the Covid-19 pandemic, in which people avoid touching fomites (surfaces that could carry infection) like playground equipment? We also need to think of new ways to imagine and experience the city for all-age play. This requires going beyond conventional definitions of play (as a fun, frivolous activity) to thinking of play as something with purpose and as a way of being. As Sicart (2016) has observed, 'Playful cities, then, need to foster the playful attitude. They need to nudge and suggest other ways of participating, or inhabiting, of traversing these spaces so that we can start thinking playfully about the environments we live in.' Play is clearly an important urban design consideration for nurturing enjoyment and immersion in city life.

Playable city examples

Berlin's Das Netz (The Net), a multi-functional play context for all ages, Germany

Das Netz (The Net), in Berlin, is a huge urban sculpture – a suspended, roped construction that forms an elevated public square, offering a multitude of functions for all ages, including an 'urban hammock', a trampoline and a climbing structure for children and adults alike (Figure 7.6). It is also used as an informal auditorium for presenting movies or theatre performances. It is a place for social events, picnics and celebrations (the adjacent café extends into the space) and also offers a belvedere, with elevated views of the city, for rest and 'being away'. Symbolically and visually, it connects and bridges a public square and is a rare example of a multi-functional designated play space for all ages.

FIGURE 7.6 *Das Netz* (The Net), Berlin, Germany. Source: NL Architects.

Frankfurt's Stadtflucht *(Urban Flight), a play-*able *context, Germany*

Curiosity is an integral component of mental wellbeing linked with motivation and meaning in life; learning to see places differently and 'taking notice' of our environment can all help catalyse mental wellbeing (NEF 2011). *Stadtflucht* (Urban Flight) is a location-based urban health game that was staged in Frankfurt as part of a research study. It increased levels of engagement and awareness in the city, including the discovery of new city attributes, raising levels of excitement and curiosity (Halblaub and Knöll 2016; Knöll 2016). The game incorporated a feedback mechanism that advised players on their heart rate and physiological stress in relation to the six game locations, helping them learn about the positive effects of healthy places by moving around in real-world locations. In this way, the game allowed participants to also play *with* the city – that is, it allowed citizens to use the data they produced to better understand what constitutes a healthy space (or not). Moreover, the game instilled a heightened interest in the urban planning process amongst the young people and served as a tool to help city planners better understand how young people perceive and experience the city. In this way, playable cities (and data flow) can be an instrument for increasing participation in urban planning for health and liveability, a central tenet of the Playable City movement (see below). Co-creating, in itself, also has health-promoting benefits for

FIGURE 7.7 Adolescents playing a location-based urban health game, *Stadtflucht* (Urban Flight), Frankfurt, Germany. Source: Martin Knöll, TU Darmstadt, Urban Health Games.

young people in several areas, including empowerment and autonomy, self-efficacy, attribution and control beliefs, and sense of coherence (Fabian 2016).

Design principles for a playable city

General principle

- The playable city should be approached through an all-age lens and facilitate both play and playfulness.

Neighbourhood scale (see Figure 7.8)

- Provide 'on-the-doorstep' designated play facilities adjacent to people's homes.
- Incorporate designed outdoor play facilities for all ages, in parks and along trails, such as linear 'green' walkways, playparks, outdoor gyms, table tennis and chess tables, and ball game areas.
- Maximize informal nature play opportunities by leveraging pockets of green space, meadow, urban forest, vacant plots and the like.

- Design contemplative spaces for 'daydreaming', particularly near water and in other nature settings.
- Design labyrinths, mazes and murals to engage curiosity.
- Implement 'play streets' (temporary closure of a street to cars), offering play right outside a child's home – for example, chalk games, moveable apparatus (bikes, inflatables, ball games), a range of surfaces (e.g. artificial turf, road painting).
- Explore urban digital gaming opportunities to link play to engagement with street artefacts/historic city landmarks/points of interest connected to a digital game (e.g. the artefacts are 'tagged' for points).

City scale (see Figure 7.9)

- Install designated play facilities for all ages in city parks and other key city locations.
- Install playful artefacts/public interactive art.
- Develop intergenerational play facilities.
- Provide pop-up spaces for self-expression by artists/entrepreneurs.
- Maximize flexible use of structures that support activities like parkour, skateboarding and free running.
- Open play and recreational facilities on school grounds and similar facilities to the wider population and expand hours of operation.

1 digital gaming infrastructure
2 mural
3 empty lot labyrinth
4 table tennis
5 green space for relaxing
6 rooftop playspace for residents
7 interactive art
8 game tables
9 active play lane
10 playground

FIGURE 7.8 The Playable City: Neighbourhood Scale.

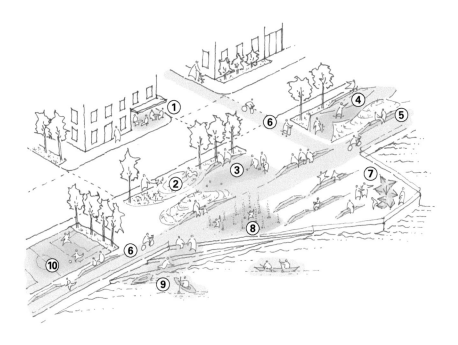

1 cafe socializing
2 hills for play + relaxing
3 slow play: bocce court
4 skate park
5 bench seating for social interaction or reflection
6 active play lane
7 interactive art
8 fountain play
9 waterfront play
10 open sports fields

FIGURE 7.9 The Playable City: City Features.

8

The inclusive city

Highlights

- Traditionally, urban planning and design professionals have developed environments targeted towards the needs and characteristics of ethnic-majority, able-bodied, working-age men, and this demographic has become a 'baseline' for urban design.
- Key demographics that should be considered in all urban design include all ages, all genders, all races and ethnicities, all sexual orientations, all socioeconomic strata, and the full diversity of physical, sensory and cognitive abilities and needs.
- Urban design can contribute to segregation, exclusion and prejudice, affecting people's self-esteem, dignity, independence and mental health, as well as their ability to access the full range of a city's educational, economic, social, cultural and health opportunities.
- Two main ways in which cities can achieve more inclusivity are by attracting people to mixed-income, mixed-age neighbourhoods offering good-quality housing, facilities and opportunities, and by making design and planning decisions that recognize the needs and characteristics of all residents, not just those with the socioeconomic resources to ensure their needs are met.
- Involvement of diverse demographic groups in every stage of planning and development can help deliver inclusive urban design that enables the whole population to thrive.
- Applying the principles of the child- and age-friendly city can deliver more inclusive urban design for the whole population.

Key concept definitions

Universal or inclusive design: Designing the built environment, including buildings and their surrounding spaces, in a way that ensures they can be accessed and used by all people, bringing difference and diversity – such as age, size (e.g. height), gender, race, ability and disability – into all stages of the design process.

Minority stress theory: The theory that minority groups experience distinct, chronic stressors related to their stigmatized identities, including victimization, prejudice and discrimination.

Residential or spatial segregation: The concentration of socioeconomic, ethnic or national-origin groups in particular neighbourhoods of a city, apart from others.

Residential or spatial co-location: People of different socioeconomic, ethnic, national-origin, gender, age and other groups sharing space in neighbourhoods.

Gender mainstreaming: The process of assessing the implications for all genders of any planned action, including legislation, policies or programmes, in all areas and at all levels so that people of all genders benefit equally and inequality is not perpetrated (ECOSOC 1997).

What is the inclusive city?

An inclusive city is one in which buildings and public places have been intentionally designed for access and use by all people. Inclusive city design brings difference and diversity – such as age, physical and cognitive variation, gender, racial and ethnic identities, and socioeconomic status – into all stages of the design process, ensuring that everybody has access to the full range of educational, economic, social, cultural and health opportunities of the city.

This does not happen automatically. Traditionally, urban planning and design has conceptualized a 'baseline' user: the young, ethnic-majority, able-bodied working man encapsulated by the 'green man' silhouette on crosswalk signs around the world. The general baseline user for urban design – particularly in emerging cities in low- and middle-income countries – is less likely to be young, old, female, disabled, unemployed, homeless or part of a minority group. However, these diverse groups together represent the majority of city residents. When their needs and characteristics are not routinely integrated from the start of design and development, these people often find themselves disadvantaged in navigating environments that were not designed for their needs.

This predicament was famously highlighted by New York industrial designer Patricia Moore. When she was in her twenties and the only woman in a design firm of 350 staff members, she asked senior staff about designing kitchen goods to enable their use by people with arthritis. She was allegedly told: 'We don't design for those people.' Concerned by the impact of places being designed by and for working-age men, Moore famously dressed up as an octogenarian woman. She plugged her ears to reduce her hearing, wore contact lenses to blur her vision, and splinted her legs and posture. Thus dressed, she visited 116 US and Canadian cities over three years to understand the experience of older women in the urban environment. Sometimes she used a walking stick or wheelchair; sometimes she appeared to be homeless, middle-class or wealthy. Many of her experiences were negative, from being unable to enter a building to being brutally attacked and left for dead. She became convinced that more inclusive design would improve people's quality of life. Moore has been dubbed the 'mother of empathy' and is considered to be one of the founders of *universal design* (Clarkson et al. 2003; Preiser and Ostroff 2001), a concept that is integral to the inclusive city.

The preceding chapters have examined how urban design can promote good mental health and wellbeing and help people thrive. But this depends on the population being able to benefit. Access to restorative urban design is rarely equal. Ethnic-majority, physically able, financially stable, working-age men often have quite a different experience of the city than those who diverge from this conceptual baseline – for instance, poorer people; older and younger people; women; people with physical or mental disabilities; and racial, ethnic, sexual and gender minorities.

Designing accessible, inclusive environments can reduce discrimination and help people feel included, valued and empowered; promote social cohesion and prevent isolation; deliver dignity; and enable everyone to access services and facilities that support mental health. Design without these different needs in mind reduces some people's access to design features that could support their mental health. And worse, the very act of excluding them can create social, cultural and economic exclusion, segregation and marginalization, reducing people's self-esteem and feelings of belongingness and putting them at even greater risk of developing mental health problems (Palis, Marchand and Oviedo-Joekes 2018). This has been highlighted, for instance, as part of the #BlackLivesMatter movement. This creates a vicious cycle: exclusion contributes to the development of mental health problems, and mental health problems contribute to exclusion.

To break out of this cycle and better support people's mental health and wellbeing, urban design must consciously address the diversity of needs that exists within a population (Wright and Stickley 2013). This should include designing cities in ways that meet the needs of everyone: people with mental health problems and disabilities, all genders, all ages and life stages, all economic statuses, all races and cultures, all sexualities and other minority groups in the city. Inclusive design acknowledges this diversity and difference and is more likely to be achieved when it is considered at every stage of the development process, from inception to completion.

For example, research tells us that cycling benefits our mental health (see the Active City chapter). But men are generally more likely than women to commute by bike, and some of the reasons for this disparity could be addressed by design:

- Women can be more risk-averse and more vulnerable than men, disproportionately deterred by perceived levels of street or traffic safety, by cycling in the dark, and by concerns about encountering aggression.
- Women may have different physical abilities than men and can be disproportionately deterred by physically challenging terrain, by long commutes (particularly in adverse weather) and by having to carry heavy belongings.
- Women around the world are subject to a host of social and cultural expectations and gender stereotypes, as well as different economic means to access a bicycle compared to men – any of which may make them feel unable to choose cycling.
- Women may be deterred by practical concerns about clothing, including what clothing feels appropriate whilst cycling, by practical challenges associated with particular types of cultural or religious clothing and by availability and appropriateness of showering/changing facilities.
- Women are more likely than men to be responsible for errands and childcare or care of older relatives – necessitating multi-stage trips/'trip chaining', including escorting others who may be unable to cycle – whereas men still largely commute directly to and from work.

And yet, particular considerations for women (and others) are rarely prioritized in designing cycling infrastructure (van Bekkum, Williams and Morris 2011). More gender-inclusive design could include increased investment in features like lighting, showering/changing facilities and safety infrastructure.

This chapter will examine how and why inclusion in urban design affects people's mental health and will explore opportunities for increasing positive impacts on population wellbeing.

Theory

There are three key pathways through which inclusion (and exclusion) can affect mental health and wellbeing (Figure 8.1).

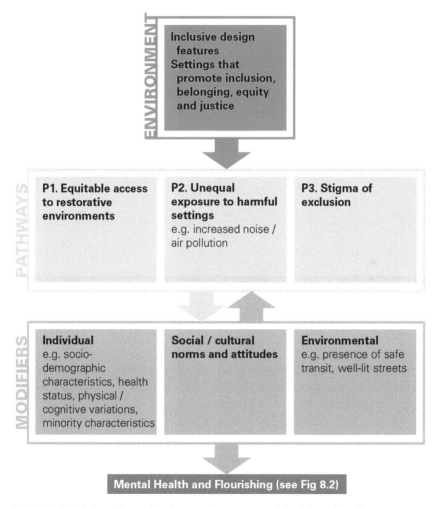

FIGURE 8.1 The effects of inclusive cities on mental health and wellbeing.

The first pathway relates to people's unequal access to settings that support mental health and wellbeing, including natural settings (see the Green City and Blue City chapters); positive sensory experience (see the Sensory City chapter); positive social interaction, conviviality and neighbourliness (the Neighbourly City chapter); and opportunities for physical activity (the Active City chapter) and play (the Playable City chapter). This pathway applies where the exclusion is geographical, often associated with socioeconomic status, and where disparities may exist in mentally protective factors such as quality of and access to housing, education, play opportunities, employment, transport, culture, social capital, healthcare, safety and security (Tunstall, Shaw and Dorling 2004). For example, poorer communities often have less access to outdoor recreational areas (including parks), which may be of poor quality (CABE 2010). The exclusion may also be based on personal characteristics, such as gender, age, race, or physical and cognitive abilities.

The second pathway is people's unequal exposure to settings that can be detrimental to mental health and wellbeing. Poorer neighbourhoods, for instance, are more likely to be located near highways, industrial areas and toxic waste sites, where land is cheaper. As a result, they may have increased noise, poorer air quality, problems with sanitation, more rubbish (trash) and neighbourhood disarray, traffic congestion, crime (Shiue 2015), increased flood risk and poorer housing quality (Gruebner et al. 2012).

The third pathway is the psychological impact associated with the stigma of exclusion. The experience of exclusion is associated with reduced self-esteem as well as hopelessness and loss of dignity, which can exacerbate the second pathway, as these feelings can lead to increased anti-social behaviour and criminal activity in poorer neighbourhoods (Wu and Wu 2012). The minority stress theory (Meyer 2003) was developed to apply to members of the LGBTQ+ community, but it is now applied to the many minority groups that experience distinct, chronic stressors related to their stigmatized identities, including victimization, prejudice and discrimination. These stressors may be personal or institutional, and they can affect physical and mental health and wellbeing both directly, by causing a stress response, and indirectly, by contributing to socioeconomic and other disadvantages, including lack of access to healthcare. The minority stress theory goes some way towards explaining why health outcomes – including depression, anxiety, substance abuse, suicide rate and life expectancy – are so often worse for minority groups.

The impact on mental health

People's divergence from a theoretical 'baseline' population affects their mental health through urban design in two main ways: spatial segregation and design for the baseline (Figure 8.2).

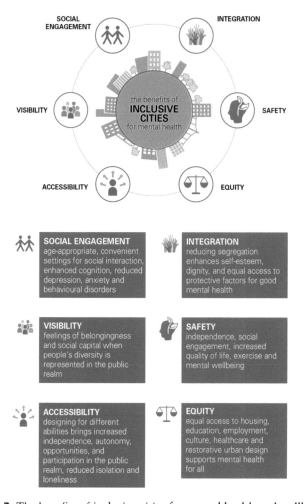

FIGURE 8.2 The benefits of inclusive cities for mental health and wellbeing.

Spatial segregation

Physical separation of people according to their place on the socioeconomic spectrum and other shared characteristics has long underpinned the development of urban neighbourhoods. Richer people tend to choose to live in attractive, economically active, amenity-rich, 'desirable' areas, whilst poorer people are, by default, often left with the 'less desirable' parts of the city. In some cities, socioeconomic spatial segregation is formalized, with slums at one end and gated communities at the other (Atkinson, Rowland and Blandy 2006; Bhalla and Anand 2018), but spatial segregation probably exists in some form in all cities. The more globalized a city and the less robust its welfare system, the more economically and spatially segregated are its citizens according to their socioeconomic status and (sometimes) their race and ethnicity, which are often (but not always) intertwined (Iceland 2014).

Poverty increases the risk of developing mental health problems, and people with mental health problems are more likely to experience poverty, creating another vicious cycle (McGovern 2014). Children in families with low socioeconomic status are two or three times more likely than their richer peers to develop mental health problems (Reiss 2013).

Urban design plays into this, mainly through spatial segregation that favours the wealthier 'baseline' with better amenities, planning and design. Neighbourhood deprivation and residential segregation are both risk factors for mental health problems (Jokela 2014; Santiago, Wadsworth and Stump 2011). The reasons are complex. As described in the Theory section, they relate to an interplay of the presence of neighbourhood factors protective of mental health, neighbourhood risk factors for poor mental health and the psychological effects of exclusion. Urban design plays an intrinsic role in upholding the effects of the minority stress theory, not only by determining what a neighbourhood looks and feels like (and what amenities it contains) but also by implementing physical and/or social segregation.

The rise of spatial segregation by neighbourhood

In many cities, socioeconomic segregation is increasing, and environmental inequity is reflected in geographical health inequalities (Musterd et al. 2017). This trend is linked to social inequalities, changing economic structures, patterns of migration, welfare regimes and housing systems (Tammaru et al. 2016). In her book *Root Shock*, Mindy Fullilove considers the development of spatial segregation in the United States: 'The problem the planners tackled was not how to undo poverty, but how to hide the poor. Urban renewal was designed to segment the city so that barriers of highways and monumental buildings protected the rich from the sight of the poor, and enclosed the wealthy centre away from the poor margin' (2016: 197).

Geography often directs socioeconomic spatial divergence (Musterd et al. 2017):

- **West-east divide:** In many cities, richer people live in the west whilst poorer people live in the east. The predominant theory relates to wind direction and air pollution, particularly in the Western Hemisphere, where the prevailing winds blow west to east, leading to more air pollution accumulating in the eastern parts of cities. Air quality disparities originally led richer people to choose to live in western areas, leaving poorer people to find housing in the less desirable, more polluted eastern areas. Even when, in some cases, the pollution abated, many of the western areas still had higher-quality amenities, such as schools and hospitals, and so continued to attract wealthier citizens (Heblich, Trew and Zylberberg 2016). This is reflected in many indicators of health. In London, for instance, a map of the Jubilee underground train route famously demonstrated that a year of average life expectancy was lost with every station from west to east (Cheshire 2012).

- **Donut-hole pattern:** The separation between those living in the urban core and those living in the surrounding suburbs varies across cities. In many, the amenity-rich urban core is home to wealthier people, with poorer communities clustered in poorly connected, but more-affordable, outer areas with fewer amenities. Conversely, in some cities, most notably in the United States, the opposite has become true: the spacious, safer suburbs became more attractive than the urban core to wealthier people, although with suburbs having poorer transport and often fewer amenities and opportunities for social interaction, this perception is not necessarily reflected in mental health benefits.

A common but inaccurate belief is that people of racial or ethnic minorities make proactive decisions to self-segregate into so-called ethnic enclaves. This may be the case for some new migrants, who may find themselves to be an ethnic minority, often for the first time, and at risk of feeling culturally, linguistically and practically excluded from the city's wider culture. Compounding their challenges may be prejudice and discrimination, uncertainties and bureaucratic hurdles associated with migration and access to services, separation issues regarding their friends and family in their place of origin, and controversy around certain cultural and religious practices in their new home. Deciding to live near people of similar races or ethnicities facilitates access to social capital and may ease the transition.

However, many migrants move to more-mixed neighbourhoods as their socioeconomic status increases. Longer-term spatial segregation associated with racial, ethnic or cultural identity is more likely to reflect a combination of socioeconomic exclusion, such as housing market discrimination, and historical oppression of certain groups. For example, Black–White spatial segregation in US cities is more pronounced than in European cities, reflecting historical patterns of racial oppression, and continues to constrain the social, educational, employment and healthcare opportunities of the oppressed group (Iceland 2014).

Segregation within shared spaces

Spatial segregation is not restricted to entire (homogeneous) neighbourhoods; it can also be fine grain within mixed places. Historically, signs have been

FIGURES 8.3A AND B Signs saying 'We Cater to White Trade Only' in a restaurant window in the United States, in 1938; and 'Japanese only' outside a bathhouse in Japan in the year 2000. Sources: a. Library of Congress, and b. Debito Arudou.

displayed that blatantly excluded certain segments of society from particular housing, public spaces or buildings – for example, the 'No coloured, No Irish' signs seen, until fairly recently, in many cities (Verma 2018, Figure 8.3). Even after legislation banned this practice in many places, such signs are still seen occasionally today.

However, more subtle indications continue to exist and may be propagated by urban design. Examples include:

- **Physical segregation in shared residential areas:** Mixed-income housing has the potential to improve social cohesion (see the Neighbourly City chapter). However, this must be done thoughtfully or else risk negative effects on mental health. The use of so-called poor doors (i.e. separate entranceways) is intended to enable integration between those living in affordable housing and those living in more-expensive homes within the same housing developments, but it also serves to create stigma and shame for those using them. Similarly, in some cases, certain facilities within mixed-income housing developments may be deemed for use only by certain residents and not by others, such as separate children's playparks for richer and poorer children (Mohdin and Michael 2019). Bringing together residents of diverse socioeconomic status can highlight income differences at close quarters. The close-up exposure of poorer people to the additional opportunities enjoyed by richer people and their exclusion from those opportunities – alongside experiences of stigma and discrimination, including racism – can have negative impacts on people's mental health through frustration, lower self-esteem and feelings of hopelessness and helplessness. For adolescent boys, in particular, run-down environments that attract crime also tend to support anti-social behaviour (Mair, Diez-Roux and Galea 2008).
- **Psychological segregation in shared residential areas:** 'Gentrification' is the transformation of a working-class or vacant area of a city into a middle-class residential and/or commercial area (Lees, Slater and Wyly 2008). Gentrification has led to longstanding residents of a previously 'undesirable' neighbourhood feeling marginalized, excluded or displaced by their neighbourhood's development or regeneration into more-expensive residences and by a change in public space design and amenities targeted to a different demographic. Whilst there may not be physical signs explicitly deterring certain people's use of spaces, implicit signs exist. For example, shops serving poorer populations and/or ethnic minorities may be replaced by gentrified stores – identifiable as, for instance, 'real coffee' shops and bars serving microbrews – which signal to their target clientele through subtle signs like prices or design aesthetic; as a result, poorer populations may feel implicitly displaced (Hubbard 2016).

  This is particularly the case when accompanied by rising rents, which can reduce the diversity and social capacity of a neighbourhood. Ruth Glass (1964: 177) who coined the term gentrification has noted, 'Any district in or near London, however dingy or unfashionable before, is likely to become expensive; and London may quite soon be a city which illustrates the principle of the survival of the fittest – the financially fittest, who can still afford to work and live there.' Fullilove's (2016) concept of 'root shock' describes people's stress reaction to the loss of their 'emotional ecosystem' (an effect not restricted to gentrification that can also apply to other changes to the fabric and social construct of a neighbourhood). Conversely, of course, people of higher socioeconomic status may feel unwelcome in areas that were traditionally working class.

- **'Defensive' or 'hostile' architecture:** Design elements intended to encourage desirable use of a space often do so by making the space inhospitable to certain groups of people. Examples include spiked or sloped benches to prevent homeless people from sleeping on them, or spikes on the ground to deter lingering in certain locations. Supporters argue that the use of defensive/hostile architecture is an effective method of promoting safe and desirable behaviours in a neighbourhood; others are concerned that such architecture or design discriminates against people with housing insecurity, reducing their dignity and sense of belonging in a place (de Fine Licht 2017). More research is needed on how to encourage safe behaviours whilst respecting and meeting the needs of vulnerable populations in the city.

Segregation also has potentially positive impacts on mental health

Despite the problems associated with spatial segregation, there are potential mental health benefits of bringing together people who share minority characteristics and feel excluded from the 'baseline' for which most cities are designed. The social capital some people develop by feeling part of a community – with shared characteristics, visibility and bespoke amenities – may help counteract their risk of developing mental health problems associated with their experiences of prejudice, discrimination, threats to safety and negative responses from neighbours, service providers, employers and even strangers in the public realm. Such examples showing both benefits and risks are well recognized.

- **The 'ethnic density hypothesis':** The research is inconclusive but suggests there may be potential mental health benefits associated with elective segregation of people according to shared race, ethnicity or culture (Halpern and Nazroo 2000). The benefits are most likely driven by reduced local exposure to prejudice, increased social support and, in some cases, a common language. Some studies involving African American and Hispanic adults in the United States found that living in neighbourhoods with a higher percentage of residents of the same minority ethnic identity can reduce both depression and anxiety in adults (Shaw et al. 2012); other studies found the opposite (Lee 2009; Mair et al. 2010). UK research found that people from similar backgrounds living near one another might help protect against developing psychosis (Cantor-Graae and Selten 2005). Overall, it would seem that there is an initial protective effect from living near people with similar backgrounds, which may diminish over time when the benefits of social and professional networks are superseded by challenges around quality of education and employment as well as levels of crime in 'majority minority areas' (Iceland 2014).

- **The 'gaybourhood':** The development of enclaves in many cities with higher-than-average LGBTQ+ density (e.g. the Castro in San Francisco) is an example of a minority group intentionally clustering together to pool social capital, express themselves without fear of prejudice through a feeling of 'safety in numbers', and develop local norms that may diverge from those of the city's 'baseline' heterosexual, cisgender majority (Ghaziani 2019). It also provides a convenient setting for targeting LGBTQ+ specific services, events and information. However, 'gaybourhoods' have also been criticized for increasing self-marginalization and 'othering' rather than integration. These enclaves often originate as deprived areas and can be associated with gentrification. Ironically, LGBTQ+ people with lower incomes may eventually find themselves marginalized or displaced from the 'gaybourhood'.

- **Age-segregated environments:** Older people tend to find themselves segregated, sometimes by choice (e.g. moving to a retirement community) and sometimes by need (e.g. living in a care home). This segregation is geographical; it may also be racial or socioeconomic, or some other factor may play a role, such as care homes for specific professionals only (e.g. actors, musicians) or for LGBTQ+ people. Whilst living with people with shared characteristics has potential benefits for mental health in terms of social opportunity, segregation can reduce people's social capital and exacerbate inequalities and inequities in the social and physical environments (Oliver, Blythe and Roe 2018).

Design for the baseline

Historically, public spaces have been the domain of ethnic-majority, able-bodied, working-age men who went to the office whilst women stayed at home, with urban planning and design prioritizing the needs and characteristics of this group as a 'baseline'.

Awareness is growing that urban design does not always intuitively meet the needs of its more diverse citizens: developments designed to meet the needs of a particular 'baseline' or 'mainstream' are likely to exclude other groups. Women, young and old people, ethnic minorities, and people with disabilities are examples of population cohorts whose needs diverge from that conceptual baseline; as a result, they are often marginalized by urban design and left to adapt to the design rather than have the design adapt to them.

The global movement towards 'age-friendly' urban design recognizes the diversity of age in the city, promotes everyone's inclusion in all aspects of civic life, respects age-related decisions and lifestyle choices, and anticipates and responds flexibly to age-related needs. The objective is to support participation, health, independence and security for all age groups in the city. Being able to do basic routine tasks, take a walk, have encounters with nature and engage socially in neighbourhoods can play pivotal roles in maintaining a person's sense of self, wellbeing and quality of life, but a baseline-focused design does not empower everyone to do so equally (Roe and Roe 2018). And this can impact people's mental health and wellbeing.

Age-friendly cities, gender mainstreaming and disability-friendly cities have all become key principles for delivering equality but remain largely underdeveloped in urban planning and design. We will explore age, gender, race and disability as key areas where disparities in needs and patterns of city use are most evident, offering significant urban design opportunities to improve mental health and wellbeing.

- **Different patterns of movement and use of the city:** Whilst a city 'baseline' of working-age men typically needs transport between home and workplace during the standard twice-daily 'rush hour', other groups have different needs that are not systematically catered to in a commuting-focused transit system. Older people who have retired from work; children with nursery, school and after-school activities; adolescents needing the freedom to get around independently; people with disabilities; and carers (primarily women, who are more likely than men to be looking after home, children and older relatives) all have multiple roles that involve diverse routing and scheduling needs. These usually require shorter, more frequent journeys throughout the entire day and evening to a wider range of destinations than the twice-daily rush hour commute, for which many cities' transport systems are designed, can adequately meet.

Younger and older people also tend to spend more time than working-age people in their immediate urban environment owing to such factors as physical, sensory and cognitive limitations; locally located amenities (schools, day centres); decreased access to transport; and development of social circles based on proximity (Garin et al. 2014). Particularly for the young, bikeability and other modes of transit, such as skateboarding and scooters, are a bigger priority than they are for older people.

Different needs for infrastructure and facilities

- **Physical accessibility:** Urban design generally prioritizes environmental accessibility for the physically able. By 2050, 15 per cent of the urban population will have a disability (United Nations 2016), and a significant proportion of the population will have other physical accessibility needs to be met in order to enable their full access to facilities/services and participation in social life. These may include the use of wheel-based mobility aids, such as prams, pushchairs, Zimmer frames and wheelchairs, that reduce people's access to both the private and the public realm. Compromised physical access can inhibit people's independence, autonomy and access to protective factors for mental health, including well-located homes; access to education, employment, healthcare, cultural, commercial and social opportunities; and access to nature and other restorative features within the urban realm.

  Key physical barriers include residential, commercial and public buildings and workplaces without step-free access or without doors wide enough to accommodate a wheelchair; exercise facilities unsuitable for wheelchairs; lack of toilets, including accessible toilets; lack of functioning hearing loops; bans on assistance dogs in public places, including parks; lack of parking for adapted bikes; inadequate time allowed by traffic lights for crossing roads; problems with navigating streets owing to street clutter, such as advertisements, or kerb changes or blockages, including by pavement parking or parking across dropped kerbs; and uneven streets owing to, for example, the use of cobbles (House of Commons 2017). Physical characteristics and needs: working-age men are, on average, taller and stronger than women, children and older people. As a result, such men tend to walk farther, longer and sometimes faster than other groups, and this can be reflected in urban design (Yang and Diez-Roux 2012). Transit times and distances – from moving between transport modalities to time afforded at a pedestrian crossing to stair access – can be harder to manage for people with different levels of walking comfort or who may need different infrastructure. For example, people with reduced mobility may depend on bench placement; women may have increased need of access to public toilets for such reasons as menstruation, menopause, more susceptibility to urinary tract infections due to anatomical differences, more susceptibility to incontinence associated with the complications of previous childbirth, and increased risk of disorders like irritable bowel syndrome. In addition, women are more likely than men to be caring for children or older people, who have increased toilet needs. Men who are caregivers may face additional barriers – for instance, when changing facilities for babies are located only in women's toilets. And some transgender people may struggle to safely access public toilets that are segregated by gender.

- **Perceptive and cognitive differences:** Inadequate design approaches to accommodate differences in people's perception and cognition create barriers to the built environment. For example, people with visual or hearing impairments need navigational and safety cues that do not depend on visual or auditory information. Exclusively written information may exclude people with dyslexia or with low levels of literacy in a given language; likewise, exclusively digital information may exclude people without digital capability. Diversity in how information is provided helps empower everyone.

  Urban design also tends to focus on the needs of neurotypical people. Certain features of urban design can be limiting to people with various neurological and mental health disorders, particularly in terms of anxiety and sensory overload. Research indicates that people with autism can become distressed and therefore be deterred from interaction in the public realm by fluorescent/flickering/buzzing lights, by noise and from feeling trapped. Inclusive urban design features can improve their experience of the public realm – for example, retreat spaces for when people begin to feel overwhelmed, shade from sunlight, wide circulation spaces, natural light, low noise levels (including good soundproofing) and low-arousal colours (Davidson and Henderson 2016).

- **Psychosocial characteristics and needs:** Children, teenagers, carers and older people have different needs for maximizing their mental health benefits of socialization. For children, this means opportunity for play and self-discovery across the urban environment and locally, especially for those living on higher floors of multi-family buildings (Evans 2003; Modi 2018). Teenagers need places to safely spend time with their friends to help foster social capital and social support, which reduces their risk of developing depression, anxiety, oppositional defiant disorder and conduct disorder (Aneshensel and Sucoff 1996). Carers need opportunities to meet peers for social support to reduce anxiety and depression. Older people need infrastructure to reduce the risk of isolation and loneliness, which doubles their risk of developing rapid cognitive decline in multiple functional domains (Mitchell and Burton 2006). This calls for design that facilitates their autonomy and independence, including social and civic participation.

- **Cultural competency and negotiating use of space:** Women, children, people with disabilities, people from ethnic minorities, and older people are less likely than able-bodied, working age men to negotiate and assert their legitimate use of spaces. For example, when women and men meet on the street, men tend to stop whilst women divert around them; and girls are less likely to use parks when they feel they have been 'taken over' by boys (see the Vienna example below).

    Cultural expectations can also limit how some people move around the city; for instance, in some cities, variables such as dress, behaviour, communication styles and rules affect some people's use of the public realm associated with their gender, culture, religion or other attributes. As an example, some cultures and religions impose restrictions and segregation within the public realm that affect urban design. Gender segregation, a cultural norm in Saudi Arabia (Doumato 2009), requires the design of gender-segregated public spaces in the cities of that country, resulting in some parts of the public realm being dominated by men; for instance, men's near-exclusive use of the roads has restricted or prevented women from being able to drive. The rise of women-only spaces, such as parks and workplaces in Saudi Arabia, has been both welcomed, for expanding women's opportunities, and criticized, for endorsing segregation, particularly when it affords one gender more opportunities than the other.

    Even where there is no formally imposed segregation, people can find their use of the public realm affected by the extent to which they see their personal characteristics reflected. For instance, one study found that Arabic immigrant women in New York City felt better able to use public space when they could see representations of their culture, such as other women wearing the Islamic headscarf, Arabic signage and the Arabic language being spoken; well-lit open spaces contributed to this visibility (Johnson and Miles 2014). Another study has proposed four principles for cultural competency in urban design: maximizing low-barrier participation, legitimizing diversity of activity, designing in micro-retreats of nearby quietness and addressing structural inequalities of open space provision and access (Rishbeth et al. 2018).

- **Safety:** Being able to navigate the city safely and independently expands opportunities for everyone. This affects certain groups disproportionately. For example, in many parts of the world, women's participation in the public realm is restricted by safety concerns. Research shows that women are more likely than men to fear crime, including sexual assault, and that this fear affects their choices of how they use the city regardless of the objective risk (Snedker 2015). Women who are caregivers may also be particularly afraid of other threats to their charges, such as traffic danger. Such safety fears – which are not confined to women and may include members of the LGBTQ+ community, ethnic minorities, people with disabilities and many others – limit such people's psychological freedom of movement, which may affect their choices concerning city places they feel able to use. This is particularly true if people feel they have a reduced ability to protect themselves and escape from dangerous situations and also have characteristics they feel may make them a more vulnerable target.

    In addition to general vulnerabilities associated with disabilities and frailty, an important safety challenge for older people with dementia is wayfinding. Dementia is characterized by symptoms that include memory loss; difficulties with thinking, orientation, problem solving, and/or language; mood or behaviour changes; and potentially wandering/roaming behaviour. Disorientation, fear and difficulty in safely moving around the public realm reduce older people's opportunities and can negatively affect their mental health. Conversely, urban design that enables people to do basic routine tasks, take a walk, have encounters with nature and engage socially in their neighbourhoods can help maintain their independence, social engagement, stimulation, exercise, and mental and physical wellbeing.

Modifiers of impact

The extent to which a city is experienced as inclusive is modified by (1) a person's characteristics, including age, gender, race/ethnicity, socioeconomic status, and physical and mental health status; (2) the extent to which these personal characteristics correspond to the predominant characteristics within a neighbourhood or city; and (3) the extent to which these characteristics confer advantage or disadvantage according to the social norms and culture of a particular place. The extent to which a city is experienced as inclusive is also modified by environmental features that confer safety and inclusion.

Design approaches for an inclusive city

For too long, designers have been content to design largely for a 'baseline' population – often, one that reflects the characteristics and needs of certain urban residents above others. This is no longer acceptable as cities expand and develop to include more and more diverse populations and as economies increasingly depend on their mental health and wellbeing. Designers have ever-increasing opportunities to embrace the principles of universal/inclusive design that meets the needs of all city users and helps empower them to thrive.

Designing an inclusive city to promote mental health and wellbeing involves two key principles:

Reducing the negative impacts of spatial segregation

Spatial segregation is most likely to occur in the context of socioeconomic gradients and different racial/ethnic/religious/sexual characteristics. Urban design should aim to maximize the benefits of people living near others with whom they have something in common – such as social capital, feelings of belongingness and perceptions of safety – whilst reducing the exclusion that affects people's mental health, self-esteem, dignity and access to opportunities, including restorative urban design within the city. This can be achieved primarily by (1) designing and redeveloping neighbourhoods to be sufficiently universally attractive to reduce the desirability gradient whilst avoiding the potential exclusion of gentrification; (2) offering affordable housing to reduce socioeconomic barriers and to be welcoming and inclusive to a diverse range of residents; (3) designing better connections between neighbourhoods, such as walking trails and safe streets, enabling people to move more easily between the neighbourhoods of their city and to feel less inclined to confine themselves to certain locations; and (4) designing neighbourhoods for conviviality, facilitating the fleeting connections between people that help create social inclusion, cultural recognition of differences, and feelings of belongingess within a place (Amin, 2018; see the Neighbourly City chapter).

Overall, reducing spatial segregation by encouraging integration of people with diverse characteristics and identities (an approach common in Europe) seems to have a more positive impact on people's mental health and wellbeing than simply seeking to improve the environment within poorer neighbourhoods that continue to be segregated, or moving people out of poorer areas (an approach common in the United States), though each approach plays an important role (Iceland 2014).

Scattered-site programmes disperse public housing within diverse neighbourhoods rather than clustering it in poorer neighbourhoods. Voucher programmes subsidize housing to increase people's choices of where to live. Both have shown modest benefits in increasing integration and opportunities. Several cities have experimented with quota allocation systems in which people were actively distributed in housing throughout the city to reduce concentrations of ethnic minorities or poverty in any one neighbourhood; this approach has not been especially successful and has been criticized for being discriminatory (Munch 2009). Similarly, housing diversification efforts – in which old housing stock is demolished and replaced with housing that varies in size, quality and cost – have not led to significant integration within neighbourhoods.

Perhaps one of the most interesting opportunities here for urban design is to help address the underlying drivers of poverty, exclusion and health inequalities by designing neighbourhoods and cities in ways that increase people's educational, economic, social and cultural opportunities. This approach focuses on locating these opportunities in accessible places and on investing in affordable, accessible and efficient transit opportunities for all.

One example of a challenge for inclusive urban planning and design is homelessness. Various estimates suggest that around 150 million people are homeless at any one time, with a further 1.6 billion lacking adequate housing, many of whom are clustered in cities (Chamie 2017). Homelessness can occur as a consequence of mental health problems associated with risk factors like poverty, unemployment and family problems. Homelessness can also contribute to mental health problems in many ways, including through stigmatization and segregation from society, with people experiencing being prohibited from begging, loitering or even resting in public–private areas of the city. Ultimately, homeless people need homes. Some of the most successful urban design approaches to addressing homelessness focus on providing homes for all. In Finland, rather than investing in temporary accommodation, the national homelessness strategy seeks to unconditionally provide permanent housing, accompanied by needs-based support, for all homeless people.

Moving from design that meets the needs of a 'baseline' population to design that meets the needs of diverse city users (inclusive/universal design)

Inclusive design means more equitable design. In the US city of Tacoma, Washington, the new Tacoma Equity Index focuses on four indicators of equity: accessibility (including transportation, parks and road quality), liveability (including crime index and tree density), economy and education. The city's analysis of how to increase equity found the priorities to be access and proximity to community facilities, services, infrastructure and employment by residents of diverse income levels and races/ethnicities. This finding is supported by the findings in Arup (2019), which highlight autonomy and independence, social connectedness, and safety and security. Some key designs include:

Walkability for all: An inclusive city invests in well-maintained pedestrian infrastructure to meet the diverse needs of its citizens, who have different routing needs, physical characteristics and abilities (see the Active City chapter). This includes design that recognizes and equally values the full diversity of people's needs and abilities, whether they use wheelchairs, prams or walking aids or whether they have physical limitations or have caring responsibilities. Inclusive walkable design approaches may include:

- Wide, well-maintained sidewalks/pavements
- Pedestrian ramps, elevators and other alternatives for those who cannot negotiate steps
- Pedestrian crossings that take into account users' different abilities when determining such factors as timing (e.g. children, older people and those who use mobility aids)
- Frequent bus stops
- Shade and shelter
- Resting places, including benches
- Access to public bathrooms
- Locating key facilities such as healthcare, day centres, grocery stores, libraries, post offices, parks and other such amenities within walking distance of homes, which can mean adaptations to zoning plans that separate residential and commercial areas
- Ensuring access for those with mobility aids and other disabilities to residences, workplaces, places of commerce, public buildings and other places, including how doors are opened, how buildings are entered and navigation within buildings

Transit for all: An inclusive city provides affordable, efficient, accessible transportation options that extend beyond rush hours and offer full geographical coverage, including to public facilities such as schools, libraries and hospitals. Urban transportation is often designed in a 'spoke and wheel' configuration to bring people from residential neighbourhoods into a commercial centre. To extend transit design beyond the commuter and meet the needs of a more diverse population that makes shorter, more frequent and more local journeys, a web configuration may be more effective. All transit options should be fully accessible to people using wheels and other mobility aids.

Safety for all: There is extensive literature on urban design to improve safety. This includes caution against 'cleaning up' a street – having eyes on the street, such as may naturally occur in a bustling street with market stalls, can increase feelings of safety for women and other vulnerable-feeling users of the public realm.

Another key element is to enable people with sensory and cognitive limitations, such as hearing and sight impairments, to move around safely and independently. Approaches may include:

- Visual cues, including diverse land use, with environmental landmarks and buildings that have visually clear, distinct uses, such as a church with a steeple or a grocery store with fruit outside. (Designers and planners should be aware of the potentially negative impact of removing longstanding landmarks – such as historic or civic buildings, clock towers, parks and other places of activity, and even street furniture like telephone boxes – that have long been used as navigational aids.)
- Clear, simple signage in locations where confusion may occur, such as T-junctions. Signs are most easily legible when the lettering contrasts with the background and the sign does not contain superfluous information. Any symbols used should be realistic. Some people with dementia report that perpendicular signs are more accessible than those parallel to walls. Conversely, non-navigational signs can be a hindrance to street legibility, and a cluttered street environment can create confusion.
- Lighting and acoustics. Lighting can mediate people's ability to navigate safely, including people who have problems with flickering lights. Persistent background noise and sudden loud noises can create confusion and disorientation, and noises that deliver signals (such as buzzers or alarms) can be lost to those who cannot hear them.
- Reducing vehicle speeds and ensuring separation between vehicles and pedestrians help reduce risk of injury. There is controversy over the concept of shared spaces where kerbs are removed. Whilst some people whose movement depends on wheels find that shared spaces without kerbs or formal crossings enhance their mobility, this design can confuse and disadvantage people who depend on the predictability of kerbs as a reliable indicator of traffic safety, including those with visual impairment and autism spectrum disorder (ASD) (House of Commons 2017). More research is needed.

Comfort for all: Concepts of design for the comfort of people with different needs are developing. This area incorporates needs such as availability of accessible toilets and particular design elements to support people with mental and neurological disorders. For instance, ASD-friendly design is developing and includes low stimulation, predictability/consistency, retreat spaces, wide circulation spaces, natural light (and avoiding flickering lights), use of low-intensity colours and shade from sunlight.

Visibility for all: Representations of a 'baseline' – such as ethnic-majority, able-bodied, heterosexual, cisgender, working-age men – are commonly encountered in cities. More diverse representation and narratives can have a powerful impact on whether people feel belongingness in a city. This may mean ensuring the presence of facilities and services in the public realm that are designed to value and meet the needs of different communities rather than creating homogeneous offerings that exclude, for example, people of lower socioeconomic class in a 'gentrifying' area. Another opportunity is naming places after people or events important to various communities represented in the area or featuring art or other representations from those communities.

Mixed-income, mixed-age residential development: Neighbourhoods with good-quality mixed-housing types, sizes and tenures; good links to services, facilities and jobs; zoning for local businesses; and walking trails connecting to other neighbourhoods (to prevent spatial segregation) help meet people's current and future needs and are most able to attract and retain diverse residents. High-quality social spaces, well-managed green spaces, communal facilities such as children's playparks serving all local residents, and local social and cultural activities can all aid development of social bonds and diverse social cohesion. And good local leadership and governance ensure sustainable diversity.

Homeless person–inclusive design: Urban design can support homeless people's basic needs and dignity by ensuring access to water, sanitation, charging stations for electronic devices, and places to rest and sleep, as well as harm-reduction facilities for drug users (e.g. safe injection sites). Urban design can also reduce stigma by avoiding hostile architecture, establishing places to seek social and practical support, and affording access to safe places to sleep – most effectively by providing permanent supportive homes for all homeless people.

Community engagement for inclusive planning and design at every stage

In order to move away from a conceptual 'baseline' population, planners and designers need to understand for whom they are designing. This means engaging with the full target community, involving as many current and future users of the place as possible. Involving diverse groups in planning and design not only improves inclusive design and avoids stereotyping or tokenism, but it also increases self-worth, purpose, social interaction, and feelings of belongingness and security in the area.

A priority is working with the target community to understand and use design to eliminate barriers to its inclusion. These barriers may be associated with physical, visual, hearing, cognitive and mental health differences, as well as gender, ethnic, racial or sexual identities, and customs and practices. Although no single design can meet every possible need, inclusive, responsive and flexible design values all users equally and provides alternatives so that everyone can use the place.

Community engagement should involve community members in consultations, working groups and evaluations. But it ought to go further, offering opportunities for the community to contribute to steering groups and forums supervising the project, to decision making (e.g. through participation in a partnership board and through consultations on strategic choices), and to helping deliver and continue the project as local successor partners.

Inclusive design for urban mental health and wellbeing depends on identifying and involving a genuine and full representation of the community: local residents and groups; local community groups; faith-based groups; racial, ethnic, cultural, age and socioeconomic groups; and others. There may be inclusive design considerations at all stages of engagement with the community, such as location and accessibility of meeting venue, timing of individual engagements, and format and language of communication. The formats of engagements may also be diverse and need to be appropriate for the objectives and participants and local context. The UN – in collaboration with WHO – has set out various participatory approaches and tools for supporting urban health planning processes, including community asset-mapping, co-creation and community engagement and community development methods (UN-Habitat and WHO 2020). Examples abound creative approaches (like giving participants cameras or art materials to capture their experience of the urban environment and explore their needs); community mapping (e.g. of safe and unsafe areas); constructing 3D models (to explore context, scale, physical frameworks); surveys; public meetings and forums; workshops and focus groups; roundtables; citizens' juries or panels; open space methods (e.g. community audit tools that capture parameters such as access and quality of space, including sensory aspects); street stalls (to engage diverse users of the area) and web-based engagement.

Inclusive city examples

Growing Up Boulder: community engagement for young people, United States

Growing Up Boulder was launched in 2009 as a child/youth-friendly city initiative in the US city of Boulder, Colorado, that was based on urban

FIGURE 8.4 Children participate in a visioning process in Boulder, Colorado, United States. Source: Donna Patterson, Growing Up Boulder.

planning participatory methods developed in the 1970s (Lynch 1977). A partnership was formed between local government, schools, universities and non-profit organizations. Growing Up Boulder has led to young people being systematically engaged in visioning processes that have helped shape major city projects, such as park design and transport planning, to be inclusive and fit for their future. Engagement methods have included community assessments, mapping, model building, photogrids, photo documentation, interviewing, participatory action research, presentations to city representatives, digital storytelling and the 'City as Play' approach for creating interactive planning models (Derr et al. 2013; Figure 8.4). The results have been greener and healthier design, increased focus on social and environmental sustainability, and an increased recognition by young people of the diverse needs of the city's population (Derr and Ildikó, 2017).

York: a dementia-friendly city, UK

The medieval walled city of York, in the UK, has a population of nearly 200,000, with rising numbers of older people. Concerns about the growing need for social care of older people led York to partner with the Joseph Rowntree

Foundation to become a dementia-friendly city. The city aims to help people with dementia stay in their homes or preferred residences for as long as possible (to maintain supportive relationships and reduce isolation), to support carers and to reduce stigma. The project enlisted the engagement and input of people with dementia and their carers and a cross-sector working group that included not only health and social care services but also others such as housing, leisure and transport services. It identified people with dementia who had various challenges in interacting with people in the city, as well as navigational challenges. Evaluation (Dean et al. 2015) has identified that the most successful changes raised awareness about dementia in the local community, including intergenerational programmes (such as between care homes and schools); training staff in local businesses; clearly identifying sports, culture and leisure options suitable for older people; and a community gardening project. York enables older people to move around the city in different ways, such as free, comfortable rickshaw rides provided as part of the Cycling without Age international movement (Figure 8.5). Much of the success in York came from involving people with dementia in planning, initiating, implementing and evaluating attempts to create a more dementia-friendly environment (Dean et al. 2015).

FIGURE 8.5 Rickshaw rides for older people, York, UK. Source: York Bike Belles Community Interest Company/image by Olivia Brabbs.

Vienna: a gender-inclusive city, Austria

In 1991, planner Eva Kail put on a photo exhibition documenting the lives of eight women in Vienna, Austria. It drew much publicity and discussion about how the city was designed for the needs of men. It raised the question: what if planning were approached from different perspectives? Kail was tasked with taking this idea forward. Only female architects (then 6 per cent of local architects) were invited to apply to design a social housing project. In 1997,

FIGURE 8.6 Representation of women in public art about the Holocaust, Vienna, Austria. Source: Emma Fullerton.

the resulting *Frauen-Werk-Stadt* (Women-Work-City) project was completed. Whilst initially this growing gender-mainstreaming approach was not universally embraced, the female perspective brought new elements to the project, such as pram storage, wider stairwells to encourage social interaction and a lower building height to enable residents to see the street, increasing safety. The new perspective was scaled up to a district size, widening pavements and creating ramps to accommodate prams and improving lighting to enhance feelings of safety. Where there were steps, ramps and elevators were added. Perhaps the most famous design intervention was the redesign of two parks in the Margareten district that were being used disproportionately by boys; girls were avoiding the parks from age nine upwards. The redesign added volleyball and badminton facilities to the male-dominated basketball courts in the parks, created seating areas and increased lighting and other safety features. The girls returned to the parks. Now scaled up across the city, gender mainstreaming is city policy, planners are held responsible for community engagement, and gender mainstreaming, along with financial incentives and sanctions, ensures that gender is addressed in all projects, including representations in public exhibitions (Figure 8.6).

Design principles for an inclusive city

General principle

- Engage with the full target community, involving diverse current and future users of the place, throughout all stages of inclusive planning, design, implementation and maintenance.

Neighbourhood scale (see Figure 8.7)

- Plan mixed-use neighbourhoods that enable walkability between homes, shops and local facilities, and provide facilities and commercial offers attractive to a diverse population.
- Provide accessible pedestrian infrastructure, such as wide streets, pedestrian ramps, timed crossings, benches for resting and full access to public transport for people with different physical abilities and mobility aids.
- Design potential subdivisions of parks and other public spaces to encourage use by different groups and to avoid one group's taking over the whole space, creating opportunities for people of diverse and shared characteristics to get together.

- Enhance wayfinding safety with clear signage, visual cues (including recognizable buildings, public art and other landmarks), and lighting and acoustics that reduce the risk of confusion.
- Reduce crime vulnerability by ensuring natural surveillance with bustling streets, good lighting and good maintenance; by avoiding opaque boundaries; and by ensuring that parks and other public spaces have visual connections with the outside area.
- Avoid stigmatizing different groups through the use of 'poor doors' and other methods of socioeconomic segregation; encourage a welcoming attitude towards all.

City scale (see Figure 8.8)

- Mandate inclusive design and development by involving diverse groups at all stages and by recognizing, engaging and empowering resident leadership.
- Ensure connectivity for all neighbourhoods – regardless of predominant socioeconomic status – to high-quality housing, education, employment, local businesses, transport, culture, healthcare and restorative features.
- Provide accessible public toilets for all genders throughout the city.
- Provide accessible public transport, including schedules beyond the standard rush hours, destinations that cover the whole city (not just residence-to-workplace routes), and access for all to educational, economic and cultural opportunities and to restorative aspects of the city; increase biking safety infrastructure.
- Provide walking trails that connect different neighbourhoods.
- Celebrate and reflect diversity throughout the city, including prominent and positive representations of the diverse population (e.g. through public art, place names, dedicated facilities, places for festivals and parades, and facilities to meet the needs of diverse groups).

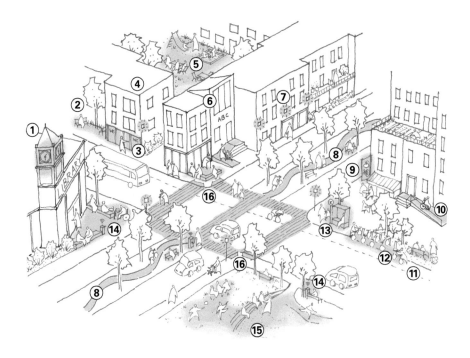

1 landmark wayfinding
2 micro-retreats
3 accessible public toilets + sanitation
4 mixed age, mixed-income housing
5 collective space for diverse groups
6 nursery + care home
7 well-designed lighting, regularly spaced, to increase feelings of safety
8 accessible pedestrian infrastructure connecting neighbourhoods
9 visual cue signage
10 ramp infrastructure
11 bike safety
12 bike share
13 bus stop: shelter + seating
14 public space amenities: drinking fountains, charging stations, seating
15 subdivisions of park/public space
16 safe intersections with timed crossings, good lighting, curb cuts

FIGURE 8.7 The Inclusive City: Neighbourhood Scale.

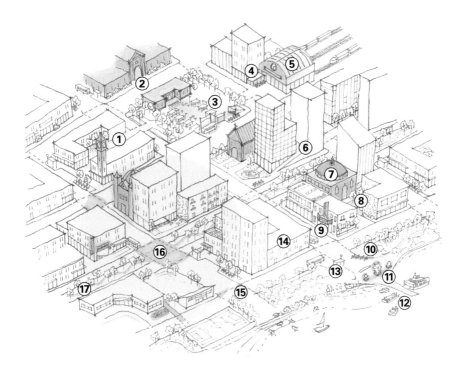

1 pedestrian mixed-use connections
2 landmarks: civic institutions
3 multi-cultural market
4 bike infrastructure
5 multi-modal transit hub
6 accessible ramp circulation
7 landmarks: multi-faith places of worship
8 pocket parks + micro-retreats
9 landmarks: theatre + entertainment
10 bike safety + infrastructure
11 public art
12 accessible blue + green space
13 accessible transit infrastructure connecting neighbourhoods
14 repurposing empty office blocks for homeless housing
15 safe intersections
16 mixed use, compact, intergenerational living
17 accessible pedestrian infrastructure connecting neighbourhoods

FIGURE 8.8 The Inclusive City: City Scale.

9

The restorative city

Restorative urbanism: implementing urban design for mental health and wellbeing

It is increasingly clear that when it comes to mental health and wellbeing at a city level, considerations extend far beyond the hospital ward and responsibility extends far beyond any psychiatrist or clinical psychologist. Urban planning and design decisions affect people's lives in many ways. Such decisions sit at the heart of whether a city will support and promote the mental health and wellbeing of its population or, conversely, whether it will contribute to the development and maintenance of mental health problems. It is time for this impact – and for the role and opportunities of the urban environment – to be formally recognized. This is restorative urbanism.

Restorative urbanism: towards a city design that is good for our mental health and wellbeing

As people around the world keep moving to cities, the impact of the urban environment on the global population's mental health and wellbeing is ever increasing. Whether this impact is positive or negative, it affects the success of cities. Mental health problems affect how people engage in the city, affecting their physical health and their ability to live a productive and satisfying life, engaged and participating in the multiple facets of a thriving urban community. There are also economic costs. The Organisation for Economic Co-operation and Development (OECD) (2014) has assessed that the direct and indirect costs of mental illness amount to over 4 per cent of gross domestic product (GDP), including costs of healthcare, social care and long-term care associated with mental illness. The OECD considers that undertreatment contributes to the high social and economic costs of mental disorders. Mental health problems are also associated with increased indirect costs, including through increased risk of developing physical illness, challenges during education, unemployment (ranging from two to seven times higher than in the general population, depending on severity of illness) and homelessness. There are also opportunity costs when family members and others are involved in informal caring roles, potentially affecting their own employment, leisure, mental and physical health, and relationships. There are many contributing factors to mental health and mental illness, but urban planning and design can help determine whether (or not) the city is a positive, supportive, nurturing place to live, with features that support people's mental health.

In this book, we have examined the role of urban planning and design in mental health and wellbeing. We have explored how cities can harness the attributes of the built environment to promote, support and enable mental health and wellbeing, whilst reducing or eliminating those factors that threaten it. We conceptualize this new way of thinking about urban planning and design as *restorative urbanism*. It is going to be vital to the future success of cities.

A restorative city is a resilient city

Resilience is the ability of people, communities, institutions, businesses and systems within a city to cope, adapt and thrive in the face of acute shocks and chronic stresses (100 Resilient Cities 2020). Resilience has to be a key objective for cities because it is integral to enabling them to thrive, no matter what challenges are thrown at them. The billions of people globally who live in cities expect that whether climate change, migration, a natural disaster, a pandemic or a terrorist attack affects their city, it will be prepared, it will be resilient and they will be safe. Policymakers, urban planners, designers, engineers and countless other urban professionals work routinely on improving cities' resilience. But their focus is often at the level of physical and social systems such as climate-resilient water systems or a strong healthcare system. A huge part of resilience planning that is often overlooked is the resilience of citizens themselves: how can people's mental health and wellbeing be optimized so they can cope, adapt and thrive in the face of acute shocks and chronic stresses? A good resilience strategy for mental health and wellbeing cannot rely solely on, for instance, a strong healthcare system. To achieve a truly resilient city, there must also be a focus on the ability of individuals and communities to cope, adapt and thrive in the face of life's challenges. And restorative urbanism has a key role to play: during periods of enforced confinement, local restrictions and social distancing arising from the Covid-19 pandemic, it has been clear that the role of public open space in supporting mental health has never been more pertinent.

Many different challenges increase our personal and community risk of developing or exacerbating mental health problems, including genetics, family and relationship problems, employment/unemployment, poverty, discrimination, housing problems, personal or family mental and physical illness, and poor access to good healthcare (WHO 2012). How people cope, adapt and thrive in the face of these challenges is affected by a range of factors. This means that supporting public mental health requires a holistic whole-systems approach. But these systems are not confined to formal healthcare. People's mental health resilience can be modulated by their social and physical environments, and these factors interact within a dynamic whole.

As urban planners, designers, geographers, public health and mental health professionals, and others involved in creating enabling environments for mental health support, we have an opportunity to plan, design, develop and deliver cities that help enable people not merely to survive but to *thrive*. Creating restorative cities is a moral imperative, an economic imperative and a sustainability imperative.

The seven pillars of restorative urbanism: a framework

Restorative urbanism means putting mental health, wellness and quality of life at the forefront of city planning and urban design. In an environment filled with cognitive, emotional and practical demands that can deplete our psychological and social resources, it leverages the urban environment to increase our mental health and wellbeing resilience. Restorative urbanism necessarily touches almost all aspects of city planning and design.

There are different ways to approach restorative urbanism. Our model comprises seven key pillars, which we have explored in depth in their own chapters (see Figure 1.4, our framework for the restorative city).

The Green City

The Green City means maximizing people's direct and indirect exposure to green space: urban spaces that include vegetation and other nature. This exposure should be near homes, in transit (including walking connections), near schools and workplaces, and throughout the public realm. This principle includes access and exposure to gardens, street trees, parks and nature views; it also incorporates the quality, maintenance and stewardship of green places. The Green City reduces depression and anxiety and improves people's mood and mental alertness, memory and ability to recover from stress. Exposure to green space also reduces the symptom severity of serious mental health problems; for example, exposure to green space in childhood reduces the symptoms of ADHD and the risk of developing mental illness in adulthood. In addition to mental health benefits, the Green City delivers a host of co-health benefits, including increased opportunities for physical activity and social interaction as well as other resilience benefits such as adaptation to climate change (e.g. mitigating heat stress and managing excess stormwater).

The Blue City

The Blue City means maximizing people's direct and indirect exposure to places that feature water prominently, including natural features like coasts and rivers and engineered features like canals and fountains. This principle incorporates both seeing and interacting with water, including water-based climate adaptation systems. The Blue City, much like the Green City, seems to reduce depression and stress and improve people's mood and other symptoms of mental illness. By mitigating heat stress and fostering more 'comfortable' environments for outdoor recreation, the Blue City can also indirectly reduce depression, agitation and anger. As more research is conducted on the benefits of the Blue City, we expect these mental health effects to be more clearly and empirically quantified.

The Sensory City

The Sensory City means maximizing benefits to mental health and wellbeing by intentionally leveraging our senses: sound, sight, smell, taste, touch and the more ephemeral sense of ambience (our 'sixth' sense; Pallasmaa, 2005). Noise stress can cause depression, anxiety, stress and anger; can affect brain function; and, by disturbing sleep, can exacerbate most mental health problems. Conversely, natural and friendly-feeling sounds can reduce stress and enhance belongingness. Visual monotony can make people more likely to dwell and ruminate on pessimistic internal thoughts, contributing to depression and anxiety; colours can affect people's emotions and help with wayfinding. Smells that are generally considered unpleasant can create stigma, whilst smells associated with nature and food can evoke positive emotions. Touch increases people's engagement with places and is part of the reason gardening and urban farming help reduce depression, anxiety and psychological distress whilst increasing mindfulness, quality of life and sense of community. Taste can evoke cultural and place belongingness, whilst access to healthy foods (and community markets) can reduce obesity – which is both a cause and a side effect of some mental health problems – and foster community and social interaction.

The Neighbourly City

The Neighbourly City means designing settings where people can develop and maintain high-quality social networks and social support that strengthen their mental resilience. Regular social interaction reduces people's risk of developing depression, anxiety, symptoms of dementia and suicidal thoughts, increases their self-esteem and feelings of belonging and can improve brain function. The Neighbourly City helps people come together through walkability, accessibility, social spaces and infrastructure, bumping places, and participatory opportunities to help people build local social networks, develop social capital, participate in community life and feel that they belong.

The Active City

The Active City integrates physical activity into everyday urban life and designs urban spaces to enable mobility for all citizens. Alongside the physical health benefits of physical activity, the Active City helps reduce depression, stress and anxiety, improve brain function and self-esteem, and strengthen social cohesion. In childhood and adolescence, regular outdoor activity, including walking to and from school, improves academic achievement. The Active City focuses on accessibility and street connectivity, with mixed land use and a safe, well-designed transit infrastructure – including benches, toilets, drinking fountains, lighting, bike infrastructure, parks and green corridors, and pedestrian precincts – to enable people to travel easily on foot or by bike in their daily activities, including with wheelchairs, mobility aids, and child prams and buggies.

The Playable City

The Playable City means designing enjoyable features within the public realm that provide people of all ages and abilities with different ways to express themselves and to experience, imagine and creatively engage with their environment. Play promotes creativity, imagination and self-confidence, reduces depression, regulates stress and emotions, and fosters social connection and belongingness. The Playable City has interactive public art installations, and places where people can retreat, daydream and think creatively. It offers age-specific play places such as parks and playgrounds (including intergenerational playgrounds) and also offers non-defined play contexts that can be appropriated in different ways by different age groups (e.g. parkour and skateboarding), as well as opportunities for 'free-range' play in pockets of wilder urban nature, wastelands and abandoned buildings.

The Inclusive City

The Inclusive City means intentionally designing all places for access and use by all people. People may be excluded from parts of the public realm practically, explicitly or implicitly owing to individual differences in such factors as age, size, physical and cognitive variation, gender, racial and ethnic identity, socioeconomic status, and mental or physical illness. Exclusion affects people's self-esteem, dignity, mood and belongingness, and restricts their opportunities to access the features of the city that support mental health. The Inclusive City reduces spatial segregation by moving away from designing for the assumed predominant group and towards an urban design that incorporates and embraces diversity at its core. The Inclusive City can reduce discrimination, promote social cohesion and prevent isolation – but success requires co-creation by bringing in diverse community participation at every step of the planning, design and stewardship processes.

Practical implementation of restorative urbanism

The seven pillars of restorative urbanism do not exist discretely. To achieve the desired support for mental health, a restorative city should incorporate elements of each pillar in the planning and design of any place. For example, safe and accessible pedestrian pathways lined with trees and flowers (the Green City) alongside a canal (the Blue City) will produce views of nature, gentle sounds of trees rustling and water flowing, the smell of flowers and textured ground (the Sensory City), will have ramps for wheelchairs and prams and link nearby neighbourhoods (the Inclusive City), will provide benches for resting and chatting and have volunteer clean-up days (the Neighbourly City), will ensure safe routes for pedestrians, cyclists and scooter users, including relevant infrastructure like bike hire and parking facilities (the Active City) and will have playparks, public art and interactive water features along the waterside (the Playable City).

Restorative urbanism can build incrementally, but it is important that the overarching masterplan be established; the masterplan can be updated or amended as new resources or opportunities emerge. Not every single pillar will be relevant for each project. But by systematically considering all seven pillars when developing a project, as many as possible can be incorporated. The result will be well-connected, accessible cities with effective wayfinding systems, nature infused into the city core, and high-quality aesthetics in urban form. These cities will have dynamic, multi-functioning neighbourhoods that support the diverse population's everyday activities, social interactions, and access to the services, facilities and features that support and promote their mental health and wellbeing. In other words, applying this framework will deliver a restorative city that leverages urban planning and design to support people's mental health and wellbeing.

Restorative urbanism can and should be implemented at all levels. Whilst an all-encompassing citywide strategy should certainly include the principles of restorative urbanism, so too should the individual designer integrate these principles into smaller projects – for example, connecting parks with green walkways, or moving beyond a cursory community consultation to actively bringing in diverse community members to co-create a new place that meets their needs and desires.

Bringing together the recommendations for each pillar will reveal clear crossovers and synergies. Whilst every project is different, with creative and diverse ways to make each one restorative, some practical commonalities in the planning and design of urban features include:

Parks

Parks are a feature of all the pillars, providing a setting for nature exposure, exercise, play and socializing. The research is clear that the more parks – and the more accessible they are from people's homes and workplaces – the better. Parks of all sizes, from pocket parks to larger ones, contribute to the restorative city. But parks are also place-specific and should serve the cultural needs of the people living in the vicinity. The research makes clear some of the ways that park design can directly support and promote the mental health and wellbeing of specific populations, and these features should be explicitly included, where possible, within the context of community engagement to meet local needs.

This approach includes subdividing large parks to increase areas for different purposes to promote engagement and inclusivity, including designated play areas for the diverse population; green connections between parks and homes/workplaces/schools; parks positioned in such a way as to provide clear views of their greenery from homes and offices; incorporation of natural water features and sensory elements; and repurposing unused urban infrastructure (e.g. parking lots and abandoned ground) to create additional accessible green space.

The public outdoor realm

As with parks, there is clear opportunity within most public spaces to apply the principles of restorative urbanism to increase the extent to which these spaces support mental health and wellbeing. How public open space can be designed and better used to support public health will be a guiding principle of urban planning and design in the post-Covid-19 city. Restorative urbanism is a key lever with which to achieve this change.

There are opportunities to consider the positioning of public social spaces – for example, co-locating them with such facilities as schools, religious buildings and markets (which people will be visiting anyway), and including new social facilities like dog parks to create bumping places.

The flexibility of public spaces can also be more creatively expanded; for example, school playing fields can be used by the public on weekends, open spaces can be used for markets and festivals, and vacant lots and underutilized infrastructure can be reclaimed to expand their public use (e.g. as community gardens or pop-up opportunities for artistic self-expression).

The inclusivity of public spaces is also a key theme. Whether designing new places – or repurposing old ones – there are opportunities to support people's mental health by making places inclusive of diverse needs and preferences so that people do not experience stigma and can fully participate in society on a level playing field.

Digital tools such as smartphone apps can also help people engage with places – for instance, apps that identify green, blue and recreational space, as well as facilities/markets, landmarks and accessible infrastructure. And urban digital games afford opportunities to explore and 'capture' attributes of the urban environment (e.g. landmarks, urban street furniture) in a competitive but playful socially interactive forum.

Synergestic thinking is also needed to understand how the attributes of restorative urbanism interact with other aspects of sustainability and resilience in a city. Pillars like the Green City can help mitigate effects of climate change and support people's use of the public realm during heat, rain, cold, storms and other types of weather by providing features such as shelters and cooling sprinklers/misters. Design can also leverage climate adaptation systems to deliver social spaces and water features – for instance, hybrid parks/ponds that support sports or social activities in dry weather and capture water to prevent flooding in wet weather, or street stormwater drainage that creates mini-waterways or ponds.

Street features

In this book, we have identified many street features that can contribute to mental health and wellbeing. The street's primary restorative health function is to be an enabling place that allows people to fully access and participate in the public realm. The accessibility of public spaces is very important for mental health; so too is accessible pedestrian and cycling infrastructure that supports movement, particularly safe, continuous routes for walkability and bikeability for people with different abilities, including those with wheels (wheelchairs, walking aids, prams, pushchairs etc.). Other street features include pedestrianized zones, short blocks and pedestrian cut-throughs in cul-de-sacs; benches, public toilets and distinctive signs and landmarks to aid intuitive navigation; bike hire, bike storage and drinking fountains; and opportunities for other modes of transport like scooters and skates. Tactical urbanism has been applied to increase opportunities for exercise (particularly walking and cycling) whilst maintaining social distancing during the Covid-19 pandemic. Some cities, including Milan, Paris and London, are experimenting with making these short-term street changes permanent fixtures to improve quality of life.

Increasing public accessibility requires understanding people's perceptions of safety, which falls into three main categories that can be modified by urban planning and design: traffic safety, wayfinding safety and safety associated with risks from other people. The research discussed in this book has made clear that safety is not binary; rather, different people have different perceptions, experiences and concerns about safety, and design solutions must include diverse populations and their needs. Design considerations include safe infrastructure for walking and cycling, safe waiting places for public transit, good lighting, natural surveillance, and good stewardship and maintenance of places to increase feelings of safety. Also included are good signposting, landmarks and other features to aid wayfinding, and safe access to sleeping and hygiene facilities for homeless people.

Making streets interesting places that arouse curiosity is clearly important to restorative health outcomes. One way is to leverage the fascination offered by natural features (e.g. street trees, gardens and waterways) by designing routes, facilities and other infrastructure to maximize people's exposure to these green and blue spaces. These can be augmented with man-made features that also promote interest and engagement, such as open shopfronts, public art, murals, stairs/bridges that feel like an 'event' (with alternatives for those with diverse mobility needs), distinctive buildings and other structures, mixed-use neighbourhoods, and participatory and playable infrastructure. Other approaches include finding ways to design interest into otherwise monotonous blocks and designing to positively engage all the senses.

Street design can increase neighbourliness, belongingness and inclusivity through community participatory opportunities, as well as through representation of diverse identities in art, buildings, amenities and more. Interactivity within the streets may include outdoor play facilities for all ages; recreational facilities for activities like sports, yoga and tai chi; structures that support parkour, skateboarding and free running; and infrastructure to facilitate water-based activities like kayaking, paddling and other play.

Transportation

The restorative city advocates for transportation that enables accessibility, connection and physical activity. Walkability and bikeability are therefore the mainstays of restorative urban design, with a focus on safety, curiosity, accessibility and connectivity – meaning not only continuous routes but also trails between neighbourhoods and between homes and key facilities, leveraging, where possible, opportunities for people's exposure to natural features whilst in transit. Easily accessible, regular and integrated public transport is also key. Public transit should be affordable, frequent, safe, comfortable and equitably distributed, with consideration given to the needs of the full population rather than prioritizing a target group (e.g. people who work 'standard' hours); there should be reliable service during and outside rush hours, serving diverse destinations. Busy roads should be routed away from pedestrian and bike routes where possible, including traffic-reducing designs such as parking underground, or outside the city centre, with integrated public transit.

Housing

People's homes should be affordable and accessible and should be integrated with social infrastructure, such as well-maintained and accessible communal places, community gardens, and mixed-income, multi-generational housing. Homes should be co-located with educational, economic, health and cultural facilities; ideally, these facilities should be safely walkable in under twenty minutes, with public transit options.

Co-creation

One of the most compelling themes running through this book is that of co-creation, of participative place making that engages the community in all its diversity at every step of the design journey to truly and sustainably meet its needs. Co-design is a tool that can be leveraged to catalyse sustained social change, support human-centred design and build social justice and equity.

Restorative urbanism: whose job is it anyway?

Historically, major urban design momentums have emerged in response to infectious disease (Ebeneezer Howard's nineteenth Century Garden City) or non-communicable disease (the recent 'walkable' city designed to tackle the growing epidemic of obesity and heart disease). From speaking with numerous architects, planners, geographers, engineers, health professionals, policymakers and others in cities around the world, we know that people's mental health and wellbeing have yet to become an explicit priority in urban planning and design. For many, it is an afterthought, or given no thought at all. Most confessed that they did not know where to begin. This excuse is no longer tenable. A new paradigm is needed. This book articulates how the new principles of restorative urbanism can help integrate people's mental health and wellbeing into all urban policy and development.

Sustainably applying the principles of restorative urbanism means that everyone involved in any aspect of city making has a role to play. From the design of the tallest skyscraper to the city's refuse management system, the effect on people's mental health, wellbeing and quality of life should be recognized, understood, considered and systematically applied. Some 'city makers' with a key role include:

Policymakers: Implement restorative urbanism as a central part of future city strategies. Recommend, incentivize or require the principles and pillars of restorative urbanism to be integrated into all urban development as a priority.

City planners: Appreciate the impact of planning decisions and developments on people's mental health and wellbeing and afford this impact equivalence with physical health considerations, in line with the city's restorative urbanism guidelines and policies.

Architects, landscape architects and urban designers: Develop an understanding of the restorative factors of design and integrate them systematically and creatively as standard across all projects.

Developers: Recognize the growing expectations and requirements to provide restorative health features within developments. Become expert on restorative urbanism and integrate its principles into developments.

Clients/business: Ascribe value to restorative urban design in commissioned projects, and explicitly require the principles of restorative design to be reflected in all proposals.

Researchers: Recognize the gaps in knowledge and the need for research in the rapidly growing field of restorative urbanism. Seek ways to evaluate the impact of new developments on people's mental health and wellbeing and disseminate this information to all stakeholders to inform new recommendations.

Public health and mental health professionals: Advocate for restorative urban design as a public mental health opportunity. Work with researchers to evidence its benefits.

City residents: Engage in all aspects of planning and design to ensure that the city is designed to meet the full diversity of needs within the population – and, as a bonus, derive mental health and wellbeing benefits just from participating. Leverage the evidence in this book to advocate for restorative urbanism in your neighbourhood.

Restorative urbanism: a new mandate for urban planning and design

Mental health and wellbeing are at the heart of a flourishing city – at a personal level and at a neighbourhood (Figure 9.1) and city (Figure 9.2) level. Urban planning and design has an important role to play. To achieve sustainable, resilient cities – where people can thrive and live 'well' alongside each other – planners, designers, developers and others involved in making cities can now contribute to the creation of green, blue, sensory, neighbourly, active, playable and inclusive cities. Now that the research increasingly demonstrates how to meaningfully contribute to – and truly improve – people's mental health and wellbeing, designing a restorative city has become an ethical imperative.

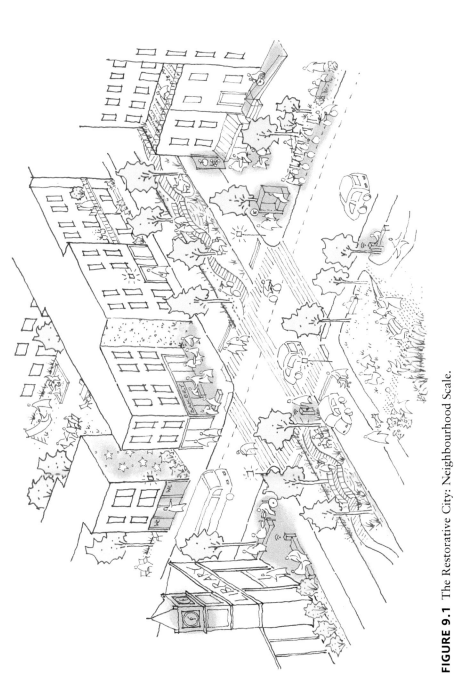

FIGURE 9.1 The Restorative City: Neighbourhood Scale.

FIGURE 9.2 The Restorative City: City Scale.

References

Chapter 1: Introduction to restorative urbanism

American Psychiatric Association (2013), *Diagnostic and Statistical Manual of Mental Disorders*, 5th edn, Philadelphia: American Psychiatric Association.

Antonovsky, A. (1979), *Health, Stress and Coping*, San Francisco: Jossey-Bass.

Blau, M. and K. L. Fingerman (2009), *Consequential Strangers: The Power of People Who Don't Seem to Matter… but Really Do*, New York: W. W. Norton.

Bulleck, P. and B. Carey (2013), 'Psychiatry's Guide Is out of Touch with Science, Experts Say', *New York Times*, 6 May.

Dye, C. (2008), 'Health and Urban Living', *Science*, 319 (5864): 766–9.

Gillibrand, K. (2015), *Off the Sidelines: Speak Up, Be Fearless, and Change Your World*, New York: Ballantine Books.

Hagerhall, C. M., T. Laike, R. P. Taylor, M. Küller, R. Küller and T. P. Martin (2008), 'Investigations of Human EEG Response to Viewing Fractal Patterns', *Perception*, 37 (10): 1488–94.

Hartig, T. (2007), 'Three Steps to Understanding Restorative Environments as Health Resources', in C. Ward Thompson and P. Travlou (eds), *Open Space, People Space*, 163–80, Oxford: Taylor and Francis.

Hartig, T., R. Catalano, M. Ong and S. L. Syme (2013), 'Vacation, Collective Restoration, and Mental Health in a Population', *Society and Mental Health*, 3 (3): 221–36.

Joiner, T. E. (2005), *Why People Die by Suicide*, Cambridge: Harvard University Press.

Kaplan, R. and S. Kaplan (1989), *The Experience of Nature: A Psychological Perspective*, New York: Cambridge University Press.

Kaplan, S. (1995), 'The Restorative Benefits of Nature: Toward an Integrative Framework', *Journal of Environmental Psychology*, 15 (3): 169–82.

Keyes, C. L. M. (1998), 'Social Well-Being', *Social Psychology Quarterly*, 61 (2): 121–40.

Keyes, C. L. M. (2002), 'The Mental Health Continuum: From Languishing to Flourishing in Life', *Journal of Health and Social Behavior*, 43 (2): 207–22.

Keyes, C. L. M. (2007), 'Promoting and Protecting Mental Health as Flourishing: A Complementary Strategy for Improving National Mental Health', *American Psychologist*, 62 (2): 95–108.

Keyes, C. L. M. (2019), 'Can Biophilic Cities Promote Flourishing?', Biophilic Leadership Summit, Serenbe, 28 April.

Kunzig, R. (2019), 'Rethinking Cities', *National Geographic* (April): 70–97.

Laugesen, K., L. M. Baggesen, S. A. J. Schmidt, M. M. Glymour, M. Lasgaard, A. Milstein, H. T. Sørensen, N. E. Adler and V. Ehrenstein (2018), 'Social Isolation and All-Cause Mortality: A Population-Based Cohort Study in Denmark', *Scientific Reports*, 8 (1): 1–8.

Lederbogen, F., P. Kirsch, L. Haddad, F. Streit, H. Tost, P. Schuch, S. Wüst, J. C. Pruessner, M. Rietschel, M. Deuschle and A. Meyer-Lindenberg (2011), 'City Living and Urban Upbringing Affect Neural Social Stress Processing in Humans', *Nature*, 474 (7352): 498–501.

Lindström, B. and M. Eriksson (2005), 'Salutogenesis', *Journal of Epidemiology and Community Health*, 59 (6): 440–2.

Mitchell, R. J. (2013), 'What Is Equigenesis and How Might It Help Narrow Health Inequities?', *Centre for Research on Environment, Society and Health (CRESH)*, 8 November. Available online: https://cresh.org.uk/2013/11/08/what-is-equigenesis-and-how-might-it-help-narrow-health-inequalities/ (accessed 5 November 2019).

Mitchell, R. J., E. A. Richardson, N. K. Shortt and J. R. Pearce (2015), 'Neighborhood Environments and Socioeconomic Inequalities in Mental Well-Being', *American Journal of Preventive Medicine*, 49 (1): 80–4.

Patel, V., S. Saxena, C. Lund, G. Thornicroft, F. Baingana, P. Bolton, D. Chisholm, P. Y. Collins, J. L. Cooper, J. Eaton and H. Herrman (2018), 'The Lancet Commission on Global Mental Health and Sustainable Development', *The Lancet*, 392 (10157): 1553–98.

Richard, A., S. Rohrmann, C. L. Vandeleur, M. Schmid, J. Barth and M. Eichholzer (2017), 'Loneliness Is Adversely Associated with Physical and Mental Health and Lifestyle Factors: Results from a Swiss National Survey', *PLOS One*, 12 (7): e0181442.

Rutter, H., N. Savona, K. Glonti, J. Bibby, S. Cummins, D. T. Finegood, F. Greaves, L. Harper, P. Hawe, L. Moore and M. Petticrew (2017), 'The Need for a Complex Systems Model of Evidence for Public Health', *The Lancet*, 390 (10112): 2602–4.

Ryan, R. M. and E. L. Deci (2001), 'On Happiness and Human Potentials: A Review of Research on Hedonic and Eudaimonic Wellbeing', *Annual Review of Psychology*, 52 (1): 141–66.

Seligman, M. E. P. (2011), *Flourish: A Visionary New Understanding of Happiness and Well-Being*, New York: Free Press.

Staats, H. (2012), 'Restorative Environments', in S. D. Clayton (ed.), *The Oxford Handbook of Environmental and Conservation Psychology*, 445, New York: Oxford University Press.

Ulrich, R. S. (1983), 'Aesthetic and Affective Responses to Natural Environment', in I. Altman and J. F. Wohlwill (eds), *Behavior and the Natural Environment, Human Behavior and Environment, Advances in Theory and Research*, vol. 6, 85–125, New York: Plenum.

Ulrich, R. S., R. F. Simons, B. D. Losito, E. Fiorito, M. A. Miles and M. Zelson (1991), 'Stress Recovery during Exposure to Natural and Urban Environments', *Journal of Environmental Psychology*, 11 (3): 201–30.

UN-Habitat and WHO (2020), *Integrating Health in Urban and Territorial Planning: A Sourcebook*. Geneva: UN-HABITAT and World Health Organization.

United Nations (2016a), Agenda for Sustainable Development, *United Nations (UN)*. Available online: http://www.un.org/sustainabledevelopment/health/ (accessed 1 November 2019).

United Nations (2016b), Sustainable Development Goal 11, *United Nations (UN)*. Available online: https://sustainabledevelopment.un.org/sdg11 (accessed (26 October 2019).

United Nations (2017), *New Urban Agenda: Quito Declaration on Sustainable Cities and Human and Human Aettlements for All*, Habitat III, Quito: United Nations.

Vos, T., R. M. Barber, B. Bell, A. Bertozzi-Villa, S. Biryukov, I. Bolliger, F. Charlson, A. Davis, L. Degenhardt, D. Dicker and L. Duan (2015), 'Global, Regional, and National Incidence, Prevalence, and Years Lived with Disability for 301 Acute and Chronic Diseases and Injuries in 188 Countries, 1990–2013: A Systematic Analysis for the Global Burden of Disease Study 2013', *The Lancet*, 386 (9995): 743–800.

WHO (2001), *Mental Health: New Understanding, New Hope*, Geneva: World Health Organization (WHO).

WHO (2004), *Promoting Mental Health: Concepts, Emerging Evidence, Practice (Summary Report)*, Geneva: World Health Organization.

WHO (2008), *Closing the Gap in a Generation: Health Equity through Action on the Social Determinants of Health*, Geneva: World Health Organization (WHO).

WHO (2016), *Global Report on Urban Health: Equitable Healthier Cities for Sustainable Development*. Geneva: World Health Organization.

WHO (2017), *International Classification of Diseases*, Geneva: World Health Organization (WHO).

Chapter 2: The green city

Alcock, I., M. P. White, B. W. Wheeler, L. E. Fleming and M. H. Depledge (2014), 'Longitudinal Effects on Mental Health of Moving to Greener and Less Green Urban Areas', *Environmental Science and Technology*, 48 (2): 1247–55.

Amin, A. (2006), 'The Good City', *Urban Studies*, 43 (5–6): 1009–23.

Astell-Burt, T. and X. Feng (2019), 'Association of Urban Green Space with Mental Health and General Health among Adults in Australia', *JAMA Network Open*, 2 (7): e198209–e198209.

Bakolis, I., R. Hammoud, M. Smythe, J. Gibbons, N. Davidson, S. Tognin and A. Mechelli (2018), 'Urban Mind: Using Smartphone Technologies to Investigate the Impact of Nature on Mental Well-Being in Real Time', *BioScience*, 68 (2): 134–45.

Berman, M. G., J. Jonides and S. Kaplan (2008), 'The Cognitive Benefits of Interacting with Nature', *Psychological Science*, 19 (12): 1207–12.

Berman, M. G., E. Kross, K. M. Krpan, M. K. Askren, A. Burson, P. J. Deldin, S. Kaplan, L. Sherdell, I. H. Gotlib and J. Jonides (2012), 'Interacting with Nature Improves Cognition and Affect for Individuals with Depression', *Journal of Affective Disorders*, 140 (3): 300–5.

Berto, R. (2005), 'Exposure to Restorative Environments Helps Restore Attentional Capacity', *Journal of Environmental Psychology*, 25 (3): 249–59.

Beyer, K. M., A. Kaltenbach, A. Szabo, S. Bogar, F. J. Nieto and K. M. Malecki (2014), 'Exposure to Neighborhood Green Space and Mental Health: Evidence from the Survey of the Health of Wisconsin', *International Journal of Environmental Research and Public Health*, 11 (3): 3453–72.

Bos, E. H., L. Van der Meulen, M. Wichers and B. F. Jeronimus (2016), 'A Primrose Path? Moderating Effects of Age and Gender in the Association between Green Space and Mental Health', *International Journal of Environmental Research and Public Health*, 13 (5): 492.

Bowler, D. E., L. M. Buyung-Ali, T. M. Knight and A. S. Pullin (2010), 'A Systematic Review of Evidence for the Added Benefits to Health of Exposure to Natural Environments', *BMC Public Health*, 10 (1): 456.

Bratman, G. N., J. P. Hamilton, K. S. Hahn, G. C. Daily and J. J. Gross (2015), 'Nature Experience Reduces Rumination and Subgenual Prefrontal Cortex Activation', *Proceedings of the National Academy of Sciences*, 112 (28): 8567–72.

CABE (2010), *Urban Green Nation: Building the Evidence Base*, London: Commission for Architecture and the Built Environment (CABE).

Calogiuri, G. and S. Chroni (2014), 'The Impact of the Natural Environment on the Promotion of Active Living: An Integrative Systematic Review', *BMC Public Health*, 14 (1): 873.

Cherrie, M. P., N. K. Shortt, R. J. Mitchell, A. M. Taylor, P. Redmond, C. W. Thompson, J. M. Starr, I. J. Deary and J. R. Pearce (2018), 'Green Space and Cognitive Ageing: A Retrospective Life Course Analysis in the Lothian Birth Cohort 1936', *Social Science & Medicine*, 196 (January): 56–65.

Dadvand, P., M. J. Nieuwenhuijsen, M. Esnaola, J. Forns, X. Basagaña, M. Alvarez-Pedrerol, I. Rivas, M. López-Vicente, M. D. C. Pascual, J. Su and M. Jerrett (2015), 'Green Spaces and Cognitive Development in Primary Schoolchildren', *Proceedings of the National Academy of Sciences*, 112 (26): 7937–42.

Dadvand, P., S. Hariri, B. Abbasi, R. Heshmat, M. Qorbani, M. E. Motlagh, X. Basagaña and R. Kelishadi (2019), 'Use of Green Spaces, Self-Satisfaction and Social Contacts in Adolescents: A Population-Based CASPIAN-V Study', *Environmental Research*, 168 (January): 171–7.

Das, K. V., Y. Fan and S. A. French (2017), 'Park-Use Behavior and Perceptions by Race, Hispanic Origin, and Immigrant Status in Minneapolis, MN: Implications on Park Strategies for Addressing Health Disparities', *Journal of Immigrant and Minority Health*, 19 (2): 318–27.

den Bosch, V., M. Annerstedt, P. O. Östergren, P. Grahn, E. Skärbäck and P. Währborg (2015), 'Moving to Serene Nature May Prevent Poor Mental Health: Results from a Swedish Longitudinal Cohort Study', *International Journal of Environmental Research and Public Health*, 12 (7): 7974–89.

De Ridder, K., V. Adamec, A. Bañuelos, M. Bruse, M. Bürger, O. Damsgaard, J. Dufek, J. Hirsch, F. Lefebre, J. M. Pérez-Lacorzana and A. Thierry (2004), 'An Integrated Methodology to Assess the Benefits of Urban Green Space', *Science of the Total Environment*, 334–335 (December): 489–97.

de Vries, S., S. M. Van Dillen, P. P. Groenewegen and P. Spreeuwenberg (2013), 'Streetscape Greenery and Health: Stress, Social Cohesion and Physical Activity as Mediators', *Social Science & Medicine*, 94 (October): 26–33.

de Vries, S., M. Ten Have, S. van Dorsselaer, M. van Wezep, T. Hermans and R. de Graaf (2016), 'Local Availability of Green and Blue Space and Prevalence of Common Mental Disorders in the Netherlands', *BJPsych Open*, 2 (6): 366–72.

Du Toit, M. J., S. S. Cilliers, M. Dallimer, M. Goddard, S. Guenat and
S. F. Cornelius (2018), 'Urban Green Infrastructure and Ecosystem Services in
Sub-Saharan Africa', *Landscape and Urban Planning*, 180 (December): 249–61.

Egorov, A. I., S. M. Griffin, R. R. Converse, J. N. Styles, E. A. Sams, A. Wilson,
L. E. Jackson and T. J. Wade (2017), 'Vegetated Land Cover near Residence
Is Associated with Reduced Allostatic Load and Improved Biomarkers of
Neuroendocrine, Metabolic and Immune Functions', *Environmental Research*,
158 (October): 508–21.

Engemann, K., C. B. Pedersen, L. Arge, C. Tsirogiannis, P. B. Mortensen and
J. C. Svenning (2019), 'Residential Green Space in Childhood Is Associated
with Lower Risk of Psychiatric Disorders from Adolescence into Adulthood',
Proceedings of the National Academy of Sciences, 116 (11): 5188–93.

Fägerstam, E. and J. Blom (2013), 'Learning Biology and Mathematics Outdoors:
Effects and Attitudes in a Swedish High School Context', *Journal of Adventure
Education and Outdoor Learning*, 13 (1): 56–75.

Gascon, M., M. Triguero-Mas, D. Martínez, P. Dadvand, J. Forns, A. Plasència and
M. J. Nieuwenhuijsen (2015), 'Mental Health Benefits of Long-Term Exposure
to Residential Green and Blue Spaces: A Systematic Review', *International
Journal of Environmental Research and Public Health*, 12 (4): 4354–79.

Gilchrist, K., C. Brown and A. Montarzino (2015), 'Workplace Settings and
Wellbeing: Greenspace Use and Views Contribute to Employee Wellbeing
at Peri-Urban Business Sites', *Landscape and Urban Planning*, 138 (June):
32–40.

Gillie, O., ed. (2006), *Sunlight, Vitamin D and Health*, Occasional Reports No. 2,
Health Research Forum, London. Available online: http://www.stjornusol.is/hfj/
images/stories/greinar/sunbook.pdf (accessed 5 March 2020).

Girma, Y., H. Terefe and S. Pauleit (2019), 'Urban Green Spaces Use and
Management in Rapidly Urbanizing Countries: The Case of Emerging Towns of
Oromia Special Zone Surrounding Finfinne, Ethiopia', *Urban Forestry & Urban
Greening*, 43 (July): 126357.

Goldy, S. P. and P. K. Piff (2019), 'Toward a Social Ecology of Prosociality: Why,
When, and Where Nature Enhances Social Connection', *Current Opinion in
Psychology*, 28 (32): 27–31.

Groenewegen, P. P., J. P. Zock, P. Spreeuwenberg, M. Helbich, G. Hoek,
A. Ruijsbroek, M. Strak, R. Verheij, B. Volker, G. Waverijn and M. Dijst (2018),
'Neighbourhood Social and Physical Environment and General Practitioner
Assessed Morbidity', *Health & Place*, 49 (January): 68–84.

Groff, E. and E. S. McCord (2012), 'The Role of Neighborhood Parks as Crime
Generators', *Security Journal*, 25 (1): 1–24.

Hamilton, J. M. (2017), *Relationships between Outdoor and Classroom Task
Settings and Cognition in Primary Schoolchildren*, Edinburgh: Heriot-Watt
University. Available online: https://www.ros.hw.ac.uk/handle/10399/3253
(accessed 18 February 2020).

Hansen, M. M., R. Jones and K. Tocchini (2017), 'Shinrin-yoku (Forest Bathing)
and Nature Therapy: A State-of-the-Art Review', *International Journal of
Environmental Research and Public Health*, 14 (8): 851.

Hartig, T., R. Catalano, M. Ong and S. L. Syme (2013), 'Vacation, Collective
Restoration, and Mental Health in a Population', *Society and Mental Health*,
3 (3): 221–36.

Helbich, M. (2018), 'Toward Dynamic Urban Environmental Exposure Assessments in Mental Health Research', *Environmental Research*, 161 (February): 129–35.

Helbich, M., D. De Beurs, M. P. Kwan, R. C. O'Connor and P. P. Groenewegen (2018), 'Natural Environments and Suicide Mortality in the Netherlands: A Cross-Sectional, Ecological Study', *The Lancet Planetary Health*, 2 (3): e134–e139.

Houlden, V., S. Weich, J. P. de Albuquerque, S. Jarvis and K. Rees (2018), 'The Relationship between Greenspace and the Mental Wellbeing of Adults: A Systematic Review', *PLOS One*, 13 (9): e0203000.

Irga, P. J., M. D. Burchett and F. R. Torpy (2015), 'Does Urban Forestry Have a Quantitative Effect on Ambient Air Quality in an Urban Environment?', *Atmospheric Environment*, 120 (November): 173–81.

Kaplan, R. and S. Kaplan (1989), *The Experience of Nature: A Psychological Perspective*, New York: Cambridge University Press.

Kaplan, S. and M. G. Berman (2010), 'Directed Attention as a Common Resource for Executive Functioning and Self-Regulation', *Perspectives on Psychological Science*, 5 (1): 43–57.

Kim, G. W., G. W. Jeong, T. H. Kim, H. S. Baek, S. K. Oh, H. K. Kang, S. G. Lee, Y. S. Kim and J. K. Song (2010), 'Functional Neuroanatomy Associated with Natural and Urban Scenic Views in the Human Brain: 3.0 T Functional MR Imaging', *Korean Journal of Radiology*, 11 (5): 507–13.

Kondo, M. C., J. M. Fluehr, T. McKeon and C. C. Branas (2018), 'Urban Green Space and Its Impact on Human Health', *International Journal of Environmental Research and Public Health*, 15 (3): 445.

Lachowycz, K. and A. P. Jones (2011), 'Greenspace and Obesity: A Systematic Review of the Evidence', *Obesity Reviews*, 12 (5): e183–e189.

Lakhani, A., M. Norwood, D. P. Watling, H. Zeeman and E. Kendall (2019), 'Using the Natural Environment to Address the Psychosocial Impact of Neurological Disability: A Systematic Review', *Health & Place*, 55 (January): 188–201.

Larson, L. R., B. Barger, S. Ogletree, J. Torquati, S. Rosenberg, C. J. Gaither, J. M. Bartz, A. Gardner, E. Moody and A. Schutte (2018), 'Gray Space and Green Space Proximity Associated with Higher Anxiety in Youth with Autism', *Health & Place*, 53 (September): 94–102.

Li, Q., M. Kobayashi, Y. Wakayama, H. Inagaki, M. Katsumata, Y. Hirata, K. Hirata, T. Shimizu, T. Kawada, B. J. Park and T. Ohira (2009), 'Effect of Phytoncide from Trees on Human Natural Killer Cell Function', *International Journal of Immunopathology and Pharmacology*, 22 (4): 951–9.

Lindley, S., S. Pauleit, K. Yeshitela, S. Cilliers and C. Shackleton (2018), 'Rethinking Urban Green Infrastructure and Ecosystem Services from the Perspective of Sub-Saharan African Cities', *Landscape and Urban Planning*, 180 (December): 328–38.

Maas, J., S. M. Van Dillen, R. A. Verheij and P. P. Groenewegen (2009), 'Social Contacts as a Possible Mechanism behind the Relation between Green Space and Health', *Health & Place*, 15 (2): 586–95.

Marin, A., Ö. Bodin, S. Gelcich and B. Crona (2015), 'Social Capital in Post-Disaster Recovery Trajectories: Insights from a Longitudinal Study of Tsunami-Impacted Small-Scale Fisher Organizations in Chile', *Global Environmental Change*, 35 (November): 450–62.

McEachan, R. R., T. C. Yang, H. Roberts, K. E. Pickett, D. Arseneau-Powell, C. J. Gidlow, J. Wright and M. Nieuwenhuijsen (2018), 'Availability, Use of, and Satisfaction with Green Space, and Children's Mental Wellbeing at Age 4 Years in a Multicultural, Deprived, Urban Area: Results from the Born in Bradford Cohort Study', *The Lancet Planetary Health*, 2 (6): e244–e254.

Neale, C., P. Aspinall, J. Roe, S. Tilley, P. Mavros, S. Cinderby, R. Coyne, N. Thin and C. Ward Thompson (2019), 'The Impact of Walking in Different Urban Environments on Brain Activity in Older People', *Cities & Health*, 4 (1) (June): 1–13.

Nutsford, D., A. L. Pearson and S. Kingham (2013), 'An Ecological Study Investigating the Association between Access to Urban Green Space and Mental Health', *Public Health*, 127 (11): 1005–11.

Ohly, H., M. P. White, B. W. Wheeler, A. Bethel, O. C. Ukoumunne, V. Nikolaou and R. Garside (2016), 'Attention Restoration Theory: A Systematic Review of the Attention Restoration Potential of Exposure to Natural Environments', *Journal of Toxicology and Environmental Health, Part B*, 19 (7): 305–43.

Özgüner, H. (2011), 'Cultural Differences in Attitudes towards Urban Parks and Green Spaces', *Landscape Research*, 36 (5): 599–620.

Pretty, J., J. Peacock, M. Sellens and M. Griffin (2005), 'The Mental and Physical Health Outcomes of Green Exercise', *International Journal of Environmental Health Research*, 15 (5): 319–37.

Pun, V. C., J. Manjourides and H. H. Suh (2018), 'Association of Neighborhood Greenness with Self-Perceived Stress, Depression and Anxiety Symptoms in Older US Adults', *Environmental Health*, 17 (1): 39.

Roberts, H., I. Kellar, M. Conner, C. Gidlow, B. Kelly, M. Nieuwenhuijsen and R. McEachan (2019), 'Associations between Park Features, Park Satisfaction and Park Use in a Multi-Ethnic Deprived Urban Area', *Urban Forestry & Urban Greening*, 46 (December): 126485.

Roe, J. (2016), 'Cities, Green Space, and Mental Well-Being', in *Oxford Research Encyclopedia of Environmental Science* (doi.org/10.1093/acrefore/9780199389414.013.93).

Roe, J. and P. Aspinall (2011a), 'The Restorative Benefits of Walking in Urban and Rural Settings in Adults with Good and Poor Mental Health', *Health & Place*, 17 (1). 103–13.

Roe, J. and P. Aspinall (2011b), 'The Restorative Outcomes of Forest versus Indoor Settings in Young People with Varying Behaviour States', *Urban Forestry & Urban Greening*, 10 (3): 205–12.

Roe, J. and C. Ward Thompson (2011), 'The Impact of Urban Gardens and Street Trees on People's Health and Well-Being', in K. Bomans, V. Dewaelheyns and H. Gulinck (eds), *The Powerful Garden*, Philadelphia: Coronet Books.

Roe, J., C. Ward Thompson, P. A. Aspinall, M. J. Brewer, E. I. Duff, D. Miller, R. Mitchell and A. Clow (2013), 'Green Space and Stress: Evidence from Cortisol Measures in Deprived Urban Communities', *International Journal of Environmental Research and Public Health*, 10 (9): 4086–103.

Roe, J., P. A. Aspinall and C. Ward Thompson (2016), 'Understanding Relationships between Health, Ethnicity, Place and the Role of Urban Green Space in Deprived Urban Communities', *International Journal of Environmental Research and Public Health*, 13 (7): 681.

Rojas-Rueda, D., M. J. Nieuwenhuijsen, M. Gascon, D. Perez-Leon and P. Mudu (2019), 'Green Spaces and Mortality: A Systematic Review and Meta-Analysis of Cohort Studies', *The Lancet Planetary Health*, 3 (11): e469–e477.

Rook, G. A. (2013), 'Regulation of the Immune System by Biodiversity from the Natural Environment: An Ecosystem Service Essential to Health', *Proceedings of the National Academy of Sciences*, 110 (46): 18360–7.

Salmond, J. A., M. Tadaki, S. Vardoulakis, K. Arbuthnott, A. Coutts, M. Demuzere, K. N. Dirks, C. Heaviside, S. Lim, H. Macintyre and R. N. McInnes (2016), 'Health and Climate Related Ecosystem Services Provided by Street Trees in the Urban Environment', *Environmental Health*, 15 (1): 95–111.

Sarkar, C., C. Webster and J. Gallacher (2018a), 'Residential Greenness and Prevalence of Major Depressive Disorders: A Cross-Sectional, Observational, Associational Study of 94,879 Adult UK Biobank Participants', *The Lancet Planetary Health*, 2 (4): e162–e173.

Sarkar, C., C. Webster and J. Gallacher (2018b), 'Neighbourhood Walkability and Incidence of Hypertension: Findings from the Study of 429,334 UK Biobank Participants', *International Journal of Hygiene and Environmental Health*, 221 (3): 458–68.

Shagdarsuren, T., K. Nakamura and L. McCay (2017), 'Association between Perceived Neighborhood Environment and Health of Middle-Aged Women Living in Rapidly Changing Urban Mongolia', *Environmental Health and Preventive Medicine*, 22 (1): 50.

South, E. C., B. C. Hohl, M. C. Kondo, J. M. MacDonald and C. C. Branas (2018), 'Effect of Greening Vacant Land on Mental Health of Community-Dwelling Adults: A Cluster Randomized Trial', *JAMA Network Open*, 1 (3): e180298–e180298.

Stigsdotter, U. K., S. S. Corazon, U. Sidenius, P. K. Nyed, H. B. Larsen and L. O. Fjorback (2018), 'Efficacy of Nature-Based Therapy for Individuals with Stress-Related Illnesses: Randomised Controlled Trial', *British Journal of Psychiatry*, 213 (1): 404–11.

Taylor, A. F. and F. E. Kuo (2011), 'Could Exposure to Everyday Green Spaces Help Treat ADHD? Evidence from Children's Play Settings', *Applied Psychology: Health and Well-Being*, 3 (3): 281–303.

Taylor, A. F., M. Kuo and W. Sullivan (2002), 'Views of Nature and Self-Discipline: Evidence from Inner City Children', *Journal of Environmental Psychology*, 22 (1): 49–63.

Taylor, M. S., B. W. Wheeler, M. P. White, T. Economou and N. J. Osborne (2015), 'Research Note: Urban Street Tree Density and Antidepressant Prescription Rates: A Cross-Sectional Study in London, UK', *Landscape and Urban Planning*, 136 (April): 174–9.

Triguero-Mas, M., P. Dadvand, M. Cirach, D. Martínez, A. Medina, A. Mompart, X. Basagaña, R. Gražulevičienė and M. J. Nieuwenhuijsen (2015), 'Natural Outdoor Environments and Mental and Physical Health: Relationships and Mechanisms', *Environment International*, 77 (April): 35–41.

Triguero-Mas, M., D. Donaire-Gonzalez, E. Seto, A. Valentín, D. Martínez, G. Smith, G. Hurst, G. Carrasco-Turigas, D. Masterson, M. van den Berg and A. Ambròs (2017), 'Natural Outdoor Environments and Mental Health: Stress as a Possible Mechanism', *Environmental Research*, 159 (November): 629–38.

Tsunetsugu, Y., B. J. Park and Y. Miyazaki (2010), 'Trends in Research Related to "Shinrin-yoku" (Taking in the Forest Atmosphere or Forest Bathing) in Japan', *Environmental Health and Preventive Medicine*, 15 (1): 27.

Twohig-Bennett, C. and A. Jones (2018), 'The Health Benefits of the Great Outdoors: A Systematic Review and Meta-Analysis of Greenspace Exposure and Health Outcomes', *Environmental Research*, 166 (October): 628–37.

Ulrich, R. S. (1983), 'Aesthetic and Affective Response to Natural Environment', in I. Altman and J. F. Wohlwill (eds), *Behavior and the Natural Environment*, 85–125, Boston: Springer.

van den Berg, A. E. and C. G. Van den Berg (2011), 'A Comparison of Children with ADHD in a Natural and Built Setting', *Child: Care, Health and Development*, 37 (3): 430–9.

van den Berg, M., W. Wendel-Vos, M. van Poppel, H. Kemper, W. van Mechelen and J. Maas (2015), 'Health Benefits of Green Spaces in the Living Environment: A Systematic Review of Epidemiological Studies', *Urban Forestry & Urban Greening*, 14 (4): 806–16.

Vemuri, A. W., J. Morgan Grove, M. A. Wilson and W. R. Burch Jr (2011), 'A Tale of Two Scales: Evaluating the Relationship among Life Satisfaction, Social Capital, Income, and the Natural Environment at Individual and Neighborhood Levels in Metropolitan Baltimore', *Environment and Behavior*, 43 (1): 3–25.

Waite, S. and B. Davis (2007), 'The Contribution of Free Play and Structured Activities in Forest School to Learning beyond Cognition: An English Case', in N. Kryger and B. Ravn (eds), *Learning beyond Cognition*, 257–74, Copenhagen: Danish University of Education Press.

Waite, S., J. Evans and S. Rogers (2013), *Educational Opportunities from Outdoor Learning as Children Begin the Primary Curriculum: Briefing Report*, Swindon ESRC.

Ward Thompson, C., P. Aspinall and J. Roe (2014), 'Access to Green Space in Disadvantaged Urban Communities: Evidence of Salutogenic Effects Based on Biomarker and Self-Report Measures of Wellbeing', *Procedia Social and Behavioral Sciences*, 153 (October): 10–22.

Ward Thompson, C., P. Aspinall, J. Roe, L. Robertson and D. Miller (2016), 'Mitigating Stress and Supporting Health in Deprived Urban Communities: The Importance of Green Space and the Social Environment', *International Journal of Environmental Research and Public Health*, 13 (4): 440.

Wells, N. M. (2000), 'At Home with Nature: Effects of "Greenness" on Children's Cognitive Functioning', *Environment and Behavior*, 32 (6): 775–95.

White, M. P., I. Alcock, J. Grellier, B. W. Wheeler, T. Hartig, S. L. Warber, A. Bone, M. H. Depledge and L. E. Fleming (2019), 'Spending at Least 120 Minutes a Week in Nature Is Associated with Good Health and Wellbeing', *Scientific Reports*, 9 (1): 1–11.

Wilson, E. O. (1984), *Biophilia*, Cambridge: Harvard University Press.

Wolch, J. R., J. Byrne and J. P. Newell (2014), 'Urban Green Space, Public Health, and Environmental Justice: The Challenge of Making Cities "Just Green Enough"', *Landscape and Urban Planning*, 125 (May): 234–44.

Wood, E., A. Harsant, M. Dallimer, A. Cronin de Chavez, R. R. McEachan and C. Hassall (2018), 'Not All Green Space Is Created Equal: Biodiversity Predicts Psychological Restorative Benefits from Urban Green Space', *Frontiers in Psychology*, 9 (November): 2320.

World Health Organization (2016), *Urban Green Spaces and Health*, Copenhagen: WHO Regional Office for Europe.

Wu, J. and L. Jackson (2017), 'Inverse Relationship between Urban Green Space and Childhood Autism in California Elementary School Districts', *Environment International*, 107 (October): 140–6.

Zacks, S. (2018), 'Soft Power in Moscow', *Landscape Architecture Magazine*, April: 160–73. Available online: https://landscapearchitecturemagazine.org/2018/04/05/soft-power-in-moscow/ (accessed 18 February 2020).

Chapter 3: The blue city

Alcock, I., M. P. White, R. Lovell, S. L. Higgins, N. J. Osborne, K. Husk and B. W. Wheeler (2015), 'What Accounts for "England's Green and Pleasant Land"? A Panel Data Analysis of Mental Health and Land Cover Types in Rural England', *Landscape and Urban Planning*, 142 (October): 38–46.

Amoly, E., P. Dadvand, J. Forns, M. López-Vicente, X. Basagaña, J. Julvez, M. Alvarez-Pedrerol, M. J. Nieuwenhuijsen and J. Sunyer (2014), 'Green and Blue Spaces and Behavioral Development in Barcelona Schoolchildren: The BREATHE Project', *Environmental Health Perspectives*, 122 (12): 1351–8.

Barker, A., N. Manning and A. Sirriyeh (2014), *'The Great Meeting Place': A Study of Bradford's City Park*, Bradford: University of Bradford. Available online: http://eprints.whiterose.ac.uk/79357/1/_The_Great_Meeting_Place_A_Study_of_Bradford_s_City_Park_Final_Report.pdf (accessed 19 November 2019).

Bell, S. L., C. Phoenix, R. Lovell and B. W. Wheeler (2015), 'Seeking Everyday Wellbeing: The Coast as a Therapeutic Landscape', *Social Science & Medicine*, 142 (October): 56–67.

Bouchama, A., M. Dehbi, G. Mohamed, F. Matthies, M. Shoukri and B. Menne (2007), 'Prognostic Factors in Heat Wave – Related Deaths: A Meta-Analysis', *Archives of Internal Medicine*, 167 (20): 2170–6.

Britton, E., G. Kindermann, C. Domegan and C. Carlin (2020), 'Blue Care: A Systematic Review of Blue Space Interventions for Health and Wellbeing', *Health Promotion International*, 35 (1): 50–69.

Burmil, S., T. C. Daniel and J. D. Hetherington (1999), 'Human Values and Perceptions of Water in Arid Landscapes', *Landscape and Urban Planning*, 44 (2–3): 99–109.

CABE (2010), *Community Green: Using Local Spaces to Tackle Inequality and Improve Health*, London: Commission for Architecture and the Built Environment (CABE).

Capaldi, C. A., R. L. Dopko and J. M. Zelenski (2014), 'The Relationship between Nature Connectedness and Happiness: A Meta-Analysis', *Frontiers in Psychology*, 5 (September): 976.

Coleman, T. and R. Kearns (2015), 'The Role of Blue Spaces in Experiencing Place, Aging and Wellbeing: Insights from Waiheke Island, New Zealand', *Health & Place*, 35 (September): 206–17.

Connolly, N. D. (2014), *A World More Concrete: Real Estate and the Remaking of Jim Crow South Florida*, vol. 114, Chicago: University of Chicago Press.

Dempsey, S., M. T. Devine, T. Gillespie, S. Lyons and A. Nolan (2018), 'Coastal Blue Space and Depression in Older Adults', *Health & Place*, 54 (November): 110–17.

Finlay, J., T. Franke, H. McKay and J. Sims-Gould (2015), 'Therapeutic Landscapes and Wellbeing in Later Life: Impacts of Blue and Green Spaces for Older Adults', *Health & Place*, 34 (July): 97–106.

Foley, R. (2010), *Healing Waters: Therapeutic Landscapes in Historic and Contemporary Ireland*, Farnham: Ashgate.

Foley, R., R. Kearns, T. Kistemann and B. Wheeler, eds (2019), 'Conclusion: New Directions', in *Blue Space, Health and Wellbeing: Hydrophilia Unbounded*, London: Routledge.

Garrett, J. K., T. J. Clitherow, M. P. White, B. W. Wheeler and L. E. Fleming (2019a), 'Coastal Proximity and Mental Health among Urban Adults in England: The Moderating Effect of Household Income', *Health & Place*, 59 (September): 102200.

Garrett, J. K., M. P. White, J. Huang, S. Ng, Z. Hui, C. Leung, L. A. Tse, F. Fung, L. R. Elliott, M. H. Depledge and M. C. Wong (2019b), 'Urban Blue Space and Health and Wellbeing in Hong Kong: Results from a Survey of Older Adults', *Health & Place*, 55 (January): 100–10.

Gascon, M., M. Triguero-Mas, D. Martínez, P. Dadvand, J. Forns, A. Plasència and M. J. Nieuwenhuijsen (2015), 'Mental Health Benefits of Long-Term Exposure to Residential Green and Blue Spaces: A Systematic Review', *International Journal of Environmental Research and Public Health*, 12 (4): 4354–79.

Gascon, M., G. Sánchez-Benavides, P. Dadvand, D. Martínez, N. Gramunt, X. Gotsens, M. Cirach, C. Vert, J. L. Molinuevo, M. Crous-Bou and M. Nieuwenhuijsen (2018), 'Long-Term Exposure to Residential Green and Blue Spaces and Anxiety and Depression in Adults: A Cross-Sectional Study', *Environmental Research*, 162 (April): 231–9.

Gesler, W. M. (1993), 'Therapeutic Landscapes: Theory and a Case Study of Epidauros, Greece', *Environment and Planning D: Society and Space*, 11 (2): 171–89.

Gesler, W. M. (1996), 'Lourdes: Healing in a Place of Pilgrimage', *Health & Place*, 2 (2): 95–105.

Grellier, J., M. P. White, M. Albin, S. Bell, L. R. Elliott, M. Gascón, S. Gualdi, L. Mancini, M. J. Nieuwenhuijsen, D. A. Sarigiannis and M. Van Den Bosch (2017), 'BlueHealth: A Study Programme Protocol for Mapping and Quantifying the Potential Benefits to Public Health and Well-Being from Europe's Blue Spaces', *BMJ Open*, 7 (6): e016188.

Haeffner, M., D. Jackson-Smith, M. Buchert and J. Risley (2017), 'Accessing Blue Spaces: Social and Geographic Factors Structuring Familiarity with, Use of, and Appreciation of Urban Waterways', *Landscape and Urban Planning*, 167 (November): 136–46.

Hancock, P. A. and I. Vasmatzidis (2003), 'Effects of Heat Stress on Cognitive Performance: The Current State of Knowledge', *International Journal of Hyperthermia*, 19 (3): 355–72.

Hsiang, S. M., M. Burke and E. Miguel (2013), 'Quantifying the Influence of Climate on Human Conflict', *Science*, 341 (6151): 1235367.

Huynh, Q., W. Craig, I. Janssen and W. Pickett (2013), 'Exposure to Public Natural Space as a Protective Factor for Emotional Well-Being among Young People in Canada', *BMC Public Health*, 13 (1): 407.

Jing, L. (2019), 'Inside China's Leading "Sponge City": Wuhan's War with Water', *Guardian*, 23 January. Available online: https://www.theguardian.com/cities/2019/jan/23/inside-chinas-leading-sponge-city-wuhans-war-with-water (accessed 21 February 2020).

Kaplan, R. and S. Kaplan (1989), *The Experience of Nature: A Psychological Perspective*, New York: Cambridge University Press.

Leeworthy, V. R. (2001), *National Survey on Recreation and Environment (NSRE): Preliminary Estimates from Versions 1–6: Coastal Recreation Participation*, U.S. Department of Commerce. Available online: http://www.elkhornsloughctp.org/uploads/files/148478105421_NSRE_Coastal_Recreation_Participation_V1-6_May-2001.pdf (accessed 12 November 2019).

MacKerron, G. and S. Mourato (2013), 'Happiness Is Greater in Natural Environments', *Global Environmental Change*, 23 (5): 992–1000.

Marshall, C. (2016), 'Story of Cities #50: The Reclaimed Stream Bringing Life to the Heart of Seoul', *Guardian*, 25 May. Available online: https://www.theguardian.com/cities/2016/may/25/story-cities-reclaimed-stream-heart-seoul-cheonggyecheon (accessed 21 February 2020).

Nutsford, D., A. L. Pearson, S. Kingham and F. Reitsma (2016), 'Residential Exposure to Visible Blue Space (but Not Green Space) Associated with Lower Psychological Distress in a Capital City', *Health & Place*, 39 (May): 70–8.

Okamoto-Mizuno, K. and K. Mizuno (2012), 'Effects of Thermal Environment on Sleep and Circadian Rhythm', *Journal of Physiological Anthropology*, 31 (1): 14.

Oldfield, P. (2018), 'What Would a Heat-Proof City Look Like?', *Guardian*, 15 August. Available online: https://www.theguardian.com/cities/2018/aug/15/what-heat-proof-city-look-like (accessed 21 February 2020).

Page, L. A., S. Hajat and R. S. Kovats (2007), 'Relationship between Daily Suicide Counts and Temperature in England and Wales', *British Journal of Psychiatry*, 191 (2): 106–12.

Pitt, H. (2018), 'Muddying the Waters: What Urban Waterways Reveal about Blue Spaces and Wellbeing', *Geoforum*, 92 (June): 161–70.

Pitt, H. (2019), 'What Prevents People Accessing Urban Bluespaces? A Qualitative Study', *Urban Forestry & Urban Greening*, 39 (March): 89–97.

Roe, J., L. Barnes, N. J. Napoli and J. Thibodeaux (2019), 'The Restorative Health Benefits of a Tactical Urban Intervention: An Urban Waterfront Study', *Frontiers in Built Environment*, 5 (June): 71.

Smith, D. G., G. F. Croker and K. A. Y. McFarlane (1995), 'Human Perception of Water Appearance: 1. Clarity and Colour for Bathing and Aesthetics', *New Zealand Journal of Marine and Freshwater Research*, 29 (1): 29–43.

Tanja-Dijkstra, K., S. Pahl, M. P. White, M. Auvray, R. J. Stone, J. Andrade, J. May, I. Mills and D. R. Moles (2018), 'The Soothing Sea: A Virtual Coastal Walk Can Reduce Experienced and Recollected Pain', *Environment and Behavior*, 50 (6): 599–625.

Triguero-Mas, M., P. Dadvand, M. Cirach, D. Martínez, A. Medina, A. Mompart, X. Basagaña, R. Gražulevičienė and M. J. Nieuwenhuijsen (2015), 'Natural Outdoor Environments and Mental and Physical Health: Relationships and Mechanisms', *Environment International*, 77 (April): 35–41.

Vert, C., M. Nieuwenhuijsen, M. Gascon, J. Grellier, L. E. Fleming, M. P. White and D. Rojas-Rueda (2019), 'Health Benefits of Physical Activity Related to an Urban Riverside Regeneration', *International Journal of Environmental Research and Public Health*, 16 (3): 462.

Völker, S. and T. Kistemann (2011), 'The Impact of Blue Space on Human Health and Well-Being – Salutogenetic Health Effects of Inland Surface Waters: A Review', *International Journal of Hygiene and Environmental Health*, 214 (6): 449–60.

White, M. P., I. Alcock, B. W. Wheeler and M. H. Depledge (2013a), 'Coastal Proximity, Health and Well-Being: Results from a Longitudinal Panel Survey', *Health & Place*, 23 (September): 97–103.

White, M. P., I. Alcock, B. W. Wheeler and M. H. Depledge (2013b), 'Would You Be Happier Living in a Greener Urban Area? A Fixed-Effects Analysis of Panel Data', *Psychological Science*, 24 (6): 920–8.

Wolch, J. and J. Zhang (2004), 'Beach Recreation, Cultural Diversity and Attitudes toward Nature', *Journal of Leisure Research*, 36 (3): 414–43.

Wood, E., A. Harsant, M. Dallimer, A. Cronin de Chavez, R. R. McEachan and C. Hassall (2018), 'Not All Green Space Is Created Equal: Biodiversity Predicts Psychological Restorative Benefits from Urban Green Space', *Frontiers in Psychology*, 9 (November): 2320.

Chapter 4: The sensory city

Abram, D. (1997), *The Spell of the Sensuous: Perception and Language in a More-Than-Human World*, New York: Vintage Publishing.

Aletta, F., T. Oberman and J. Kang (2018), 'Associations between Positive Health-Related Effects and Soundscapes Perceptual Constructs: A Systematic Review', *International Journal of Environmental Research and Public Health*, 15 (11): 2392.

Ardiel, E. L. and C. H. Rankin (2010), 'The Importance of Touch in Development', *Paediatrics and Child Health*, 15 (3): 153–6.

Barker, E., K. Kolves and D. De Leo (2017), 'Rail-Suicide Prevention: Systematic Literature Review of Evidence-based Activities', *Asia Pacific Psychiatry*, 9 (3): e12246.

Basner, M., W. Babisch, A. Davis, M. Brink, C. Clark, S. Janssen and S. Stansfeld (2014), 'Auditory and Non-auditory Effects of Noise on Health', *The Lancet*, 383(9925): 1325–32.

Basner, M. and S. McGuire (2018), 'WHO Environmental Noise Guidelines for the European Region: A Systematic Review on Environmental Noise and Effects on Sleep', *International Journal of Environmental Research and Public Health*, 15 (3): E519.

Basner, M., U. Müller and E. M. Elmenhorst (2011), 'Single and Combined Effects of Air, Road, and Rail Traffic Noise on Sleep and Recuperation', *Sleep*, 34: 11–23.

Billot, P. E., P. Andrieu, A. Biondi, S. Vieillard, T. Moulin and J. L. Millot (2017), 'Cerebral Bases of Emotion Regulation toward Odours: A First Approach', *Behavioural Brain Research*, 317: 37–45.

Bingley, A. (2003), 'In Here and Out There: Sensations between Self and Landscape', *Social and Cultural Geography*, 4 (3): 329–45.

Bissell, D. (2010), 'Passenger Mobilities: Affective Atmospheres and the Sociality of Public Transport'. *Environment and Planning D: Society and Space*, 28 (2): 270–89.

Brino, G. and F. Rosso (1980), *Colore e città. Il piano del colore di Torino: 1800–1850*, 1st edn, Milan: Idea Editions.

Brown, K. M. (2017), 'The Haptic Pleasures of Ground-Feel: The Role of Textured Terrain in Motivating Regular Exercise', *Health and Place*, 46: 307–14.

Chalfin, A., B. Hansen, J. Lerner and L. Parker (2019), 'Reducing Crime through Environmental Design: Evidence from a Randomized Experiment of Street Lighting in New York City', *National Bureau of Economic Research*. Available online: https://urbanlabs.uchicago.edu/attachments/e95d751f7d91d0bcfeb209ddf6adcb4296868c12/store/cca92342e666b1ffb1c15be63b484e9b9687b57249dce44ad55ea92b1ec0/lights_04242016.pdf (accessed 4 June 2020).

Chesney, E., G. M. Goodwin and S. Fazel (2014), 'Risks of All-Cause and Suicide Mortality in Mental Disorders: A Meta-review', *World Psychiatry*, 13: 153–60.

Cozens, P., G. Saville and D. Hiller (2005), 'Crime Prevention through Environmental Design (CPTED): A Review and Modern Bibliography', *Property Management*, 23 (5): 328–56.

Diaz-Roux, A., J. Nieto, L. Caulfield, H. Tyroler, R. Watson and M. Szklo (1999), 'Neighborhood Differences in Diet: The Atherosclerosis Risk in Communities (ARIC) Study'. *Journal of Epidemiology and Community Health*, 53(1):55–63.

Dzhambov, A. M. (2015), 'Long-term Noise Exposure and the Risk for Type 2 Diabetes: A Meta-analysis', *Noise and Health*, 17 (74): 23–33.

Echevarria, G. (2016), 'Bridging the Gap between Architecture/City Planning and Urban Noise Control', *INTER-NOISE and NOISE-CON Congress and Conference Proceedings, InterNoise16, Hamburg GERMANY*, pages 5848–6840, pp. 6579–85 (7). Available online: https://pdfs.semanticscholar.org/3f24/b6ca281012b6538992b425ad55ce730fa9b1.pdf (accessed 4 June 2020).

Ellard, C. (2017), 'A New Agenda for Urban Psychology: Out of the Laboratory and Onto the Streets', *Journal of Urban Design and Mental Health*, 2: 3.

Engelhart, M. J., M. I. Geerlings, A. Ruitenberg, J. C. van Swieten, A. Hofman, J. C. Witteman and M. M. Breteler (2002), 'Dietary Intake of Antioxidants and Risk of Alzheimer Disease', *JAMA*, 287 (24): 3223–9.

Firth, J., W. Marx, S. Dash, R. Carney, S. B. Teasdale, M. Solmi, B. Stubbs, F. B. Schuch, A. F. Carvalho, F. Jacka and J. Sarris (2019), 'The Effects of Dietary Improvement on Symptoms of Depression and Anxiety – A Meta-Analysis of Randomized Controlled Trials', *Psychosomatic Medicine*, 81 (3): 265–80.

Gehl, J. (1996), *Life between Buildings: Using Public Space*, Washington, DC: Island Press.

Gehl, J. (2011), *Cities for People*, Washington, DC: Island Press.

Gillis, K. and B. Gatersleben (2015), 'A Review of Psychological Literature on the Health and Wellbeing Benefits of Biophilic Design', *Buildings*, 5 (3): 948–63.

Gilroy, P. (2005), *Postcolonial Melancholia*, London: Routledge.

Gonzalez, M. T. and M. Kirkevold (2015), 'Clinical Use of Sensory Gardens and Outdoor Environments in Norwegian Nursing Homes: A Cross-Sectional E-mail Survey', *Issues in Mental Health Nursing*, 36: 35–43.

Gorman, R. (2017), 'Smelling Therapeutic Landscapes: Embodied Encounters within Spaces of Care Farming', *Health and Place*, 47: 22–8.

Hanada, M. (2018), 'Correspondence Analysis of Color–Emotion Associations', *Color Research and Application*, 43: 224–37.

Hansen, M. M., R. Jones and K. Tocchini (2017), 'Shinrin-Yoku (Forest Bathing) and Nature Therapy: A State-of-the-Art Review', *International Journal of Environmental Research and Public Health*, 14 (8): 851.

Hanssen, I. and B. M. Kuven (2016), 'Moments of Joy and Delight: The Meaning of Traditional Food in Dementia Care', *Journal of Clinical Nursing*: 25: 5–6.

Henshaw, V. (2014), *Urban Smellscapes: Understanding and Designing Urban Smell Environments*, New York: Routledge.

Hiss, T. (1991), *The Experience of Place*, New York: Random House.

Hong, J. Y. and J. Y. Jeon (2013), 'Designing Sound and Visual Components for Enhancement of Urban Soundscapes', *The Journal of the Acoustical Society of America*, 134: 2026–36.

Howes, D. (2014), 'Introduction to Sensory Museology', *The Senses and Society*, 9 (3): 259–67.

Hughes, R. W. and D. M. Jones (2003), 'Indispensable Benefits and Unavoidable Costs of Unattended Sound for Cognitive Functioning', *Noise Health*; 6: 63–76.

Hussein, H. (2014), 'Experiencing and Engaging Attributes in a Sensory Garden as Part of a Multi-sensory Environment', *Journal of Special Needs Education*, 2: 38–50.

Jaśkiewicz, M. (2015), 'Place Attachment, Place Identity and Aesthetic Appraisal of Urban Landscape', *Polish Psychological Bulletin*, 46 (4): 573–8.

Jeon, J. Y., P. J. Lee and J. You (2012), 'Acoustical Characteristics of Water Sounds for Soundscape Enhancement in Urban Open Spaces', *The Journal of the Acoustical Society of America*, 131 (3):10.1121/1.3681938.

Kohli, P., Z. M. Soler, S. A. Nguyen, J. S. Muus and R. J. Schlosser (2016), 'The Association between Olfaction and Depression: A Systematic Review', *Chemical Senses*, 41 (6): 479–86.

Kolotkin, R. L., P. K. Corey Lisle, R. D. Crosby, J. M. Swanson, A. V. Tuomari, G. J. L'Italien and J. E. Mitchell (2012), 'Impact of Obesity on Health-related Quality of Life in Schizophrenia and Bipolar Disorder', *Obesity*, 16 (4): 749–54.

Lenclos, J. P. and D. Lenclos (1999), *Couleurs de L'Europe. Geographie de La Couleur.* Paris: Editions Le Moniteur.

Lindstrom, M. (2005), 'Broad Sensory Branding', *Journal of Product and Brand Management*, 14 (2): 84–7.

Luppino, F. S., L. M. de Wit, P. F. Bouvy, T. Stijnen, P. Cuijpers and B. W. J. H. Penninx (2010), 'Overweight, Obesity, and Depression: A Systematic Review and Meta-Analysis of Longitudinal Studies', *Archives of General Psychiatry*, 67: 220–9.

McGregor, J. A., I. Jones, S. C. Lee, J. T. R. Walters, M. J. Owen, M. O'Donovan, M. Delpozo-Banos, D. Berridge and K. Lloyd (2018), 'Premature Mortality among People with Severe Mental Illness – New Evidence from Linked Primary Care Data', *Schizophrenia Research*, 199: 154–62.

Ministry for the Environment. (2016), *Good Practice Guide for Assessing and Managing Odour*, Wellington: Ministry for the Environment.

Mitchell, L. and E. Burton (2006), 'Neighbourhoods for Life: Designing Dementia-friendly Outdoor Environments', *Quality in Ageing and Older Adults*, 7: 26–33.

Moughtin, C. (1992), *Urban Design Street and Square*, Oxford: Butterworth Architecture.

Münzel, T., F. P. Schmidt, S. Steven, J. Herzog, A. Daiber and M. Sørensen (2018), 'Environmental Noise and the Cardiovascular System', *Journal of the American College of Cardiology*, 71: 688–97.

Nasar, J. L. (1994), 'Urban Design Aesthetics: The Evaluative Qualities of Building Exteriors'. *Environment and Behavior*, 26, 377–401.

Nia, H. A. and R. Atun (2015), 'Aesthetic Design Thinking Model for Urban Environments: A Survey Based on a Review of the Literature', *Urban Design International*, 21: 10.1057/udi.2015.25.

Nicell, J. A. (2009), 'Assessment and Regulation of Odour Impacts', *Atmospheric Environment*, 43: 196–206.

Ohiduzzaman, M. D., O. Sirin, E. Kassem and J. L. Rochat (2016), 'State-of-the-Art Review on Sustainable Design and Construction of Quieter Pavements – Part 1: Traffic Noise Measurement and Abatement Techniques', *Sustainability*, 8:742.

O'Neil, A., S. E. Quirk, S. Housden, S. L. Brennan, L. J. Williams, J. A. Pasco and F. N. Jacka (2014), 'Relationship between Diet and Mental Health in Children and Adolescents: A Systematic Review', *American Journal of Public Health*, 104(10),e31–e42.

Orban, E., K. McDonald and R. Sutcliffe (2015), 'Residential Road Traffic Noise and High Depressive Symptoms after Five Years of Follow-up: Results from the Heinz Nixdorf Recall Study', *Environmental Health Perspectives*, 124: 5.

Orians, G. (1986), 'An Ecological and Evolutionary Approach to Landscape Aesthetics', in E. C. Penning-Rowsell and D. Lowenthal (eds), *Landscape Meaning and Values*, 3–25, London: Allen and Unwin.

Pallasmaa, J. (2014), 'Space, Place and Atmosphere. Emotion and Peripheral Perception in Architectural Experience', *Lebenswelt: Aesthetics and Philosophy of Experience*, 10.13130/2240-9599/4202.

Park, B. J., Y. Tsunetsugu, T. Kasetani, T. Kagawa and Y. Miyazaki (2010), 'The Physiological Effects of Shinrin-yoku (Taking in the Forest Atmosphere or Forest Bathing): Evidence from Field Experiments in 24 Forests across Japan', *Environmental Health and Preventive Medicine* 15: 18–26.

Paul, K. C., M. Haan, E. R. Mayeda and B. R. Ritz (2019), 'Ambient Air Pollution, Noise, and Late-Life Cognitive Decline and Dementia Risk', *Annual Review of Public Health* 40 (1): 203–20.

Payne, S. R. (2010), 'Urban Park Soundscapes and Their Perceived Restorativeness', *Proceedings of the Institute of Acoustics*, 3 (32): 264–71.

Payne, S. R. (2013), The Production of a Perceived Restorativeness Soundscape Scale. *Applied Acoustics*, 74 (2): 255–63.

Perron, S., C. Plante, M. S. Ragettli, D. J. Kaiser, S. Goudreau and A. Smargiassi (2016), 'Sleep Disturbance from Road Traffic, Railways, Airplanes and from Total Environmental Noise Levels in Montreal', *International Journal of Environmental Research and Public Health*, 13 (8): 809.

Pheasant, R. J., M. N. Fisher, G. R. Watts, D. J. Whitaker and K. V. Horoshenkov (2010), 'The Importance of Auditory-Visual Interaction in the Construction of "Tranquil Space"', *Journal of Environmental Psychology*, 30: 501–09.

Porteous, J. (1990), *Landscapes of the Mind: Worlds of Sense and Metaphor*. Toronto; Buffalo; London: University of Toronto Press.

Quercia, D., L. M. Aiello and R. Schifanella (2016), 'The Emotional and Chromatic Layers of Urban Smells', *Proceedings of the Tenth International AAAI Conference on Web and Social Media*, 309–18.

Quercia, D., L. M. Aiello and S. Schifanella (2017), 'Mapping towards a Good City Life', *Journal of Urban Design and Mental Health*, 3: 3.

Rapoport, A. (1990), *History and Precedent in Environmental Design*, New York: Springer.

Ratcliffe, E., B. Gatersleben and P. T. Sowden (2018), 'Predicting the Perceived Restorative Potential of Bird Sounds through Acoustics and Aesthetics', *Environment and Behavior*, 52 (4): 371–400.

Rhys-Taylor, A. (2013), 'The Essences of Multiculture: A Sensory Exploration of an Inner-City Street Market', *Identities*, 20 (4): 393–406.

Soga, M., K. J. Gasrton and Y. Yamaurax (2017), 'Gardening Is Beneficial for Health: A Meta-Analysis', *Preventive Medicine Reports*, 5: 92–9.

Spencer, J. and R. Alwani (2018), 'Using Art and Design to Create Shared Safe Space in Urban Areas: A Case Study of the Banks and Bridges of the River Foyle in Derry/Londonderry Northern Ireland', *Journal of Urban Design and Mental Health*, 5: 6.

Stansfeld, S. A. and M. P. Matheson (2003), 'Noise Pollution: Non-auditory Effects on Health', *British Medical Bulletin*, 68 (1): 243–57.

Stansfeld, S. and C. Clark (2015), 'Health Effects of Noise Exposure in Children', *Early Life Environmental Health*; 2: 171–8.

Taylor, R. P. and B. Spehar (2016), 'Fractal Fluency: An Intimate Relationship between the Brain and Processing of Fractal Stimuli', in A. Di Leva (ed.), *The Fractal Geometry of the Brain*, New York: Springer, 485–96.

The Japan Times (2001), 'Ministry Compiles List of Nation's 100 Best-Smelling Spots', 31 October 2001, retrieved from https://www.japantimes.co.jp/news/2001/10/31/national/ministry-compiles-list-of-nations-100-best-smelling-spots/.

Thibaud, J. P. (2011), 'The Sensory Fabric of Urban Ambiances', *The Senses and Society*, 6 (2): 203–15.

Thombre, L. and C. Kapshe (2020), 'Conviviality as a Spatial Planning Goal for Public Open Spaces', *International Journal of Recent Technology and Engineering*, 8(5): 10.35940/ijrte.e7038.018520.

Vianna, K.Md.P., M. R. A. Cardoso and R. M. C. Rodrigues (2015), 'Noise Pollution and Annoyance: An Urban Soundscapes Study', *Noise and Health*, 17 (76): 125–33.

Winz, M. (2018), 'An Atmospheric Approach to the City-psychosis Nexus. Perspectives for Researching Embodied Urban Experiences of People Diagnosed with Schizophrenia', *Ambiances*, 10.4000/ambiances.1163.

Wright, B., E. Peters, U. Ettinger, E. Kuipers and V. Kumari (2014), 'Understanding Noise Stress-Induced Cognitive Impairment in Healthy Adults and Its Implications for Schizophrenia', *Noise Health*, 16 (70): 166–76.

Xiao, J., M. Tait and J. Kang (2018), 'A Perceptual Model of Smellscape Pleasantness', *Cities*, 76: 105–15.

Chapter 5: The neighbourly city

Arentshorst, M. E., R. R. Kloet and A. Peine (2019), 'Intergenerational Housing: The Case of Humanitas Netherlands', *Journal of Housing for the Elderly*, 33 (3): 244–56.

Attree, P., B. French and B. Milton (2011), 'The Experience of Community Engagement for Individuals', *Health and Social Care in the Community*, 19: 250–60.

Baba, Y. (2017), 'Case Study: Developing Comprehensive Community Care in Japan – Urban Planning Implications for Long Term Dementia Care', *Journal of Urban Design and Mental Health*, 3: 6.

Badcock, J. C., S. Shah, A. Mackinnon, H. J. Stain, C. Galletly, A. Jablensky and V. A. Morgan (2015), 'Loneliness in Psychotic Disorders and Its Association with Cognitive Function and Symptom Profile', *Schizophrenia Research*, 169: 268–73.

Bagnall, A. M., J. South, S. Di Martino, B. Mitchell, G. Pilkington and R. Newton (2017), *A Systematic Scoping Review of Reviews of the Evidence for 'What Works to Boost Social Relations' and Its Relationship to Community Wellbeing*, London: What Works Centre for Wellbeing.

Barros, P., L. N. Fat, L. M. Garcia, A. D. Slovic, N. Thomopoulos, T. H. de Sá and J. S. Mindell (2019), 'Social Consequences and Mental Health Outcomes of Living in High-Rise Residential Buildings and the Influence of Planning, Urban Design and Architectural Decisions: A Systematic Review', *Cities*, 93: 263–72.

Bennett, K., T. Gualtieri and B. Kazmierczyk (2018), 'Undoing Solitary Urban Design: A Review of Risk Factors and Mental Health Outcomes Associated with Living in Aocial Isolation', *Journal of Urban Design and Mental Health*, 4:7.

Bentley, R., E. Baker, K. Simons, J. A. Simpson and T. Blakely (2018), 'The Impact of Social Housing on Mental Health: Longitudinal Analyses Using Marginal Structural Models and Machine Learning-Generated Weights', *International Journal of Epidemiology*, 47 (5): 1414–22.

Beutel, M. E., E. M. Klein, E. Brähler, I. Reiner, C. Jünger, M. Michal, J. Wiltink, P. S. Wild, T Münzel, K. J. Lackner and A. N. Tibubos (2017), 'Loneliness in the General Population: Prevalence, Determinants and Relations to Mental Health', *BMC Psychiatry*, 17: 97.

Bierman, A., E. M. Fazio and M. A. Milkie (2006), 'A Multifaceted Approach to the Mental Health Advantage of the Married. Assessing How Explanations Vary by Outcome Measure and Unmarried Group', *Journal of Family Issues*, 27 (4): 554–82.

Brackertz, N., A. Wilkinson and J. Davison (2018), 'Housing, Homelessness and Mental Health: Towards System Change', *Australian Housing and Urban Research Institute*, 10.31235/osf.io/48ujp.

Buonfino, A. and P. Hilder (2006), *Neighbouring in Contemporary Britain*, York: Joseph Rowntree Foundation.

Celata, F., C. Y. Hendrickson and V. S. Sanna (2017), 'The Sharing Economy as Community Marketplace? Trust, Reciprocity and Belonging in Peer-to-Peer Accommodation Platforms', *Cambridge Journal of Regions, Economy and Society*, 10 (2): 349–63.

Clark, C., R. Myron, S. Stansfeld and B. Candy (2006), 'A Systematic Review on the Effect of the Built and Physical Environment on Mental Health', *Journal of Public Mental Health*, 6 (2): 14–27.

Cohen-Cline, H., S. A. Beresford, W. Barrington, R. Matsueda, J. Wakefield and G. E. Duncan (2018), 'Associations between Social Capital and Depression: A Study of Adult Twins', *Health and Place*, 50: 162–7.

Courtin, E. and M. Knapp (2015), Social Isolation, Loneliness and Health in Old Age: A Scoping Review, *Health and Social Care in the Community*, 3: 799–812.

Cruwys, T., S. A. Haslam and G. A. Dingle (2014), 'Depression and Social Identity: An Integrative Review', *Personality and Social Psychology Review*, 18: 215–38.

Dempsey, N., H. Smith and M. Burton (2014), *Place-Keeping: Open Space Management in Practice*, Oxford: Routledge.

Dines, N. and V. Cattell (2006), *Public Spaces, Social Relations and Well-Being in East London*, Joseph Rowntree Foundation, Plymouth, GB: Latimer Trend Printing Group.

Ehsan, A. M. and M. J. De Silva (2015), 'Social Capital and Common Mental Disorder: A Systematic Review', *Journal of Epidemiology and Community Health*, 69: 1021–8.

Ellard, C. (2015), 'Streets with No Game'. *Aeon*, 1 September. Available online: https://aeon.co/essays/why-boring-streets-make-pedestrians-stressed-and-unhappy (accessed 4 June 2020).

Evans, G. W. (2003), 'The Built Environment and Mental Health', *Journal of Urban Health: Bulletin of the New York Academy of Medicine*, 80: 4.

Garin, N., B. Olaya, M. Miret, J. L. Ayuso-mateos, M. Power, P. Bucciarelli and J. M. Haro (2014), 'Built Environment and Elderly Population Health : A Comprehensive Literature Review', *Clinical Practice and Epidemiology in Mental Health*, 10: 103–15.

Gehl, J. (1987), *Life between Buildings-Using Public Spaces*, New York: Van Nostrand Reinhold Company Inc.

Generaal, E., E. Timmermans, J. Dekkers, J. Smit and B. Penninx (2019), 'Not Urbanization Level but Socioeconomic, Physical and Social Neighbourhood Characteristics Are Associated with Presence and Severity of Depressive and Anxiety Disorders', *Psychological Medicine*, 49 (1): 149–61.

Gillespie, S., M. T. LeVasseur and Y. L. Michael (2017), 'Neighbourhood Amenities and Depressive Symptoms in Urban-Dwelling Older Adults', *Journal of Urban Design and Mental Health*, 2: 4.

Hatcher, S. and O. Stubbersfield (2013), 'Sense of Belonging and Suicide: A Systematic Review', *Canadian Journal of Psychiatry*, 58: 432.

Heinz, A., L. Deserno and U. Reininghaus (2013), 'Urbanicity, Social Adversity and Psychosis', *World Psychiatry*, 12 (3): 187–97.

Holvast, F., H. Burger, M. M. W. de Waal, H. W. J. van Marwijk, H. C. Comijs and P. F. M. Verhaak (2015), 'Loneliness Is Associated with Poor Prognosis in Late-life Depression: Longitudinal Analysis of the Netherlands Study of Depression in Older Persons', *Journal of Affective Disorders*, 185: 1–7.

Horn, E. E., Y. Xu, C. R. Beam, E. Turkheimer and R. E. Emery (2013), 'Accounting for the Physical and Mental Health Benefits of Entry into Marriage: A Genetically Informed Study of Selection and Causation', *Journal of Family Psychology*, 27 (1): 30–41.

Kawachi, I. and L. F. Berkman (2001), 'Social Ties and Mental Health', *Journal of Urban Health*, 78: 458–67.

Kuiper, J. S., M. Zuidersma, R. C. O. Voshaar, S. U. Zuidema, E. R. van den Heuvel and R. P. Stolk (2015), 'Social Relationships and Risk of Dementia: A Systematic Review and Meta-Analysis of Longitudinal Cohort Studies', *Ageing Research Review*, 22: 39e57.

Krieger, J. and D. L. Higgins (2002), 'Housing and Health: Time Again for Public Health Action', *American Journal of Public Health*, 92 (5), 758–68.

Johnson, G. and C. Chamberlain (2011), 'Are the Homeless Mentally Ill?', *Australian Journal of Social Issues*, 46 (1): 29–48.

Joiner, T. (2009), 'The Interpersonal-Psychological Theory of Suicidal Behavior: Current Empirical Status'. *Psychological Science Agenda, American Psychological Association*. Available online: https://www.apa.org/science/about/psa/2009/06/sci-brief (accessed 4 June 2020).

Lai, L. and P. Rios (2017), 'Housing Design for Socialisation and Wellbeing', *Journal of Urban Design and Mental Health*, 3: 12.

Lasgaard, M., K. Friis and M. Shevlin (2016), 'Where Are All the Lonely People? A Populationbased Study of High-Risk Groups across the Life Span', *Social Psychiatry and Psychiatric Epidemiology*, 51 (10): 1373–84.

Law, C. K., Y. C. Wong, E. Chui, K. M. Lee, Y. Y. Pong, R. Yu and V. Lee (2009), *A Study on Tin Shui Wai New Town*, Hong Kong: Hong Kong University.

Leigh-Hunt, N., D. Bagguley, K. Bash, V. Turner, S. Turnbull, N. Valtorta and W. Caan (2017), 'An Overview of Systematic Reviews on the Public Health Consequences of Social Isolation and Loneliness', *Public Health*, 152: 157–71.

Madanipour, A. (2004), 'Marginal Public Spaces in European Cities', *Journal of Urban Design*, 9 (3): 267–86.

McCay, L. and L. Lai (2018), 'Urban Design and Mental Health in Hong Kong: A City Case Study', *Journal of Urban Design and Mental Health*, 4: 9.

Meltzer, H., P. Bebbington, M. S. Dennis, R. Jenkins, S. McManus and T. S. Brugha (2013), 'Feelings of Loneliness among Adults with Mental Disorder', *Social Psychiatry and Psychiatric Epidemiology*, 48 (1): 5–13.

Milton, B., P. Attree, B. French, S. Povall, M. Whitehead and J. Popay (2011), 'The Impact of Community Engagement on Health and Social Outcomes: A Systematic Review', *Community Development Journal*, 47: 316–34.

Mitchell, L. and E. Burton (2006), 'Neighbourhoods for Life: Designing Dementia-Friendly Outdoor Environments', *Quality in Ageing and Older Adults*, 7: 1:26–33.

Muennig, P., B. Jiao and E. Singer (2017), 'Living with Parents or Grandparents Increases Social Capital and Survival: 2014 General Social Survey-National Death Index', *SSM – Population Health*, 4: 71–5.

Newman, O. (1976), *Design Guidelines for Creating Defensible Space*, United States: National Institute of Law Enforcement and Criminal Justice.

NICE Guideline (NG44) (2016), *Community Engagement: Improving Health and Wellbeing and Reducing Health Inequalities*, United Kingdom: National Institute for Health and Care Excellence.

Nikkhah, H., M. Nia, S. Sadeghi and M. Fani (2015), 'The Mean Difference of Religiosity between Residents of Rural Areas and Urban Areas of Mahmoudabad City', *Asian Social Science*, 11: 10.5539/ass.v11n2p144.

Osborne, C., C. Baldwin and D. Thomsen (2016), 'Contributions of Social Capital to Best Practice Urban Planning Outcomes', *Urban Policy and Research*, 34: 212–24.

Peplau, L. A. and D. Perlman (1982), *Loneliness: A Sourcebook of Current Theory, Research, and Therapy*, New York: Wiley Interscience.

Petty, J. (2016), 'The London Spikes Controversy: Homelessness, Urban Securitisation and the Question of "Hostile Architecture"', *International Journal for Crime, Justice and Social Democracy*, 5 (1): 67–81.

Putnam, R. (1993), *Making Democracy Work: Civic Traditions in Modern Italy*, Princeton, NJ: Princeton University Press.

Rico-Uribe, L. A., F. F. Caballero, N. Martín-Marín, M. Cabello, J. L. Ayuso-Mateos and M. Miret (2018), 'Association of Loneliness with All-Cause Mortality: A Meta-Analysis', *PloS One*, 13 (1): e0190033.

Santini, Z. I., A. Koyanagi, S. Tyrovolas, C. Mason and J. M. Haro (2015), 'The Association between Social Relationships and Depression: A Systematic Review', *Journal of Affective Disorders*, 175: 53–65.

Shaw, M. (2004), 'Housing and Public Health', *Annual Review of Public Health*, 25: 397–418.

Sorensen, A., H. Koizumi and A. Miyamoto (2009), 'Machizukuri, Civil Society, and Community Space in Japan', *Political Science*. 10.4324/9780203892770-11.

Srinivasan, S., L. R. O'Fallon and A. Dearry (2003), 'Creating Healthy Communities, Healthy Homes, Healthy People: Initiating a Research Agenda on the Built Environment and Public Health', *American Journal of Public Health*, 93 (9): 1446–50.

Stahl, S. T., S. R. Beach, D. Musa and R. Schulz (2017), 'Living Alone and Depression: The Modifying Role of the Perceived Neighborhood Environment', *Ageing and Mental Health*, 21(10): 1065–71.

Teo, A. R., R. Lerrigo and M. A. M. Rogers (2013), 'The Role of Social Isolation in Social Anxiety Disorder: A Systematic Review and Metaanalysis', *Journal of Anxiety Disorders*, 27: 353e64.

Thombre, L. and C. Kapshe (2020), 'Conviviality as a Spatial Planning Goal for Public Open Spaces', *International Journal of Recent Technology and Engineering*, 8(5): 10.35940/ijrte.e7038.018520.

Umberson, D. and J. K. Montez (2010), 'Social Relationships and Health: A Flashpoint for Health Policy', *Journal of Health and Social Behaviour*, 51(1): 54–66.

United Nations, Department of Economic and Social Affairs, Population Division, UNDESA (2018), *World Urbanization Prospects: The 2018 Revision (ST/ESA/ SER.A/420)*, New York: United Nations.

UN-Habitat (2009), *State of the World's Cities Report 2008/9: Harmonious Cities*, London: Earthscan.

UN-Habitat and WHO (2020), *Integrating Health in Urban and Territorial Planning: A Sourcebook*, Geneva: UN-HABITAT and World Health Organization.

Visentini, C., M. Cassidy, V. J. Bird and S. Priebea (2018), 'Social Networks of Patients with Chronic Depression: A Systematic Review', *Journal of Affective Disorders*, 241: 571–8.

Wang, J., F. Mann, B. Lloyd-Evans, R. Ma and S. Johnson (2018a), 'Associations between Loneliness and Perceived Social Support and Outcomes of Mental Health Problems: A Systematic Review', *BMC Psychiatry*, 18: 156.

Wang, R., D. Xue, Y. Liu, H. Chen and Y. Qui (2018b), 'The Relationship between Urbanization and Depression in China: The Mediating Role of Neighborhood Social Capital', *International Journal for Equity in Health*, 17: 105.

Wilson, C. and B. Moulton (2010), *Loneliness among Older Adults: A National Survey of Adults 45+*, Washington, DC: AARP.

Wirth, L. (1938), 'Urbanism as a Way of Life', *American Journal of Sociology*, 44 (1): 1–24.

Wright, P. A. and B. Kloos (2007), 'Housing Environment and Mental Health Outcomes: A Levels of Analysis Perspective', *Journal of Environmental Psychology*, 27 (1): 79–89.

Wood, L., K. Martin, H. Christian, A. Nathan, C. Lauritsen, S. Houghton,
    I. Kawachi and S. McCune (2015), 'The Pet Factor – Companion Animals as a
    Conduit for Getting to Know People, Friendship Formation and Social Support',
    PLOS ONE, 10 (4): e0122085.
Yeung, J. W. K., Z. Zhang and T. Y. Kim (2018), 'Volunteering and Health Benefits
    in General Adults: Cumulative Effects and Forms', *BMC Public Health*, 18 (8):
    10.1186/s12889-017-4561-8.

Chapter 6: The active city

Age UK (2011), *Healthy Aging Evidence Review*, London: Age UK.
Ahmadi, E. and G. Taniguchi (2007), 'Influential Factors on Children's Spatial
    Knowledge and Mobility in Home – School Travel: A Case Study in the City
    of Tehran', *Journal of Asian Architecture and Building Engineering*, 6 (2):
    275–82.
Arup (2017), *Cities Alive: Designing for Urban Childhoods*, London: Arup Group.
    Available online: https://www.arup.com/perspectives/publications/research/
    section/cities-alive-designing-for-urban-childhoods (accessed 20 February
    2020).
Badland, H. M., G. M. Schofield and N. Garrett (2008), 'Travel Behavior and
    Objectively Measured Urban Design Variables: Associations for Adults
    Traveling to Work', *Health & Place*, 14 (1): 85–95.
Bakolis, I., R. Hammoud, M. Smythe, J. Gibbons, N. Davidson, S. Tognin and
    A. Mechelli (2018), 'Urban Mind: Using Smartphone Technologies to
    Investigate the Impact of Nature on Mental Well-Being in Real Time',
    BioScience, 68 (2): 134–45.
Barbour, K. A., T. M. Edenfield and J. A. Blumenthal (2007), 'Exercise as a
    Treatment for Depression and Other Psychiatric Disorders: A Review', *Journal
    of Cardiopulmonary Rehabilitation and Prevention*, 27 (6): 359–67.
Barros, P., L. N. Fat, L. M. Garcia, A. D. Slovic, N. Thomopoulos, T. H. de Sá,
    P. Morais and J. S. Mindell (2019), 'Social Consequences and Mental Health
    Outcomes of Living in High-Rise Residential Buildings and the Influence of
    Planning, Urban Design and Architectural Decisions: A Systematic Review',
    Cities, 93 (October): 263–72.
Barton, J. and J. Pretty (2010), 'What Is the Best Dose of Nature and Green
    Exercise for Improving Mental Health? A Multi-Study Analysis', *Environmental
    Science and Technology*, 44 (10): 3947–55.
Besser, L. M., M. Marcus and H. Frumkin (2008), 'Commute Time and Social
    Capital in the US', *American Journal of Preventive Medicine*, 34 (3): 207–11.
Biddle, S. J. and M. Asare (2011), 'Physical Activity and Mental Health in Children
    and Adolescents: A Review of Reviews', *British Journal of Sports Medicine*,
    45 (11): 886–95.
Blackwell, D. L. and T. C. Clarke (2018), *State Variation in Meeting the 2008
    Federal Guidelines for Both Aerobic and Muscle-Strengthening Activities
    through Leisure-Time Physical Activity among Adults Aged 18–64: United
    States, 2010–2015*, National Health Statistics Report No. 112, Hyattsville:
    Centers for Disease Control and Prevention.

Booth, F. W., C. K. Roberts and M. J. Laye (2011), 'Lack of Exercise Is a Major Cause of Chronic Diseases', *Comprehensive Physiology*, 2 (2): 1143–211.

Bornioli, A., G. Parkhurst and P. L. Morgan (2018), 'Psychological Wellbeing Benefits of Simulated Exposure to Five Urban Settings: An Experimental Study from the Pedestrian's Perspective', *Journal of Transport & Health*, 9 (June): 105–16.

Bornioli, A., G. Parkhurst and P. L. Morgan (2019), 'Affective Experiences of Built Environments and the Promotion of Urban Walking', *Transportation Research Part A: Policy and Practice*, 123 (May): 200–15.

Center for Active Design (2010), *Civic Design Guidelines*. Available online: https://centerforactivedesign.org/guidelines/ (accessed 22 February 2020).

Center for Active Design (2016), *Designed to Move Active Cities* (available from alr@ucsd.edu).

Chalmin-Pui, L. S., A. Griffiths, J. J. Roe and R. W. Cameron (2019), 'Bringing Fronts Back: A Research Agenda to Investigate the Health and Well-Being Impacts of Front Gardens', *Challenges*, 10 (2): 37.

Christian, T. J. (2012), 'Automobile Commuting Duration and the Quantity of Time Spent with Spouse, Children, and Friends', *Preventive Medicine*, 55 (3): 215–18.

Dale, L. P., L. Vanderloo, S. Moore and G. Faulkner (2019), 'Physical Activity and Depression, Anxiety, and Self-Esteem in Children and Youth: An Umbrella Systematic Review', *Mental Health and Physical Activity*, 16 (March): 66–79.

Delmelle, E. C., E. Haslauer and T. Prinz (2013), 'Social Satisfaction, Commuting and Neighborhoods', *Journal of Transport Geography*, 30 (April): 110–16.

Donnelly, J. E., C. H. Hillman, D. Castelli, J. L. Etnier, S. Lee, P. Tomporowski, K. Lambourne and A. N. Szabo-Reed (2016), 'Physical Activity, Fitness, Cognitive Function, and Academic Achievement in Children: A Systematic Review', *Medicine and Science in Sports and Exercise*, 48 (6): 1197.

Durand, C. P., M. Andalib, G. F. Dunton, J. Wolch and M. A. Pentz (2011), 'A Systematic Review of Built Environment Factors Related to Physical Activity and Obesity Risk: Implications for Smart Growth Urban Planning', *Obesity Reviews*, 12 (5): e173–e182.

Erickson, K. I., M. W. Voss, R. S. Prakash, C. Basak, A. Szabo, L. Chaddock, J. S. Kim, S. Heo, H. Alves, S. M. White and T. R. Wojcicki (2011), 'Exercise Training Increases Size of Hippocampus and Improves Memory', *Proceedings of the National Academy of Sciences*, 108 (7): 3017–22.

Faber Taylor, A. and F. E. Kuo (2009), 'Children with Attention Deficits Concentrate Better after Walk in the Park', *Journal of Attention Disorders*, 12 (5): 402–9.

Falck, R. S., J. C. Davis, J. R. Best, R. A. Crockett and T. Liu-Ambrose (2019), 'Impact of Exercise Training on Physical and Cognitive Function among Older Adults: A Systematic Review and Meta-Analysis', *Neurobiology of Aging*, 79 (July): 119–30.

GDCI (2016), *Global Street Design Guide*, New York: Global Designing Cities Initiative (GDCI). Available online: https://globaldesigningcities.org/publication/global-street-design-guide/ (accessed 22 February 2020).

Gehl, J. (1986), '"Soft Edges" in Residential Streets', *Scandinavian Housing and Planning Research*, 3 (2): 89–102.

Gorelick, P. B., K. L. Furie, C. Iadecola, E. E. Smith, S. P. Waddy, D. M. Lloyd-Jones, H. J. Bae, M. A. Bauman, M. Dichgans, P. W. Duncan and M. Girgus (2017), 'Defining Optimal Brain Health in Adults: A Presidential Advisory from the American Heart Association/American Stroke Association', *Stroke*, 48 (10): e284–e303.

Gössling, S., A. Choi, K. Dekker and D. Metzler (2019), 'The Social Cost of Automobility, Cycling and Walking in the European Union', *Ecological Economics*, 158 (April): 65–74.

Hajrasouliha, A. and L. Yin (2015), 'The Impact of Street Network Connectivity on Pedestrian Volume', *Urban Studies*, 52 (13): 2483–97.

Handy, S., R. G. Paterson and K. S. Butler (2003), *Planning for Street Connectivity: Getting from Here to There*, APA Planning Advisory Service Report 515, Chicago: American Planning Association (APA).

Hillier, B. and J. Hanson (1989), *The Social Logic of Space*, Cambridge: Cambridge University Press.

Hillier, B., J. Hanson and H. Graham (1987), 'Ideas Are in Things: An Application of the Space Syntax Method to Discovering House Genotypes', *Environment and Planning B: Planning and Design*, 14 (4): 363–85.

Hillman, C. H., M. B. Pontifex, L. B. Raine, D. M. Castelli, E. E. Hall and A. F. Kramer (2009), 'The Effect of Acute Treadmill Walking on Cognitive Control and Academic Achievement in Preadolescent Children', *Neuroscience*, 159 (3): 1044–54.

Hipp, J., A. Eyler and J. Kuhlberg (2013), 'Target Population Involvement in Urban Ciclovias: A Preliminary Evaluation of St. Louis Open Streets', *Journal of Urban Health*, 90 (6): 1010–15.

Holt-Lunstad, J., T. B. Smith and J. B. Layton (2010), 'Social Relationships and Mortality Risk: A Meta-Analytic Review', *PLOS Med*, 7 (7): e1000316.

Hörder, H., L. Johansson, X. Guo, G. Grimby, S. Kern, S. Östling and I. Skoog (2018), 'Midlife Cardiovascular Fitness and Dementia: A 44-Year Longitudinal Population Study in Women', *Neurology*, 90 (15): e1298–e1305.

Javadi, A. H., B. Emo, L. R. Howard, F. E. Zisch, Y. Yu, R. Knight, J. P. Silva and H. J. Spiers (2017), 'Hippocampal and Prefrontal Processing of Network Topology to Simulate the Future', *Nature Communications*, 8 (1): 1–11.

Jensen, O. B., M. Sheller and S. Wind (2015), 'Together and Apart: Affective Ambiences and Negotiation in Families' Everyday Life and Mobility', *Mobilities*, 10 (3): 363–82.

Jones, A., A. Goodman, H. Roberts, R. Steinbach and J. Green (2013), 'Entitlement to Concessionary Public Transport and Wellbeing: A Qualitative Study of Young People and Older Citizens in London, UK', *Social Science & Medicine*, 91 (August): 202–9.

Kamijo, K., M. B. Pontifex, K. C. O'Leary, M. R. Scudder, C. T. Wu, D. M. Castelli and C. H. Hillman (2011), 'The Effects of an Afterschool Physical Activity Program on Working Memory in Preadolescent Children', *Developmental Science*, 14 (5): 1046–58.

Kibbe, D. L., J. Hackett, M. Hurley, A. McFarland, K. G. Schubert, A. Schultz and S. Harris (2011), 'Ten Years of TAKE 10!®: Integrating Physical Activity with Academic Concepts in Elementary School Classrooms', *Preventive Medicine*, 52 (June): S43–S50.

Knöll, M., M. H. Miranda, T. Cleff and A. Rudolph-Cleff (2019), 'Public Space and Pedestrian Stress Perception: Insights from Darmstadt, Germany', in A. Pearson, A. Gershim, G. DeVerteuil and A. Allen (eds), *Handbook of Global Urban Health*, 269, London: Routledge.

Kondo, M. C., S. F. Jacoby and E. C. South (2018), 'Does Spending Time
  Outdoors Reduce Stress? A Review of Real-Time Stress Response to Outdoor
  Environments', *Health & Place*, 51 (May): 136–50.
Koohsari, M. J., T. Sugiyama, K. E. Lamb, K. Villanueva and N. Owen (2014),
  'Street Connectivity and Walking for Transport: Role of Neighborhood
  Destinations', *Preventive Medicine*, 66 (September): 118–22.
Koohsari, M. J., K. Oka, N. Owen and T. Sugiyama (2019), 'Natural Movement:
  A Space Syntax Theory Linking Urban Form and Function with Walking for
  Transport', *Health & Place*, 58 (July): 102072.
Kweon, B. S., W. C. Sullivan and A. R. Wiley (1998), 'Green Common Spaces and
  the Social Integration of Inner-City Older Adults', *Environment and Behavior*,
  30 (6): 832–58.
Lerman, Y., Y. Rofè and I. Omer (2014), 'Using Space Syntax to Model Pedestrian
  Movement in Urban Transportation Planning', *Geographical Analysis*, 46 (4):
  392–410.
Lindal, P. J. and T. Hartig (2013), 'Architectural Variation, Building Height, and
  the Restorative Quality of Urban Residential Streetscapes', *Journal of
  Environmental Psychology*, 33 (March): 26–36.
Livingston, G., A. Sommerlad, V. Orgeta, S. G. Costafreda, J. Huntley, D. Ames,
  C. Ballard, S. Banerjee, A. Burns, J. Cohen-Mansfield and C. Cooper (2017),
  'Dementia Prevention, Intervention, and Care', *The Lancet*, 390 (10113):
  2673–734.
Lubans, D., J. Richards, C. Hillman, G. Faulkner, M. Beauchamp, M. Nilsson,
  P. Kelly, J. Smith, L. Raine and S. Biddle (2016), 'Physical Activity for Cognitive
  and Mental Health in Youth: A Systematic Review of Mechanisms', *Pediatrics*,
  138 (3): e20161642.
Lynch, K. (1960), *The Image of the City*, Boston: MIT Press.
Maas, J., S. M. Van Dillen, R. A. Verheij and P. P. Groenewegen (2009), 'Social
  Contacts as a Possible Mechanism behind the Relation between Green Space
  and Health', *Health & Place*, 15 (2): 586–95.
MacKerron, G. and S. Mourato (2013), 'Happiness Is Greater in Natural
  Environments', *Global Environmental Change*, 23 (5): 992–1000.
Macpherson, H., W. P. Teo, L. A. Schneider and A. E. Smith (2017), 'A Life-
  Long Approach to Physical Activity for Brain Health', *Frontiers in Aging
  Neuroscience*, 9 (May): 147.
Martinsen, E. W. (2008), 'Physical Activity in the Prevention and Treatment of
  Anxiety and Depression', *Nordic Journal of Psychiatry*, 62 (47): 25–9.
Mattisson, K., C. Håkansson and K. Jakobsson (2015), 'Relationships between
  Commuting and Social Capital among Men and Women in Southern Sweden',
  Environment and Behavior, 47 (7): 734–53.
Mazumdar, S., V. Learnihan, T. Cochrane and R. Davey (2018), 'The Built
  Environment and Social Capital: A Systematic Review', *Environment and
  Behavior*, 50 (2): 119–58.
Mondschein, A. (2018), 'Healthy Transportation: A Question of Mobility or
  Accessibility', in T. Beatley, C. Jones and R. Rainey (eds), *Healthy Environments,
  Healing Spaces*, Charlottesville: University of Virginia Press, 11–30.
Mueller, N., D. Rojas-Rueda, H. Khreis, M. Cirach, D. Andrés, J. Ballester,
  X. Bartoll, C. Daher, A. Deluca, C. Echave and C. Milà (2020), 'Changing
  the Urban Design of Cities for Health: The Superblock Model', *Environment
  International*, 134 (January): 105132.

Neale, C., P. Aspinall, J. Roe, S. Tilley, P. Mavros, S. Cinderby, R. Coyne, N. Thin and C. Ward Thompson (2019), 'The Impact of Walking in Different Urban Environments on Brain Activity in Older People', *Cities & Health*, 4 (1) (June): 94–106.

North, T. C., P. McCullagh and Z. V. Tran (1990), 'Effect of Exercise on Depression', *Exercise and Sport Sciences Reviews*, 18 (1): 379–416.

Panter, J., C. Guell, D. Humphryes and D. Ogilvie (2019), 'Can Changing the Physical Environment Promote Walking and Cycling? A Systematic Review of What Works and How', *Health & Place*, 58 (July): 102161.

Pesce, C., C. Crova, L. Cereatti, R. Casella and M. Bellucci (2009), 'Physical Activity and Mental Performance in Preadolescents: Effects of Acute Exercise on Free-Recall Memory', *Mental Health and Physical Activity*, 2 (1): 16–22.

Pollard, E. L. and P. D. Lee (2003), 'Child Well-Being: A Systematic Review of the Literature', *Social Indicators Research*, 61 (1): 59–78.

Powers, M. B., G. J. Asmundson and J. A. Smits (2015), 'Exercise for Mood and Anxiety Disorders: The State-of-the Science', *Cognitive Behaviour Therapy*, 44 (4): 237–9.

Ramanathan, S., C. O'Brien, G. Faulkner and M. Stone (2014), 'Happiness in Motion: Emotions, Well-Being, and Active School Travel', *Journal of School Health*, 84 (8): 516–23.

Roberts, D. (2019), 'Cars Dominate Cities Today. Barcelona Has Set Out to Change That', *Vox*, 8 April. Available online: https://www.vox.com/energy-and-environment/2019/4/8/18273893/barcelona-spain-urban-planning-cars (accessed 20 February 2020).

Roe, J. and A. Roe (2019), 'Urban Design for Adolescent Mental Health', in D. Bhugra (ed.), *Urban Mental Health*, 189–203, Oxford: Oxford University Press.

Roe, J. and P. A. Aspinall (2011), 'The Restorative Benefits of Walking in Urban and Rural Settings in Adults with Good and Poor Mental Health', *Health & Place*, 17 (1): 103–13.

Romero, V. (2010), 'Children's Views of Independent Mobility during Their School Travels', *Children, Youth and Environments*, 20 (2): 46–66.

Rovio, S., I. Kåreholt, E. L. Helkala, M. Viitanen, B. Winblad, J. Tuomilehto, H. Soininen, A. Nissinen and M. Kivipelto (2005), 'Leisure-Time Physical Activity at Midlife and the Risk of Dementia and Alzheimer's Disease', *The Lancet Neurology*, 4 (11): 705–11.

Sallis, J. F., M. F. Floyd, D. A. Rodríguez and B. E. Saelens (2012), 'Role of Built Environments in Physical Activity, Obesity, and Cardiovascular Disease', *Circulation*, 125 (5): 729–37.

Sallis, J. F., C. Spoon, N. Cavill, J. K. Engelberg, K. Gebel, M. Parker, C. M. Thornton, D. Lou, A. L. Wilson, C. L. Cutter and D. Ding (2015), 'Co-Benefits of Designing Communities for Active Living: An Exploration of Literature', *International Journal of Behavioral Nutrition and Physical Activity*, 12 (1): 30.

Sallis, J. F., E. Cerin, T. L. Conway, M. A. Adams, L. D. Frank, M. Pratt, D. Salvo, J. Schipperijn, G. Smith, K. L. Cain and R. Davey (2016), 'Physical Activity in Relation to Urban Environments in 14 Cities Worldwide: A Cross-Sectional Study', *The Lancet*, 387 (10034): 2207–17.

Smith, J. C., K. A. Nielson, P. Antuono, J. A. Lyons, R. J. Hanson, A. M. Butts, N. C. Hantke and M. D. Verber (2013), 'Semantic Memory Functional MRI and Cognitive Function after Exercise Intervention in Mild Cognitive Impairment', *Journal of Alzheimer's Disease*, 37 (1): 197–215.

Smits, J. A., A. C. Berry, D. Rosenfield, M. B. Powers, E. Behar and M. W. Otto (2008), 'Reducing Anxiety Sensitivity with Exercise', *Depression and Anxiety*, 25 (8): 689–99.

Spartano, N. L., K. L. Davis-Plourde, J. J. Himali, C. Andersson, M. P. Pase, P. Maillard, C. DeCarli, J. M. Murabito, A. S. Beiser, R. S. Vasan and S. Seshadri (2019), 'Association of Accelerometer-Measured Light-Intensity Physical Activity with Brain Volume: The Framingham Heart Study', *JAMA Network Open*, 2 (4): e192745–e192745.

Stroth, S., K. Hille, M. Spitzer and R. Reinhardt (2009), 'Aerobic Endurance Exercise Benefits Memory and Affect in Young Adults', *Neuropsychological Rehabilitation*, 19 (2): 223–43.

Tinker, A. and J. Ginn (2015), *An Age Friendly City: How Far Has London Come?*, London: King's College London.

UNICEF (2018), *Child Friendly Cities and Communities Handbook*, New York: UNICEF.

van den Berg, P., A. Kemperman, B. de Kleijn and A. Borgers (2016), 'Ageing and Loneliness: The Role of Mobility and the Built Environment', *Travel Behaviour and Society*, 5 (September): 48–55.

van Vliet, W. (1983), 'Children's Travel Behavior', *Ekistics*, 50 (298): 61–5.

Ward Thompson, C., P. Aspinall, J. Roe, L. Robertson and D. Miller (2016), 'Mitigating Stress and Supporting Health in Deprived Urban Communities: The Importance of Green Space and the Social Environment', *International Journal of Environmental Research and Public Health*, 13 (4): 440.

Waygood, E. O. D., M. Friman, L. E. Olsson and A. Taniguchi (2017), 'Transport and Child Well-Being: An Integrative Review', *Travel Behaviour and Society*, 9 (October): 32–49.

Westman, J., M. Johansson, L. E. Olsson, F. Mårtensson and M. Friman (2013), 'Children's Affective Experience of Every-Day Travel', *Journal of Transport Geography*, 29 (May): 95–102.

WHO (2007), *Global Age-Friendly Cities: A Guide*, Geneva: World Health Organization (WHO). Available online: https://www.who.int/ageing/publications/Global_age_friendly_cities_Guide_English.pdf (accessed 22 February 2020).

WHO (2011), *Global Recommendations on Physical Activity for Health*, Geneva: World Health Organization (WHO). Available online: https://www.who.int/dietphysicalactivity/pa/en/ (accessed 22 February 2020).

Won, J., A. J. Alfini, L. R. Weiss, C. S. Michelson, D. D. Callow, S. M. Ranadive, R. J. Gentili and J. C. Smith (2019), 'Semantic Memory Activation after Acute Exercise in Healthy Older Adults', *Journal of the International Neuropsychological Society*, 25 (6): 557–68.

Wood, L., L. D. Frank and B. Giles-Corti (2010), 'Sense of Community and Its Relationship with Walking and Neighborhood Design', *Social Science & Medicine*, 70 (9): 1381–90.

Chapter 7: The playable city

Ackermann, J., A. Rauscher and D. Stein, eds (2016), 'Introduction', in 'Playin' the City: Artistic and Scientific Approaches to Playful Urban Arts', special issue, *Navigationen*, 16 (1): 7–24.

Age UK (2018), 'How Care Homes and Nurseries Are Coming Together for Good', Age UK, 26 April. Available online: https://www.ageukmobility.co.uk/mobility-news/article/intergenerational-care (accessed 20 February 2020).

Arup (2017), *Cities Alive: Designing for Urban Childhoods*, London: Arup Group. Available online: https://www.arup.com/perspectives/publications/research/section/cities-alive-designing-for-urban-childhoods (accessed 20 February 2020).

Baggini, J. (2014), 'Playable Cities: The City That Plays Together, Stays Together', *Guardian*, 4 September. Available online: https://www.theguardian.com/cities/2014/sep/04/playable-cities-the-city-that-plays-together-stays-together (accessed 20 February 2020).

Barnett, T. A., A. S. Kelly, D. R. Young, C. K. Perry, C. A. Pratt, N. M. Edwards, G. Rao and M. B. Vos (2018), 'Sedentary Behaviors in Today's Youth: Approaches to the Prevention and Management of Childhood Obesity: A Scientific Statement from the American Heart Association', *Circulation*, 138 (11): e142–e159.

Berk, L. E. (2013) *Child Development*, 9th edn, New Jersey: Pearson.

Brussoni, M., R. Gibbons, C. Gray, T. Ishikawa, E. B. H. Sandseter, A. Bienenstock, G. Chabot, P. Fuselli, S. Herrington, I. Janssen and W. Pickett (2015), 'What Is the Relationship between Risky Outdoor Play and Health in Children? A Systematic Review', *International Journal of Environmental Research and Public Health*, 12 (6): 6423–54.

Chawla, L. (2015), 'Benefits of Nature Contact for Children', *Journal of Planning Literature*, 30 (4): 433–52.

Cortinez-O'Ryan, A., A. Albagli, K. P. Sadarangani and N. Aguilar-Farias (2017), 'Reclaiming Streets for Outdoor Play: A Process and Impact Evaluation of "Juega en Tu Barrio" (Play in Your Neighborhood), an Intervention to Increase Physical Activity and Opportunities for Play', *PLOS One*, 12 (7): e0180172.

Csikszentmihalyi, M. (2008), *Flow: The Psychology of Optimal Experience*, New York: Harper Perennial Modern Classics.

D'Haese, S., D. Van Dyck, I. De Bourdeaudhuij, B. Deforche and G. Cardon (2015), 'Organizing "Play Streets" during School Vacations Can Increase Physical Activity and Decrease Sedentary Time in Children', *International Journal of Behavioral Nutrition and Physical Activity*, 12 (1): 14.

Donoff, G. and R. Bridgman (2017), 'The Playful City: Constructing a Typology for Urban Design Interventions', *International Journal of Play*, 6 (3): 294–307.

El-hage, T. (2011), 'Sébastien Foucan: Founder of Free Running', *Guardian*, 20 July. Available online: https://www.theguardian.com/lifeandstyle/2011/jul/20/sebastien-foucan-founder-free-running (accessed 20 February 2020).

Erikson, E. H. (1968), *Identity: Youth and Crisis*, New York: W. W. Norton.

Fabian, C. (2016), 'Der Beitrag partizipativer Prozesse bei der Freiraumentwicklung für die Gesundheit von Kindern', *Umweltpsychologie*, 20 (2): 112–36.

Fearn, M. and J. Howard (2011), 'Play as a Resource for Children Facing Adversity: An Exploration of Indicative Case Studies', *Children and Society*, 26 (6): 456–68.

Frost, J. L. (1988) 'Neuroscience, play and brain development'. Paper presented at: IPA/USA Triennial National Conference; Longmont, CO; 18–21 June. Available at: www.eric.ed.gov/ERICDocs/data/ericdocs2/content_storage_01/0000000b/80/11/56/d6.pdf.

Gibson, J. J. (1979), *The Ecological Approach to Visual Perception*, Boston: Houghton Mifflin.

Gill, T. (2005), 'Let Our Children Roam Free', *Ecologist*, 35 (8). Available online: https://theecologist.org/2005/sep/23/let-our-children-roam-free (accessed 20 February 2020).

Gill, T. (2014), 'The Benefits of Children's Engagement with Nature: A Systematic Literature Review', *Children, Youth and Environments*, 24 (2): 10–34.

Ginsburg, K. R. (2007), 'The Importance of Play in Promoting Healthy Child Development and Maintaining Strong Parent-Child Bonds', *Paediatrics*, 119 (1): 182–91.

Graham, K. L. and G. M. Burghardt (2010), 'Current Perspectives on the Biological Study of Play: Signs of Progress', *Quarterly Review of Biology*, 85 (4): 393–418.

Gray, P. (2011), 'The Decline of Play and the Rise of Psychopathology in Children and Adolescents', *American Journal of Play*, 3 (4): 443–63.

Halblaub, M. M. and M. Knöll (2016), 'Stadtflucht: Learning about Healthy Places with a Location-Based Game', in J. Ackermann, A. Rauscher and D. Stein (eds), 'Playin' the City: Artistic and Scientific Approaches to Playful Urban Arts', special issue, *Navigationen*, 16 (1): 101–18.

Harris, M. A. (2018), 'Beat the Street: A Pilot Evaluation of a Community-Wide Gamification-Based Physical Activity Intervention', *Games for Health Journal*, 7 (3): 208–12.

Hart, R. (1978), *Children's Experience of Place*, New York: Irvington Publishers.

Heft, H. (1988), 'Affordances of Children's Environments: A Functional Approach to Environmental Description', *Children's Environments Quarterly*, 5 (3): 29–37.

Huizinga, J. (1938), *Homo Ludens. A Study of the Play-Element in Culture*, New York: Angelico Press.

Hutchinson, S. L., C. M. Yarnal, J. Staffordson and D. L. Kerstetter (2008), 'Beyond Fun and Friendship: The Red Hat Society as a Coping Resource for Older Women', *Ageing and Society*, 28 (7): 979–99.

Jensen, S. A., J. N. Biesen and E. R. Graham (2017), 'A Meta-Analytic Review of Play Therapy with Emphasis on Outcome Measures', *Professional Psychology: Research and Practice*, 48 (5): 390–400.

Kashdan, T. B. and P. J. Silvia (2009), 'Curiosity and Interest: The Benefits of Thriving on Novelty and Challenge', in S. J. Lopez and C. R. Snyder (eds), *Oxford Handbook of Positive Psychology*, 367–74, Oxford: Oxford University Press.

Knöll, M. (2016), 'Bewertung von Aufenthaltsqualität durch Location-Based-Games: Altersspezifische Anforderungen in der Studie "Stadtflucht" in Frankfurt am Main', in G. Marquardt (ed.), *MATI: Mensch–Architektur–Technik–Interaktion für demografische Nachhaltigkeit*, 266–77, Dresden: Fraunhofer IRB Verlag.

Knöll, M. and J. Roe (2016), 'Pokemon Go: A Tool to Help Urban Design Improve Mental Health?', Centre for Urban Design and Mental Health (July). Available online: https://www.urbandesignmentalhealth.com/blog/archives/07-2016 (accessed 20 February 2020).

Kyttä, M. (2006), 'Environmental Child-Friendliness in the Light of the Bullerby Model', in C. Spencer and M. Blades (eds), *Children and Their Environments: Learning, Using and Designing Spaces*, 141–58, Cambridge: Cambridge University Press.

Lester, S. and W. Russell (2008), *Play for a Change, Play Policy and Practice: A Review of Contemporary Perspectives*, London: Play England.

Lester, S. and W. Russell (2010), *Children's Right to Play: An Examination of the Importance of Play in the Lives of Children Worldwide*, The Hague: Bernard van Leer Foundation.

Louv, R. (2008), *Last Child in the Woods: Saving Our Children from Nature-Deficit Disorder*, 2nd edn, Chapel Hill: Algonquin.

Magnuson, C. D. and L. A. Barnett (2013), 'The Playful Advantage: How Playfulness Enhances Coping with Stress', *Leisure Sciences*, 35 (2): 129–44.

Mahdjoubi, L. and B. Spencer (2015), 'Healthy Play for All Ages in Public Open Spaces', in H. Barton, S. Thompson, S. Burgess and M. Grant (eds), *The Routledge Handbook of Planning for Health and Well-being*, 136–49, London: Routledge.

Miller, M. H. (2019), 'Tyree Guyton Turned a Detroit Street into a Museum. Why Is He Taking It Down?', *New York Times*, 9 May. Available online: https://www.nytimes.com/2019/05/09/magazine/tyree-guyton-art-detroit.html?action=click andmodule=Editors%20Picksandpgtype=Homepage (accessed 20 February 2020).

Moss, S. (2012), *Natural Childhood*, Swindon: National Trust.

Murray, J. and C. Devecchi (2016), 'The Hantown Street Play Project', *International Journal of Play*, 5 (2): 196–211.

Natural England (2010), *Wild Adventure Space*, Worcester: Natural England.

NEF (2011), *Five Ways to Wellbeing: New Applications, New Ways of Thinking*, London: New Economics Foundation (NEF).

Nijhof, S. L., C. H. Vinkers, S. M. van Geelen, S. N. Duijff, E. M. Achterberg, J. Van Der Net, R. C. Veltkamp, M. A. Grootenhuis, E. M. van de Putte, M. H. Hillegers and A. W. van der Brug (2018), 'Healthy Play, Better Coping: The Importance of Play for the Development of Children in Health and Disease', *Neuroscience and Biobehavioral Reviews*, 95 (December): 421–9.

O'Sullivan, F. (2016), 'The Problem with "Playable" Cities', *City Lab*, 7 November. Available online: https://www.citylab.com/design/2016/11/playable-cities-projects-crosswalk-party/506528/ (accessed 20 February 2020).

Panksepp, J. (2007), 'Can PLAY Diminish ADHD and Facilitate the Construction of the Social Brain?', *Journal of the Canadian Academy of Child and Adolescent Psychiatry*, 16 (2): 57.

Pellis, S. M. and V. C. Pellis (2010), *The Playful Brain: Venturing to the Limits of Neuroscience*, London: Oneworld Publications.

Proyer, R. T. (2017), 'A Multidisciplinary Perspective on Adult Play and Playfulness', *International Journal of Play*, 6 (3): 241–3.

Roe, J. and A. Roe (2019), 'Urban Design for Adolescent Mental Health', in D. Bhugra (ed.), *Urban Mental Health*, Oxford: Oxford University Press, 189–203.

Roe, J. J. and P. A. Aspinall (2012), 'Adolescents' Daily Activities and the Restorative Niches That Support Them', *International Journal of Environmental Research and Public Health*, 9 (9): 3227–44.

Sakaki, M., A. Yagi and K. Murayama (2018), 'Curiosity in Old Age: A Possible Key to Achieving Adaptive Aging', *Neuroscience & Biobehavioral Reviews*, 88 (May): 106–16.

Shonkoff J. P. and D. A. Phillips, eds (2000), *From Neurons to Neighborhoods: The Science of Early Childhood Development*. Washington, DC: National Academy Press

Sicart, M. (2014), *Play Matters*, Boston: MIT Press.

Sicart, M. (2016), 'Play and the City', in J. Ackermann, A. Rauscher and D. Stein (eds), *'Playin' the City: Artistic and Scientific Approaches to Playful Urban Arts'*, special issue, *Navigationen*, 16 (1): 25–40.

Stein, D. (2016), 'Playing the City: The Heidelberg Project in Detroit', in J. Ackermann, A. Rauscher and D. Stein (eds), 'Playin' the City: Artistic and Scientific Approaches to Playful Urban Arts', special issue, *Navigationen*, 16 (1): 53–70.

Sutton-Smith, B. (2008) 'Play Theory – A Personal Journey of New Thoughts', *Am. J. Play*, 1: 80–123

Tamis-LeMonda, C. S., J. D. Shannon, N. J. Cabrera and M. E. Lamb (2004), 'Fathers and Mothers at Play with Their 2- and 3-Year-Olds: Contributions to Language and Cognitive Development', *Child Development*, 75 (6): 1806–20.

Thomas, M. (2017), 'Public Art as Public Health', *Public Health Post*, 3 March. Available online: https://www.publichealthpost.org/research/public-art-as-public-health/ (accessed 20 February 2020).

Umstattd-Meyer, M. R. U., C. N. Bridges, T. L. Schmid, A. A. Hecht and K. M. P. Porter (2019), 'Systematic Review of How Play Streets Impact Opportunities for Active Play, Physical Activity, Neighborhoods, and Communities', *BMC Public Health*, 19 (1): 335.

United, Generations and Eisner Foundation (2019), *The Best of Both Worlds: A Closer Look at Creating Spaces That Connect Young and Old*, Washington, DC: Generations United/Eisner Foundation. Available online: https://www.gu.org/app/uploads/2019/06/Intergenerational-Report-BestofBothWorlds.pdf (accessed 20 February 2020).

UN (1989), *Convention on the Rights of the Child*, New York: United Nations (UN).

UN (2013), *General Comment No. 17 (2013) on the Right of the Child to Rest, Leisure, Play, Recreational Activities, Cultural Life and the Arts (Art. 31)*, CRC/C/GC/17, New York: UN Committee on the Rights of the Child. Available online: https://www.refworld.org/docid/51ef9bcc4.html (accessed 20 February 2020).

UN-Habitat (2013), 'Streets as Public Spaces and Drivers of Urban Prosperity', United Nations Human Settlements Programme, Nairobi: UN-Habitat.

United for All Ages (2019), *The Next Generation: How Intergenerational Interaction Improves Life Chances of Children and Young People*, Norfolk: United for All Ages.

Whitebread, D. (2017), 'Free Play and Children's Mental Health', *The Lancet Child and Adolescent Health*, 1 (3): 167–9.

World Health Organization (2010) Global Recommendations on Physical Activity for Health, https://www.who.int/publications/i/item/9789241599979 (accessed 15 January 2021).

Zieff, S. G., A. Chaudhuri and E. Musselman (2016), 'Creating Neighborhood Recreational Space for Youth and Children in the Urban Environment: Play (ing in the) Streets in San Francisco', *Children and Youth Services Review*, 70 (November): 95–101.

Chapter 8: The inclusive city

Aneshensel, C. S. and C. Sucoff (1996), 'The Neighborhood Context of Adolescent Mental Health', *Journal of Health and Social Behavior*, 37 (4): 293–310.

Amin, A. (2018), 'Collective Culture and Urban Public Space', *City*, 12(1): 5–24.

Arup (2019), *Cities Alive: Designing for Ageing Communities*, London: Arup.

Atkinson, R. and S. Blandy (2006), *Gated Communities: International Perspectives*, London: Routledge.

Bhalla, A. and S. Anand (2018), 'A City of Happy Captives: A Study of Perceived Liveability in Contemporary Urban Gurgaon, India', *Journal of Urban Design and Mental Health*, 4:8.

CABE (2010), *Urban Green Nation: Building the Evidence Base*, London: CABE.

Cantor-Graae, E. and J. P. Selten (2005), 'Schizophrenia and Migration: A Meta-Analysis and Review', *American Journal of Psychiatry*, 162: 12–24.

Chamie, J. (2017), 'As Cities Grow, So Do the Numbers of Homeless', *Yale Global Online*, 13 July. Available online: https://yaleglobal.yale.edu/content/cities-grow-so-do-numbers-homeless (accessed 4 June 2020).

Cheshire, J. (2012), 'Featured Graphic. Lives on the Line: Mapping Life Expectancy along the London Tube Network', *Environment and Planning A*, 44: 1525–28.

Clarkson, P. J., R. Coleman and S. Keates (2003), *Inclusive Design: Design for the Whole Population*, New York: Springer.

Davidson, J. and V. L. Henderson (2016), 'The Sensory City: Autism, Design and Care', in C. Bates, R. Imrie and K. Kullman, *Care and Design: Bodies, Buildings, Cities*, Chichester: Wiley, 74–94.

Dean, J., K. Silversides, J. Crampton and J. Wrigley (2015), *Evaluation of the York Dementia Friendly Communities Programme*, York: Joseph Rowntree Foundation.

de Fine Licht, K. P. (2017), 'Hostile Urban Architecture: A Critical Discussion of the Seemingly Offensive Art of Keeping People Away', *Nordic Journal of Applied Ethics*, 11 (2): 27–44.

Derr, V. and G. K. Ildikó (2017), 'How Participatory Processes Impact Children and Contribute to Planning: A Case Study of Neighborhood Design from Boulder, Colorado, USA', *Journal of Urbanism*, 10:1, 29–4.

Derr, V., L. Chawla, M. Mintzer, D. Cushing and W. Vliet (2013), 'A City for All Citizens: Integrating Children and Youth from Marginalized Populations into City Planning', *Buildings*, 3: 482–505.

Doumato, E. (2009), 'Obstacles to Equality for Saudi Women', in *The Kingdom of Saudi Arabia, 1979–2009: Evolution of a Pivotal State*, Washington, DC: The Middle East Institute, https://www.mei.edu/publications/obstacles-equality-saudi-women (accessed 15 January 2021).

ECOSOC (1997), 'Gender Mainstreaming', in *Report of the Economic and Social Council, A/52/3*, 18 September, New York: United Nations.

Evans, G. W. (2003), 'The Built Environment and Mental Health', *Journal of Urban Health*, 80: 4.

Fullilove, M. T. (2016), *Root Shock: How Tearing Up City Neighborhoods Hurts America, and What We Can Do about It*, New York: New Village Press.

Garin, N., B. Olaya, M. Miret, J. L. Ayuso-Mateos, M. Power, P. Bucciarelli and J. M. Haro (2014), 'Built Environment and Elderly Population Health : A Comprehensive Literature Review', *Clinical Practice and Epidemiology in Mental Health*, 10: 103–15.

Ghaziani, A. (2019), 'Cultural Archipelagos: New Directions in the Study of Sexuality and Space', *City and Community*, 18: 4–22.

Glass, R. (1964), 'Introduction', in *Centre for Urban Studies, Aspects of Change*, London: MacGibbon and Kee, xiii, xvii–xix.

Gruebner, O., M. M. Khan, S. Lautenbach, D. Müller, A. Krämer, T. Lakes and P. Hostert (2012), 'Mental Health in the Slums of Dhaka – A Geoepidemiological Study', *BMC Public Health*, 12 (177): 10.1186/1471-2458-12-177.

Halpern, D. and J. Nazroo (2000), 'The Ethnic Density Effect: Results from a National Community Survey of England and Wales', *International Journal of Social Psychiatry*, 46 (1): 34–46.

Heblich, S., A. Trew and Y. Zylberberg (2016), 'East Side Story: Historical Pollution and Persistent Neighborhood Sorting', *Discussion Paper Series, School of Economics and Finance, University of St Andrews*.

House of Commons Women and Equalities Committee (2017), *Building for Equality: Disability and the Built Environment*, UK: House of Commons.

Hubbard, P. (2016), 'Hipsters on Our High Streets: Consuming the Gentrification Frontier', *Sociological Research Online*, 21 (3): 10.5153/sro.3962.

Iceland, J. (2014), *Residential Segregation: A Transatlantic Analysis*, Washington: Migration Policy Institute.

Johnson, A. M. and R. Miles (2014), 'Toward More Inclusive Public Spaces: Learning from the Everyday Experiences of Muslim Arab Women in New York City', *Environment and Planning A*, 46 (8): 1892–907.

Jokela, M. (2014), 'Are Neighborhood Health Associations Causal? A 10-year Prospective Cohort Study with Repeated Measurements', *American Journal of Epidemiology*, 180 (8): 776–84.

Lee, M. A. (2009), 'Neighborhood Residential Segregation and Mental Halth: A Multilevel Analysis on Hispanic Americans in Chicago', *Social Science and Medicine*, 68 (11): 1975–84.

Lees, L., T. Slater and E. Wyly (2008), *Gentrification*, New York: Routledge.

Lynch, K. (1977), *Growing Up in Cities: Study of the Spatial Environment of Adolescence in Cracow, Melbourne, Mexico City, Salta and Warszawa*. Boston: MIT Press.

Mair, C., A. V. Diez Roux, T. L. Osypuk, S. R. Rapp, T. Seeman and K. E. Watson (2010), 'Is Neighborhood Racial/Ethnic Composition Associated with Depressive Symptoms? The Multi-ethnic Study of Atherosclerosis', *Social Science and Medicine*, 71 (3): 541–50.

Mair, C., A. V. Diez Roux and S. Galea (2008), 'Are Neighbourhood Characteristics Associated with Depressive Symptoms? A Review of Evidence', *Journal of Epidemiology and Community Health*, 62 (11): 940–6.

McGovern, P. (2014), 'Why Should Mental Health Have a Place in the Post-2015 Global Health Agenda?', *International Journal of Mental Health Systems*, 118 (1): 38.

Meyer, I. H. (2003), 'Prejudice, Social Stress, and Mental Health in Lesbian, Gay, and Bisexual Populations: Conceptual Issues and Research Evidence', *Psychological Bulletin*, 129: 674–97.

Mitchell, L. and E. Burton (2006), 'Neighbourhoods for Life: Designing DementiaFriendly Outdoor Environments', *Quality in Ageing and Older Adults*, 7(1): 26–33.

Modi, S. (2018), 'An Analysis of High-Rise Living in Terms of Provision of Appropriate Social Spaces for Children', *Journal of Urban Design and Mental Health*, 5: 4.

Mohdin, H. G. A. and C. Michael (2019), 'More Segregated Playgrounds Revealed: "We Just Play in the Car Park"', *The Guardian*, 30 March. Available online: https://www.theguardian.com/cities/2019/mar/30/we-just-play-in-the-carpark-more-segregated-playgrounds-revealed (accessed 4 June 2020).

Munch, S. (2009), 'It's All in the Mix: Constructing Ethnic Segregation as a Social Problem in Germany', *Journal of Housing and the Built Environment*, 24: 441–55.

Musterd, S., S. Marcińczak, M. van Ham and T. Tammaru (2017), 'Socioeconomic Segregation in European Capital Cities. Increasing Separation between Poor and Rich', *Urban Geography*, 38 (7): 1062–83.

Oliver, C., M. Blythe and J. Roe (2018), 'Negotiating Sameness and Difference in Geographies of Older Age', *Area*, 50 (4): 444–51.

Palis, H., K. Marchand and E. Oviedo-Joekes (2018), 'The Relationship between Sense of Community Belonging and Self-rated Mental Health among Canadians with Mental or Substance Use Disorders', *Journal of Mental Health*, 9 (2): 168–75.

Preiser, W. F. E. and E. Ostroff (2001), *Universal Design Handbook*, New York: McGraw-Hill.

Reiss, F. (2013), 'Socioeconomic Inequalities and Mental Health Problems in Children and Adolescents: A Systematic Review', *Social Science and Medicine*, 90: 24–31.

Rishbeth, C., F. Ganji and G. Vodicka (2018), 'Ethnographic Understandings of Ethnically Diverse Neighbourhoods to Inform Urban Design Practice', *Local Environment*, 23 (1): 36–53.

Roe, J. and A. Roe (2018), 'Restorative Environments and Subjective Wellbeing and Mobility Outcomes in Older People', in S. R. Nyman, A. Barker, T Haines, K. Horton, C. Musselwhite, G. Peeters, C. R. Victor and J. K. Wolff (eds), *The Palgrave Handbook of Ageing and Physical Activity Promotion*, Palgrave Macmillan, 485–506.

Santiago, C. D., M. E. Wadsworth and J. Stump (2011), 'Socioeconomic Status, Neighborhood Disadvantage, and Poverty-Related Stress: Prospective Effects on Psychological Syndromes among Diverse Low-Income Families', *Journal of Economic Psychology*, 32(2): 218–30.

Shaw, R. J., K. Atkin, L. Bécares, C. B. Albor, M. Stafford, K. E. Kiernan, J. Y. Nazroo, R. G. Wilkinson and K. E. Pickett (2012), 'Impact of Ethnic Density on Adult Mental Disorders: Narrative Review', *British Journal of Psychiatry*, 201 (1): 11–19.

Shiue, I. (2015), 'Neighborhood Epidemiological Monitoring and Adult Mental Health: European Quality of Life Survey, 2007–2012', *Environmental Science and Pollution Research*, 22 (8): 6095–103.

Snedker, K. A. (2015), 'Neighborhood Conditions and Fear of Crime: A Reconsideration of Sex Differences', *Crime and Delinquency*, 61(1): 45–70.

Tammaru, T., S. Musterd, M. van Ham and S. Marcińczak (2016), 'A Multi-factor Approach to Understanding Socio-Economic Segregation in European Capital Cities', in T. Tammaru, S. Marcińczak, M. van Ham and S. Musterd (eds), *Socio-economic Segregation in European Capital Cities. East Meets West*, London: Routledge, 1–29.

Tunstall, H. V. Z., M. Shaw and D. Dorling (2004), 'Places and Health', *Journal of Epidemiology and Community Health*, 58: 6–10.

United Nations (2016), *Good Practices of Accessible Urban Development*. ST/ESA/364.

Van Bekkum, J., J. M. Williams and P. G. Morris (2011), 'Cycle Commuting and Perceptions of Barriers: Stages of Change, Gender and Occupation', *Health Education*, 111 (6): 476–97.

Verma, R. (2018). 'It Was Standard to See Signs Saying, "No Blacks, No Dogs, No Irish"', *Each Other*. Available online: https://eachother.org.uk/racism-1960s-britain/ (accessed 13 December 2019).

Wright, N. and T. Stickley (2013), 'Concepts of Social Inclusion, Exclusion and Mental Health: A Review of the International Literature', *Journal of Psychiatric and Mental Health Nursing*, 20: 71–81.

Wu, D. and Z. Wu (2012), 'Crime, Inequality and Unemployment in England and Wales', *Applied Economics*, 44: 3765–75.

Yang, Y. and A. V. Diez-Roux (2012), 'Walking Distance by Trip Purpose and Population Subgroups', *American Journal of Preventative Medicine*, 43(1): 11–19.

Yeh, J. C., J. Walsh, C. Spensley and M. Wallhagen (2016), 'Building Inclusion: Toward an Aging- and Disability-Friendly City', *American Journal of Public Health*, 106: 1947–49.

Chapter 9: The restorative city

100 Resilient Cities (2020), 'What Is Urban Resilience?' Available online: https://www.100resilientcities.org/resources/ (accessed 14 March 2020).

OECD (2014), 'Focus on Mental Health: Making Mental Health Count', *OECD*. Available online: https://www.oecd.org/els/health-systems/Focus-on-Health-Making-Mental-Health-Count.pdf (accessed 4 June 2020).

Pallasmaa, J. (2005), *The Eyes of the Skin. Architecture and the Senses*, New York: John Wiley.

WHO (2012), *Risks to Mental Health: An Overview of Vulnerabilities and Risk Factors*, Background paper by WHO Secretariat for the Development of a Comprehensive Mental Health Action Plan. Available online: https://www.who.int/mental_health/mhgap/risks_to_mental_health_EN_27_08_12.pdf (accessed 4 June 2020).

Index

Page numbers in *italic* refer to figures.

Abram, David 65
accessibility
    active cities 123
    blue cities and water settings
        50–1, 53–4
    to green space 12, 17, 31, 38, 121
    and inclusive cities 160–1, 164, 179
    physical accessibility 173–4
    to restorative soundscapes 76–7
Accessible Natural Greenspace
        Standard (ANGSt) (Natural
        England) 31
active cities 113–33, 195
    accessibility 123
    active living 114
    active travel 114, 119–20, 125–7
    all-age active cities, urban design
        characteristics 125
    Barcelona (Spain) 127–9, *128*
    brain health 114
    characteristics and features 114–15
    city scale 130–2, *133*
    cognitive function 114
    dementia, reduction of 120
    design approaches 122–7
    design principles and guidelines
        129–33, *132*, *133*
    examples of 127–9
    exercise and sleep 117
    impact on mental health 117,
        118–21, *118*
    improvements in children's
        and young people's mental
        wellbeing 119–20
    key concepts 114
    mixed land use 114, 123–4, 130
    modifiers of impact 122

mood and physical activity 117
multi-modal street design 114, 121
neighbourhood scale 130–2, *132*
neurobiological mechanism
    hypothesis 116–17
parks and street trees 124–5
place aesthetics 126
policy and promotion 132
and positive mental health/
    wellbeing 116–17, *116*
reducing depression, anxiety and
    stress 119
residential density 122, 123, 124
safe routes 123
social wellbeing improvements 121
space syntax 127
spatial cognition and wayfinding
    120
street connectivity 114, 122, 123, 127
addiction 51
adolescents. *See* children and young
    people
affective atmosphere 75
air quality 8, 9, 21, 99, 164, 166–7
allotments 81, *81*
ambience 64, 67, 75, 194
Antonovsky, Aaron 8
anxiety 4, 5, 6, 17, 25, 27, 33, 91, 96,
    195
    reduction of, in active cities 119
    and sensations 67
    and touch 72–3
attention deficit hyperactivity disorder
    (ADHD) 6, 17, 26, 119, 143, 194
attention restoration theory (ART)
    10–11, 20, 44, 66, 79
Australia 32, 97–8

Austria
  Vienna, gender inclusiveness
    185–6, *185*
autism spectrum disorder (ASD) 6,
  26–7, 174, 180–1

Barcelona (Spain) 53, 127–9, *128*
Beijing (China) 1
belongingness 67, *68*, 73–4, 75, 77,
  85, 91, 96, 98, 161, 177, 181
  belonging-in-place 90
  and smell 78
  and taste 80–1, *81*, 195
Berlin (Germany) 30
  Das Netz (The Net) 153, *154*
Bilbao (Spain) 50
biochemical mechanisms 20
biodiversity 17, 33, *47*
biophilia hypothesis 20
Biophilic Cities network 20
bipolar disorder 6, 74
birdsong 24, 69
black and minority ethnic people
    (BME) 29, 53–4, 74, 91, 175
  ethnic density hypothesis 170–1
  self-segregation notion 167
#BlackLivesMatter movement 161
blue cities and water settings 41–61, 194
  accessibility 50–1, 53–4
  Blue Active Tool 53
  blue care interventions 41, 42, 46, 51
  Bradford (UK) 54–5, *55*
  canals and inland waterways 49,
    50–1, 194
  characteristics and features 42–3
  children and young people 45
  city scale 60, *61*
  coasts/coastal cities 46, 48, 49,
    50, 54
  compared with green space 43
  depression and mood
    improvement 47–8, 51
  design approaches 50–4, *52*
  design principles and guidelines
    59–61, *60*, *61*
  examples of 54–9
  fountains 14, 35–6, 42–3, 50, 52,
    55–6, *56*, 60, 69, 147, 151, 194
  freshwater blue space 46

heat island effect 42
heat stress and mental health
    51–2, *52*
inclusive environments 53–4
key concepts 42
life span experiential variations 45
mental health, impact on 46–9, *47*
Middelfart, Denmark 56–7, *57*
modifiers of impact 49
multisensory experiences 43, *47*
neighbourhood scale 59, *60*
older people 46, 47–8
physical activities 43, 45, 51, 53
physical contact with water 45
relationship with mental health,
    theory of 43–6, *44*
rivers 35–6, *36*, 42, 50–1, 53, 58–9,
    58, 194
safety fears 45
Seoul (South Korea) 58–9, *58*
Sheffield (UK) 55–6, *56*
social health, support for 49
stress reduction 48
sustainability and economic drivers
    of development 53
therapeutic blue space design 51
unhealthy aspects 49
urban blue space 42–3
water contact, type of 44–5
water cure facilities 42
water misters 52, *52*, 198
water quality 49
water sensitive urban design
    (WSUD) 42
Bogotá (Colombia) *146*
Boulder (US), Growing Up Boulder
    initiative 182–3, *183*
Bradford (UK) 54–5, *55*, 151
brain activity. *See* cognitive function
Brazil 151
bumping places 74, 81, 86, 89, 94,
    101, 102, 105, 109, 195, 198

Canada 67–8
carers 174, 175, 176
Chicago (US), *Cloud Gate* 138, 147–8,
    148
children and young people 17, 29, 82,
    166, 172, 195

adverse childhood experiences and
    play 143
attention deficit hyperactivity
    disorder (ADHD) 6, 17, 26, 119,
    143, 194
behavioural problems 26, 175
child-friendly city initiative
    (UNICEF) 125, 136
child-friendly urban design 136
cognitive function 27–8, 119
community engagement for 182–3,
    183
Declaration of the Rights of the
    Child (UN) 140
free play 144, 148
green cities and space, benefits
    of 23
intergenerational play 152, 153,
    154
loneliness 97
mental wellbeing improvements in
    active cities 119–20
multi-generational living 100–1,
    107
and nature 17, 148
noise and sound, effects of 69
play, importance for adolescents
    140
social cohesion 29
social/emotional development and
    play 140
socialization needs 174–5
water experiences 45, 48
China 2, 96
    Beijing 1
    Chongqing 52
    Shanghai 52
churches and spiritual places 77, 102,
    109, 198
    church bells 69
city typologies. See active cities;
    blue cities and water settings;
    green cities and space; inclusive
    cities/inclusion; neighbourly
    cities; playable cities; restorative
    urbanism/cities; sensory cities
    garden cities 2, 18
    regenerative cities 10
    resilient cities 10, 34, 42, 192–3
    vertical cities 2, 3

climate 33, 46, 194, 198–9
coasts. See water settings
cognitive function 17, 20, 26, 45, 51,
    64, 65, 91, 96, 113, 114, 120,
    141, 152, 194
    children and young people 27–8,
    119
    cognitive overload 124–5
    electroencephalograms (EEG) 27
    green cities, effects on brain
    activity 27–8
    magnetic resonance imaging (MRI)
    27
    memory 27, 45, 64, 69, 91, 116–17,
    119, 120, 152, 176, 194
    neurobiological mechanism
    hypothesis 116–17
    noise and sound, effects of 69–70
    and physical accessibility 174
    and playful cities 142
Colombia 146
colour geography and planning 70–1,
    84–5, 85, 194
community engagement 105–6,
    200–1
    for inclusive planning and design
    181–2
    for young people 182–3, 183
consequential strangers 11–12
conviviality 90, 102, 177
Covid-19 1, 9, 31, 32, 80, 123, 153,
    193, 199
crime 94, 164, 169, 171, 176, 187
Crime Prevention Through
    Environmental Design (CPTED)
    79–80
culture 29, 29–30, 74, 81, 122, 143,
    167
    cultural competency and
    negotiating use of space 175–6
cycling 36, 53, 80, 86, 115, 119, 122,
    123, 126, 130–1, 199
    Cycling without Age movement
    184, 184
    and women 162

Darmstaft (Germany) 127
dementia 5, 6, 17, 28, 53, 70, 72, 74,
    79, 82, 142, 175, 180, 195
    and active cities 120

and neighbourly cities 96
   York (UK): a dementia friendly city
      183–4, *184*
demography 29
Denmark 23, 24–5
   Middelfart 56–7, *57*
density, residential density 122, 123,
      124
depression 1, 4, 5–6, 8, 17, 22, 33, 91,
      114, 195
   blue cities and water settings,
      effects of 47–8, 51
   green cities and space, effects of
      23–4
   neighbourly cities and reduction of
      depression 96
   and noise 69
   and obesity 73–4
   reduction of, in active cities 119
   reduction of, in playable cities 141,
      142
   and sense of smell 72
   sight, and the reduction of
      depression 70–1
   and touch 72–3
Derry/Londonderry (Northern Ireland,
      UK) 82–3, *82*
design principles and guidelines
   active cities 129–33, *132*, *133*
   blue cities and water settings
      59–61, *60*, *61*
   green cities and space 37–9, *38*, *39*
   inclusive cities 186–7, *188*, *189*
   neighbourly cities 108–11, *110*, *111*
   playable cities 155–6, *157*, *158*
   sensory cities 85–8, *87*, *88*
Detroit (US), Heidelberg Project *149*,
      150
Deventer (Netherlands) 107
disability-adjusted life years (DALYS) 53
disease 8–9, 18, 21, 25, 49, 53, 73,
      114, 144, 201, 202
dose-response relationship 18, 23–4,
      26, 34

Ebbsfleet (UK) 2
ecological momentary assessments
      (EMAs) 24
education 8, 12, 27, 82, 119–20, 171,
      192

electroencephalogram (EEG) 27
employment 164, 167, 171, 173, 179,
      192, 193
Epidauros (Greece) 51
equigenesis 12
ethnic density hypothesis 170–1
ethnic enclaves 91
evidence-based practice (EBP) 14
evidence-informed practice (EIP) 14,
      41
evolutionary psychology 65
exclusion. *See* inclusive cities
exercise and physical activity 20, 199
   in blue space 43, 45, 51, 53
   green exercise 8, 34, 117, 119 (*see
      also* active cities)
Exeter (UK) 34

families 90, 91, 94, 97, 108, 121, 146,
      152, 166, 167, 178, 192, 193
Finland 178
flourishing 5, 6–7
fomites 80, 153
food/foodscapes 63, 73–4, 80–1, 86
forest bathing (*shinrin yoku*) 25, 82
Foucan, Sébastien 150
fountains. *See* blue cities and water
      settings
France
   Lourdes 51
   Paris 30, 34, *35*, 199
Frankfurt (Germany), *Stadtflucht*
      (Urban Flight) 149, 154–5, *155*
Fullilove, Mindy, *Root Shock* 168, 170

garden cities 2, 18
gardens 9, 17, 29, 73, 74, 109, 121,
      194, 195
   sensory gardens 82, 86
Geddes, Patrick 18
Gehl, Jan 2, 66, 79
gender aspects 122, 160
   gender inclusiveness 185–6, *185*
   gender segregation 175
   women and cycling 162
gentrification 30, 50, 53, 129, 169–70,
      171, 177
Germany 149
   Berlin 30, 153, *154*
   Darmstaft 127

Frankfurt, *Stadtflucht* (Urban Flight) 149, 154–5, *155*
Glass, Ruth 170
graffiti 80
Granada (Spain) 52
Greece 51
green cities and space 7, 8, 17–39, 124–5, *126*, 193–4, 198
  accessibility 12, 17, 31, 38, 121
  amount of space 31
  biodiversity quality 33
  brain activity, effects on 27–8
  characteristics and features 18
  children, effects on 23
  city scale 37, *39*
  climate and seasonability 33
  compared with blue space 43
  cultural aspects 29–30
  demographic and socioeconomic factors 29
  depression 23–4
  design approaches 31–3
  design principles and guidelines 37–9, *38*, *39*
  examples of 34–7, *35*, *36*
  gardens 9, 17, 29
  green prescribing 33–4
  green walls 17
  health equity 30
  key concepts 17–18
  mental health, impact on 21–2, *22*
  modifiers of impact 29–30
  mood and emotional regulation 23–4
  Moscow (Russia) 35–7, *36*
  neighbourhood scale 37, *38*
  Paris (France) 34, *35*
  quality perceptions 32–3
  relationship with mental health, theory of 19–21, *19*
  schizophrenia/psychotic disorders, mitigation of 25–7
  and social cohesion 28–9
  stress disorders, reduction of 24–5
  time spent 33
  types of space 31–2
  urban green space 17
  views 32
grey (built-up) space 27
Guyton, Tyree 150

Happy City's Happy Home Toolkit 101
heat stress 21, 27, 34, 42, 45, 46, *47*, 103, 194
  and mental health 51–2, *52*
homelessness 53, 97–8, 192, 199
  anti-homeless spikes 98, 170
  homeless person-inclusive design 181
  and housing affordability/availability 98–9
  and urban design 178
Hong Kong 2, 47–8, 103
  sitting out area concept 104, *104*
housing 12, 54, 89, 98–101, 178, 193, 200–1
  adequacy and quality 99
  availability/affordability 98–9
  cohousing/cooperative housing 100–1, 107–8, *108*
  design for social opportunity 101
  high-rise living 101, 124
  homeless person-inclusive design 181
  location 99–100
  mixed-income, mixed-age residential development 181
  multi-generational living 100–1, 107
  privacy 101
  social housing 99, 100, 129, 185–6
  stigma 100
Howard, Ebenezer 2, 18

Illinois University 26
inclusive cities/inclusion 53–4, 94, 159–89, 196
  accessibility 160–1, 164
  age-friendly urban design 172
  age-segregated environments 171
  characteristics and features 160–3
  city scale 187, *189*
  comfort for all 180–1
  community engagement for inclusive planning and design 181–2
  cultural competency and negotiating use of space 175–6
  defensive or hostile architecture 170
  design approaches 177–82

design for the baseline 172–3
design principles and guidelines
  186–7, *188*, *189*
different needs for infrastructure
  and facilities 173–6
ethnic density hypothesis 170–1
examples of 182–6
exposure to inferior settings 164
gaybourhoods 171
gender mainstreaming 160
geographical exclusion 164, 166–7
Growing Up Boulder 182–3, *183*
impact on mental health 164–76,
  165
key concepts 160
mental health and positive impacts
  of segregation 170–1
minority stress theory 160, 164
mixed-income, mixed-age
  residential development 181
modifiers of impact 175–6
movement and use of the city,
  patterns of 172–3
neighbourhood scale 186–7, *188*
neighbourhood spatial segregation,
  rise of 166–7
perceptive and cognitive
  differences 174
physical accessibility 173–4
physical segregation in shared
  residential areas 169
psychological segregation in shared
  residential areas 169–70
psychosocial characteristics and
  needs 174–5
residential/spatial location 160
safety 176, 177, 180
segregation 159, 160, 161, 165–71
shared spaces and segregation
  167–70, *168*
spatial segregation 165–6, 177–8
stigma of exclusion 164
theory of relationship with mental
  health 163–4, *163*
transit for all 179
universal/inclusive design 160, 161,
  178–81
Vienna (Austria) and gender
  inclusiveness 185–6, *185*

visibility of minorities 181
walkability for all 179
York (UK): a dementia friendly city
  183–4, *184*
intergenerational aspects
  housing 100–1, 107
  intergenerational longevity 94
  play 152, 153, *154*
investment 89, 94
Iran 29
Ireland 48
isolation 1, 7, 89, 90, 91, 93, 161, 175
Italy
  Milan 199
  Rome 136
  Turin 71, 84–5, *85*

Japan 25, 33, 65, 78, *168*
  machizukuri 106
  Tokyo 83–4, *83*, 99–100
Joseph Rowntree Foundation 183–4

Kail, Eva 185
Kaplan, Rachel 10–11, 20
Kaplan, Stephen 10–11, 20
Kapoor, Anish 147
Keyes, Corey L.M. 5–6

land use 102, 123–4, 130, 195
Le Corbusier 2
LGBTQ+ people 171, 175
libraries 94, 102, 103, 109, 179
life expectancy 73, 167
lighting 20, 70, 79–80, 83, 86, 162,
  174, 180
  blue light 83–4, *83*
litter 49, 94
live-work space 114
London (UK) 18, 34, 54, 136, 151, 167,
  170, 199
loneliness 1, 7, 12, 28, 89, 90, 91, 93,
  96, 97, 121, 175
Los Angeles (US) 53
Lourdes (France) 51
low- and middle-income countries 14,
  30, 122, 160

magnetic resonance imaging (MRI) 27
markets 74, 80, 81, 86, 103, 104, 198

marriage 100
Melbourne (Australia) 97–8
mental health and illness 1
   blue space, impact on mental
      health 46–9, *47*
   costs of mental illness 191–2
   definition of 5–7
   design for mental health and
      wellbeing 191–2
   and green prescribing 33–4
   green space, impact on mental
      health 21–2, *22*
   and heat stress 51–2, *52*
   impact of physical activity 117,
      118–21, *118*
   inclusive cities, impact of 164–76,
      165
   life expectancy 73
   nature, benefits of *19*, 20, 24
   neighbourly cities, impact on
      mental health 95–7, *95*
   playable cities, benefits of 139–41,
      139
   playable cities, impact of 141–3,
      142
   relationship with inclusive cities
      161–2, 163–4, *163*
   sensory cities, impact of 64–5
   sensory cities, relationship with
      65–8, *66*
   systems approach to 8–9
   theory of relationship with active
      cities 116–17, *116*
   theory of relationship with blue
      space 43–6, *44*
   theory of relationship with
      neighbourly cities 92–4, *93*
   theory of relationship with urban
      green space 19–21, *19*
   urban paradigm for 4–5
Middelfart (Denmark) 56–7, *57*
migration 91, 97, 167
Milan (Italy) 199
minority stress theory 160, 164
Mongolia 30
monotony 70, 73, 76, 79, 194
Montreal (Canada) 67–8
mood and emotional regulation 23–4,
   48

noise and sound, effect of 69–70
and physical activity 117
sight, effects of 70–1
smell, effects of 71–2
Moore, Patricia 161
Moscow (Russia) 35–7, *36*
multi-generational living 100–1, 107
multisensory experiences 43, *47*
murals 80, 200
museums 11, 73

National Trust 144
nature 2, *4*, 7, 10–11, 17, 18, 79, 94,
   194, 196
   benefits for mental health *19*, 20,
      24
   birdsong 69
   brain activity, effects on 27–8
   and children 17, 148
   incidental nature exposure 18
   intentional nature exposure 18
   nature deficit disorder 148
   nature immersion 81–2
   and sensations 66–7
   and stress disorders 24–5
   views 32
neighbourly cities 89–111, 195
   age 97
   anxiety reduction 96
   bumping places 74, 81, 86, 89, 101,
      102, 105, 109, 195, 198
   characteristics and features 90–2
   city scale 109–10, *111*
   community 90
   conviviality 90, 102
   dementia symptoms 96
   depression, reduction of 96
   design approaches 98–107
   design principles and guidelines
      108–11, *110*, *111*
   Deventer (Netherlands) 107
   examples of 107–8
   homelessness 97–8
   housing 98–101
   key concepts 90
   loneliness 90, 91, 93, 96, 97
   machizukuri (Japan) 106
   mental health, impact on 95–7, *95*
   migration 91, 97

modifiers of impact 97–8
neighbourhood scale 109, *110*
neighbourliness 90, 94, 98, 99
participatory settings in the
    neighbourhood 105–6
pets 105, 109
protection against psychosis 96
relationship with mental health,
    theory of 92–4, *93*
shared services 103
social capital 90, 92–3, 96, 98, 106
social cohesion 90, 92, 96, 98, 99,
    106
social isolation 90, 91, 93, 97
social overload 92
social support 90, 91, 92
stewardship of meeting places 103
and suicide 97
third spaces 103–4, 109
transit design 106–7
wider neighbourhood social
    settings 102–4, *104*
Zurich (Switzerland) 107–8, *108*
Netherlands 23–4, 28
Deventer 107
neurobiological mechanism
    hypothesis 116–17
New York City (US) 18, 30, 79, 136, 175
NIMBYism 106
noise and sound 63, 64, 66, 67, 174,
    194
effects on mood, stress and
    cognitive function 69–70
noise management 77
salutogenic soundscapes 64, 77,
    85–6
sleep disruption 67–8
unwanted noise reduction
    and access to restorative
    soundscapes 76–7

obesity 73–4, 114, 149
older people 17, 20, 28, 29, 32, 45, 82,
    96, 121, 142, 172, 175
age-segregated environments 171
and exercise 115, 120
housing 99–100
intergenerational play 152, 153,
    154

loneliness 97, 175
multi-generational living 100–1, 107
noise and sound, effects of 69
urban environment experiences 161
and water settings 46, 47–8
Organisation for Economic Co-
    operation and Development
    (OECD) 191–2

Pallasmaa, Juhani 64
Paris (France) 30, 199
Isles of Coolness 34, *35*
parkour 36, 137, 138, 150–1, 196, 200
parks 7, 9, 17, 18, 27–8, 29, 30, 33, 77,
    89, 104, 121, 130, 194
biodiversity 33
Moscow (Russia) 35–7, *36*
Paris (France) 34, *35*
redesign of, for female use 186
and restorative design 196–7
people with disabilities 51, 53, 160,
    161, 172, 175
physical accessibility needs 173–4,
    179
and street design 180
perception 64, 65
pets 105, 109
Philadelphia (US) 32
physical activities. *See* active cities
physiological biomarkers 25
place attachment/identity 28–9, 71, 74
playable cities 135–8, 195–6, 200
adult play 136–7, *137*, 140
adverse childhood experiences,
    risk reduction 143
appropriative play 136, 144, 149,
    150–1
Beat the Street 149
benefits for mental and physical
    health 139–41, *139*
Berlin (Germany) *Das Netz* (The
    Net) 153, *154*
brain function improvement 142
characteristics and features 136–8
city scale 156, *158*
curiosity and novelty seeking 141,
    154
depression and stress reduction
    141, *142*

design approaches 143–53
design principles and guidelines
    155–6, *157*, *158*
digital play 144, 148–9, 156, 198
examples of 153–5
flow 137
Frankfurt (Germany) *Stadtflucht*
    (Urban Flight) 149, 154–5, *155*
free play 144, 148
future developments 152
Heidelberg Project, Detroit (US)
    149, 150
impact on mental health 141–3,
    142
interactive art 147–8, *148*
intergenerational play 152, 153,
    154
key concepts 135–6
ludic urban design 144
and mental freedom 138
modifiers of impact 143
neighbourhood scale 155–6, *157*
new play movements and playable
    technologies 151–2
non-defined play contexts 148
parkour 36, 137, 138, 150–1, 196,
    200
and physical activity 141
play 135, 137
play-*able* context 136, 147–9, *147*
play affordance 135
play areas/playgrounds 17, 26, 94,
    145
playfulness 135, 137–8, 140–1,
    149–51, *149*
playful rebellion *149*, 150
play streets 145–6, *146*, 152, 156
Pokémon Go 138, 149
pure-play contexts 136, 145–6
resilience 140–1, 143
safety fears 143, 144
social and emotional development
    of young people 140
trash, use of *149*, 150
urban play settings, impact of 141
water play 45
Playable City movement 151, 154
pollution 27, 166–7
post-traumatic stress disorder (PTSD)
    4, 6, 25, 41, 51, 143

poverty 8, 12, 166, 178, 193
preferenda 11
privacy 101
psychosis 25, 93, 96, 171
public art 79, 80, 83, 86, 138, 141, 196
    gender inclusiveness 185–6, *185*
    interactive art 147–8, *148*

racism 54, 169
randomized controlled trials (RCTs)
    14, 32
regenerative city concept 10
religion 51, 91, 93, 175
resilience 6, 8, 29, 46, 92
    and play 140–1, 143
    resilient city concept 10, 34, 42,
        192–3
restorative environment theory 3, 9,
    10–12, 124–5
    attention restoration theory (ART)
        10–11, 20, 44, 66, 79
    collective restoration 11–12, 28
    dyad restoration 11, 28
    individual restoration 28
    stress reduction theory (SRT) 10,
        11, 20, 44
restorative urbanism/cities 9–13
    city scale *204*
    co-creation 199
    design for mental health and
        wellbeing 191–2
    framework for 12–13, *13*, 193–6
    and health inequity 12
    housing 199
    neighbourhood scale *203*
    parks 197–8
    practical implementation of
        196–201
    public open space 197–8
    reasons for 1–4, *3*, *4*
    research and evidence 13–14
    responsibility for creation of
        201–2
    street features 198–9
    transportation 199
    urban paradigm for mental health
        4–5
    urban planning and design, new
        mandate for 201–2
Rio de Janeiro (Brazil) 151

rivers. *See* blue cities and water settings
Rome (Italy) 136
Russia
   Moscow 35–7, *36*

safety 45, 70, 79–80, 94, 103, 123, 143, 144, 162, 176, 177, 180, 199
salutogenesis theory 3, 6, 8–9
   smellscapes 78, 85–6
   soundscapes 64, 77, 85–6
San Francisco (US) 171
Saudi Arabia 175
savanna hypothesis 65
schizophrenia 4, 5, 6, 17, 23, 74, 75, 96
   green cities and space, effects of 25–6
schools 82, 119–20, 131, 179, 198
Scotland 27–8
seating 38, 48, 49, 56, 57, 103, 104, *104*, 109, 110, 125, 174
segregation 12, 100, 159, 161, 165–71, 196
   age-segregated environments 171
   defensive or hostile architecture 170
   donut-hole pattern 167
   ethnic density hypothesis 170–1
   gaybourhoods 171
   gender segregation 175
   neighbourhood spatial segregation, rise of 166–7
   poor doors 169, 187
   and positive impacts on mental health 170–1
   psychological segregation in shared residential areas 169–70
   self-segregation notion 167
   shared residential areas 169
   in shared spaces 167–70, *168*
   spatial segregation 165–6, 177–8
   west-east divide 166–7
sensory cities 63–88, 194–5
   ambience 64, 75
   characteristics and features 64–5
   city scale *88*
   cognition 64, 65, 69–70
   colour geography and planning 70–1, 84–5, *85*, 194
   combined sensory design 81–2

   Derry/Londonderry (Northern Ireland, UK) 82–3, *82*
   design approaches 76–82
   design principles and guidelines 85–8, *87*, *88*
   examples of 82–5
   ground-feel 72–3, 80, 86
   key concepts 63–4
   lighting 70, 79–80, 82–4, *82*, *83*, 86
   mental health, impact on 64–5, 68, *68*
   modifiers of impact 75–6
   monotony 70, 73, 76, 79, 194
   neighbourhood scale *87*
   noise management 77
   perception 64, 65
   public art 79, 80, 83, 86
   reducing exposure to unpleasant sensations 86–7
   reducing unpleasant smells 78
   relationship with mental health, theory of 65–8, *66*
   salutogenic soundscape/ smellscape 64, 77, 78, 85–6
   savanna hypothesis 65
   sensation 63, 65
   sight and reduction of depression 70–1
   smell and belongingness 78
   smells and mood disorders 71–2
   sounds, effects of 69–70, 194
   street views 70
   tastes, physical health and belongingness 73–4, 80–1, *81*, 195
   Tokyo (Japan) 83–4, *83*
   touch and haptic experience 80
   touch, effects of on depression and anxiety 72–3, 194–5
   Turin (Italy) 84–5, *85*
   unwanted noise reduction and access to restorative soundscapes 76–7
   visual impact of cities 78–80
Seoul (South Korea) 50, 58–9, *58*
Shanghai (China) *52*
Sheffield (UK) 49, 55–6, *56*
shinrin yoku (forest bathing) 25, 82
shops/stores 74, 79, 80, 86, 103
Sicart, Miguel 137, 144, 149, 153

sight
  reducing monotony 79
  and reduction of depression 70–1
  visual impact of cities 78–80
Singapore 2, *3*
Situationist movement 136
sleep 45, 63, 67–8, 117, 194
smartphones 24, 48, 126–7, 198
smell 63, 64, 67, 194
  and creation of belongingness 78
  and mood disorders 71–2
  reducing unpleasant smells 78
  salutogenic smellscapes 78, 85–6
social capital 7, 81, 89, 90, 92–3, 96,
    98, 106, 167, 170, 171, 177
social cohesion 7, 28–9, 90, 92, 96,
    99, 106, 121, 161, 169
social health 7, 29, 43, 49, 121, 124
social networks 1, 9, 29, 90, 91, 92–3,
    95, 96, 97, 98, 105, 144, 195
social prescribing 8, 33–4
socioeconomic aspects 12, 29, 94,
    100, 164
  and segregation 165–7, 177
solistalgia 53
South Korea
  Seoul 50, 58–9, *58*
space syntax 127
Spain
  Barcelona 53, 127–9, *128*
  Bilbao 50
  Granada 52
  Valencia 50
spatial cognition 120
stigma 100, 101, 160, 169, 178, 181,
    187
  of exclusion 164
streets/street views 70, 77, 104, 130
  multi-modal street design 114, 121
  play streets 145–6, *146*, 152, 156
  and restorative principles 199–200
  safety aspects 180
  street connectivity 114, 122, 123,
    127, 195
stress 1, 17
  green cities and space, effects of
    24–5
  noise and sound, effects of 69–70
  reduction of, in active cities 119

reduction of, in playable cities 141,
    142
stress reduction theory (SRT) 10,
    11, 20, 44
substance abuse 6, 146, 181
suicide 7, 23, 45, 73, 91
  prevention 82–4, *82*, *83*, 97
superblock model (Barcelona) 127–9,
    128
Sustainable Development Goals
  (SDGs) 9
Sweden 31
Switzerland
  Zurich 107–8, *108*

Tacoma (US) 178–9
tactical urbanism 128, 129, 132, 199
tastes 73–4
  and belongingness 80–1, *81*, 195
third spaces 103–4, 109
toilets. *See* washing and hygiene/
  toilets
Tokyo (Japan) 83–4, *83*
  Daily Activity Areas 99–100
touch 194–5
  effects on depression and anxiety
    72–3
  and haptic experience 80
traffic 10, 56, 68, 69, 77, 86–7, 121,
    122, 126, 180
  superblock model (Barcelona)
    127–9, *128*
travel
  active travel 114, 119–20, 125–7
  movement and use of the city,
    patterns of 172–3
  public transport 121, 122, 131,
    172–3, 179, 187, 195, 200
trees 17, 20, 26, 32, 33, 124–5, 194
Turin (Italy) 71, 84–5, *85*

Ulaanbaatar (Mongolia) 30
Ulrich, Roger S. 11
unemployment 97, 178, 192, 193
UNICEF, child-friendly city initiative
    125, 136
United Kingdom (UK) 2, 14, 23, 24, 29,
    33–4, 81, 115, 145–6, 149, 171
  Bradford 54–5, *55*, 151

Derry/Londonderry 82–3, *82*
Ebbsfleet 2
Exeter 34
London 18, 34, 54, 136, 151, 167, 170, 199
Sheffield 49, 55–6, *56*
Welwyn Garden City 2
York, help for people with dementia 183–4, *184*
United Nations (UN)
Agenda for Sustainable Development 9
Declaration of the Rights of the Child 140
Habitat III Quito Conference 9
New Urban Agenda 9
tools for supporting urban health planning 182
United States 2, 12, 26, 29, 32, 33, 42, 48, 53–4, 115, 129, 144, 145, 166, 167, *168*, 171, 178
Boulder, Growing Up Boulder initiative 182–3, *183*
Chicago, *Cloud Gate* 138, 147–8, *148*
Detroit, Heidelberg Project *149*, 150
Illinois University 26
Los Angeles 53
New York City 18, 30, 79, 136, 175
Philadelphia 32
San Francisco 171
Tacoma 178–9
West Palm Beach, Florida 48
urban farms 73, 81, 82, 195

Valencia (Spain) 50
vertical cities 2, *3*
Vienna (Austria), gender inclusiveness 185–6, *185*
Ville Radieuse (Le Corbusier) 2
volunteering 89, 105–6

walking/walkability 8, 11, 20, 24, 25–6, 27, 33, 37–8, 45, 48, 89, 99–100, 101, 109–10, 115, 119, 121, 179, 199
physical accessibility 173–4

safe routes 123
urban walking 126–7
washing and hygiene/toilets 80, 98, 111, 125, 162, 173, 174, 180–1, 187
water misters 52, *52*, 198
water settings. *See* blue cities and water settings
wayfinding 120, 175, 199
We Are Undefeatable campaign 115
wellbeing *68*
curiosity and novelty seeking 141
eudaimonic wellbeing 5, 6
gross national wellbeing 7
hedonic wellbeing 5, 6
links with green space 18
psychological wellbeing/health 5, 6, 7, 96, 174–5
social wellbeing 5, 6, 7, 121
Welwyn Garden City (UK) 2
West Palm Beach, Florida (US) 48
Wirth, Louis, *Urbanism as a Way of Life* 91
women 29, 31, 54, 122, 141, 143, 161, 172, 174
and cycling 162
gender inclusiveness in Vienna (Austria) 185–6, *185*
gender segregation 175
safety concerns 176
World Health Organization (WHO) 5, 6, 69
age-friendly city initiative 125
global strategy on physical activity and health 141
Health Cities Program 9
tools for supporting urban health planning 182

York (UK), help for people with dementia 183–4, *184*
young people. *See* children and young people

Zurich (Switzerland) 107–8, *108*